Harold P. Nebelsick, Professor of Doctrinal Theology at Louisville Presbyterian Theological Seminary, Louisville, Kentucky, and a member of the Center of Theological Inquiry, Princeton, New Jersey, has spent the past ten years concentrating on the discussion of Theology and Natural Science. Following his work, *Theology and Science in Mutual Modification*, the book, *Circles of God* continues his contribution to the current ecumenical dialogue about the relationship of our knowledge of God to our knowledge of the world.

THEOLOGY AND SCIENCE AT THE FRONTIERS OF KNOWLEDGE

NUMBER TWO

CIRCLES OF GOD
THEOLOGY AND SCIENCE
FROM
THE GREEKS TO COPERNICUS

THEOLOGY AND SCIENCE AT THE FRONTIERS OF KNOWLEDGE

THEOLOGY AND SCIENCE AT THE FRONTIERS OF KNOWLEDGI

GENERAL EDITOR—T. F. TORRANCE

CIRCLES OF GOD

THEOLOGY AND SCIENCE
FROM
THE GREEKS TO COPERNICUS

HAROLD P. NEBELSICK

SCOTTISH ACADEMIC PRESS
EDINBURGH
1985

Published in association with the
Center of Theological Inquiry
and
The Templeton Foundation Inc.
by
SCOTTISH ACADEMIC PRESS
33 Montgomery Street, Edinburgh EH7 5JX

First published 1985

ISBN 0 7073 0448 2

© H. P. Nebelsick

British Library Cataloguing in Publication Data

Nebelsick, Harold P.
  Circles of God : Theology and Science
  from the Greeks to Copernicus.
  1. Religion and science———1946–
  I. Title
  215   BL240.2

  ISBN 0-7073-0448-2

Printed in Great Britain by
Clark Constable, Edinburgh, London, Melbourne

To My Children
Louis, Mary, and James
in love and gratitude

CONTENTS

GENERAL FOREWORD

A VAST shift in the perspective of human knowledge is taking place, as a unified view of the one created world presses for realisation in our understanding. The destructive dualisms and abstractions which have disintegrated form and fragmented culture are being replaced by unitary approaches to reality in which thought and experience are wedded together in every field of scientific inquiry and in every area of human life and culture. There now opens up a dynamic, open-structured universe, in which the human spirit is being liberated from its captivity in closed deterministic systems of cause and effect, and a correspondingly free and open-structured society is struggling to emerge.

The universe that is steadily being disclosed to our various sciences is found to be characterised throughout time and space by an ascending gradient of meaning in richer and higher forms of order. Instead of levels of existence and reality being explained reductionistically from below in materialistic and mechanistic terms, the lower levels are found to be explained in terms of higher, invisible, intangible levels of reality. In this perspective the divisive splits become healed, constructive syntheses emerge, being and doing become conjoined, an integration of form takes place in the sciences and the arts, the natural and the spiritual dimensions overlap, while knowledge of God and of his creation go hand in hand and bear constructively on one another.

We must now reckon with a revolutionary change in the generation of fundamental ideas. Today it is no longer philosophy but the physical and natural sciences which set the pace in human culture through their astonishing revelation of the rational structures that pervade and underly all created reality. At the same time, as our science presses its inquiries to the very boundaries of being, in macrophysical and microphysical dimensions alike, there is being brought to light a hidden traffic between theological and scientific ideas of the most far-reaching significance for both theology and science. It is in that situation where theology and science are found to have deep mutual relations, and increasingly cry out for each other, that our authors have been at work.

The different volumes in this series are intended to be geared into this fundamental change in the foundations of knowledge. They do not present "hack" accounts of scientific trends or theological fashions, but are intended to offer interdisciplinary and creative interpretations which will themselves share in and carry forward the new synthesis transcending the gulf in popular understanding between faith and reason, religion and life, theology and science. Of special concern is the mutual modification and cross-fertilisation between natural and theological science, and the creative integration of all human thought and culture within the universe of space and time.

What is ultimately envisaged is a reconstruction of the very foundations of modern thought and culture, similar to that which took place in the early centuries of the Christian era, when the unitary outlook of Judaeo-Christian thought transformed that of the ancient world, and made possible the eventual rise of modern empirico-theoretic science. The various books in this series are written by scientists and by theologians, and by some who are both scientists and theologians. While they differ in training, outlook, religious persuasion, and nationality, they are all passionately committed to the struggle for a unified understanding of the one created universe and the healing of our split culture. Many difficult questions are explored and discussed, and the ground needs to be cleared of often deep-rooted misconceptions, but the results are designed to be presented without technical detail or complex argumentation, so that they can have their full measure of impact upon the contemporary world.

In an earlier work, *Theology and Science in Mutual Modification*, 1981, Professor Harold P. Nebelsick set out to clarify the tangled connections between theology and natural science that have characterised Western thought since Isaac Newton. Here, however, he offers the results of a further probing into those interconnections by tracing them from the very rise of science in ancient times to the "Copernican revolution" in the sixteenth century. This is a fascinating account of cosmological inquiry in which it is shown that from the very beginning science (thought about the world) and theology (thought about God or the gods) were so intermingled that science took the field as a basically religious quest and has remained throughout its long development subtly influenced, rightly as well as wrongly, by theological ideas. While the ancients held that the way we think about nature bears on what we think about God, it has also become clear that the way we think about God profoundly affects the way we think about nature. The specific theme of this book, pursued with detective-like persistence, relates to the way in which a wrong conception of circularity linked with divine rationality helped and hindered the progress of science. It was only with a deep change in the understanding of God at work in European culture that science was enabled to shake off harmful Greek theological and scientific ideas and develop as an autonomous field of knowledge on its own. Yet that is not the whole story, as Dr. Nebelsick shows, for there remains an inevitable if subtle kind of symbiosis at work in which scientific and theological inquiry, in autonomy and openness to one another, give rise to an underlying harmony which may be fruitful to both inquiries.

Thomas F. Torrance

Edinburgh,
Advent, 1984

PREFACE

THE argument in the present volume underscores Professor Thomas F. Torrance's statement in the General Foreword to this series of books: "A vast shift in the perspective of human knowledge is taking place as a unified view of the one created world presses for realisation in our understanding". We are beginning to comprehend that theological science and natural science are interdependent. Indeed, as the study of the history of science shows, from the very beginnings of the development of scientific thinking in the ancient world, first in Babylon and then in Greece, thought about God or the gods — *theology* — and thought about the world — *natural science* — were so intermingled that often it was quite impossible to differentiate between the two. The study of nature was a cultic discipline pursued for the sake of knowing the divine before it developed into a procedure for knowing the world. Even when it became the study of nature, science continued to be dependent upon theological ideas. These at one and the same time motivated those who pursued it to attempt to understand nature and prevented them from perceiving the world in appropriate terms.

Thus in the following pages which trace the development of science from its beginnings in the ancient world through Copernicus, I shall argue that the main motivating force behind the pursuit of natural knowledge from the time of Babylon and Greece in the East to the time of the Renaissance in the West was *theological* rather than *scientific*. It was primarily for religious reasons that people from the unnamed Babylonians through the pre-Socratics, the Pythagoreans, Plato, and Aristotle attempted to understand the heavens, to trace their geometry and calculate their ratios. Divinity was thought to be known by the regularity and harmony of the heavens right up through the Renaissance and including Copernicus.

At the same time the perfect regularity of heavenly harmony was countermanded by a contradictory motif which made the planets subject to living and divine principles. These ancient "astral divinities" which were thought to be responsible both for the motion of the planets and for the events of nature and humankind were brought to the Renaissance world by the writings of Aristotle, Pseudo-Dionysius, and the *Hermetic Corpus*. Hence, along with Greek science, the Renaissance West inherited the belief in capricious divine forces which compromised cosmic dependability and continued the mythicisation of reality.

Our thinking about God and his relationship to the world, our "theology", is therefore decisive not only for our religious beliefs; equally important, our theology is quite determinative of the way we understand the world as well. Our thoughts about God and about the world in relationship to him will have a quite crucial effect on how we are enabled to know nature and interact with it. Our faith will have a significant influence on the way we see and understand the world whether we attribute to its reality qualifications which stem from theological, humanistic, or even presupposed scientific predilections or whether by allowing ourselves to be subjected to nature's own inner structures we will be drawn to penetrate below the phenomena into the revealing relationships within nature itself. It is when we allow the objects of nature to speak to us in ways which are appropriate to them, when we who are subjects subject ourselves to the objects under investigation and thus by an *epistemological inversion* allow these objects to become subjects that denote the terms by which they may be perceived and known that nature will disclose *itself* to us in ways that are appropriate.[1] Following Albert Einstein (1879–1955) who has reminded us that the whole of science is nothing more than a refinement of everyday thinking we can say that any discoveries we make regarding the way we understand nature will apply to the way we think on all levels.[2] Thus the "epistemological inversion" of which we spoke, not only points the way to an appropriate understanding of nature, it becomes paradigmatic for all objective thinking whatsoever.

The following pages give an account of that fascinating era of human history when, by and large, theological thought and its implications dominated science often in such subtle ways that the "scientists" least of all realised the source of their bondage. For the most part these students of nature were quite convinced that the world they saw through the theologically deformed lenses of the glasses they wore was the world that was really there. They were quite successful according to their own criteria. This was at one and the same time the measure of their achievement and the cause of their failure. The same presuppositions which precluded seeing reality with the kind of "objectivity" we think necessary and stopped science from developing beyond a rudimentary level nevertheless carried them far enough into the rationality of nature for the rudiments of science to come into being.

My attempt to clarify both the positive and negative aspects of the interrelationships of theological science and natural science has two purposes. On the one hand, it is hoped that the evidence brought forth will put us on guard against the danger of permitting the presuppositions of either of the two sciences to dominate each other. On the other hand, one may trust that such a discussion will expose the torpitude which results from thinking that theology and natural science are so disparate that the one has nothing to do with the other. What we believe will eventually have to do with what we think about the world and the way we interact with it. If we believe in God, the way we know and treat nature will eventually expose our relationship to God and define the kind of God we believe in. As the question regarding God more often than not is, not whether we believe in God, but what kind of a God do we believe in, so with regard to the world, it is not, do we have an understanding of it, but how do we understand it.

Although I am personally quite convinced of the interrelational aspects of theological thought and thought about the world, the point of a study such as this is not to advise conflating the two. Each of the sciences has its own object, its own method, and its own body of knowledge. Naïvely to transfer knowledge from one to the other would be crassly unscientific. What is wanted is for us to see that false theological conceptualities entail false scientific ones and that proper theology will allow the world to be seen as having both the kind of value and contingent freedom which makes knowing it worthwhile and demands that it be known according to an appropriate rationality. At the same time, it is to be hoped that the methodological characteristics of openness, integrity, and critical consistency which are the *sine qua non* of all scientific thinking will be shared by natural scientists and theologians alike.

We cannot nor would we desire to reduplicate the mediaeval synthesis or even the earlier Hellenistic one in which theological thought and thought about the world were so interimpinging as to be indistinguishable. Much as that kind of thinking gave a unity to the understanding of existence which we in our time find sadly wanting, the effect of such a synthesis was, and will likely always be, the inevitable dominance of one area of thought over the other to the detriment of both. In contrast, what is desired is the realisation by the scientist that, as all scientific systems depend upon values and structures which are antecedent to their systems and beyond their comprehensibility, so what is desired for the theologian is the realisation that theological structures too depend on metastructures of thought which allow systematisation to take place.

It is also to be hoped that, just as theologians realise that there is no thinking about God without thinking about the world, they will take it for granted that they must be just as rigorous, just as critical, and just as systematic in their thinking about God as are natural scientists in their thinking about nature. Knowledge and method in the one area, therefore, do not duplicate one another; rather they complement each other and may be mutually corrective. Dialogue between the *two sciences*, both through literature and by way of the personal encounter of their practitioners, may help keep the natural sciences from wandering off into the grounds of rationalistic positivism and may prevent theology from slipping into idealistic mythology. By allowing ourselves to be constrained by one another's discipline we may hope that we may be open to the revelation that awaits us in nature, on the one hand, and from God, on the other.

Once more I wish to express my gratitude to Louisville Presbyterian Theological Seminary, which has generously granted me sabbatical leave to finish this project; to the University of Edinburgh, where I began research for it; to Princeton Theological Seminary and Princeton University for opening their facilities for my further research; to The Center of Theological Inquiry at Princeton and its director, Dr. James I. McCord, which in granting me membership made the finishing of the book possible; to Professor Thomas F. Torrance, who as a friend continues to encourage me, not least as editor of this series; and to the late Mr. Eyre Crowe of Edinburgh and Professor Ernest White of Louisville who helped me in preparing the typescript.

I am most grateful to my wife, Melissa, who made visit after visit to the libraries in Edinburgh and Princeton to borrow and return books, checked references and quotations, and typed draft after draft of text from its early beginnings from a dictating machine or from hastily handwritten pages to the final draft. Her interest in and knowledge of the subject has also enabled her to become a helpful critic so that she has prevented many an egregious error.

A word about foreign language publications. Where I have used an English translation, I have cited the English title of the book and followed the English text, correcting it only on occasion as indicated in the footnotes. With the exception of certain publications whose Latin titles have become standard, if the title of a non-English work is given in the original language, the translation is my own.

Harold P. Nebelsick

Princeton,
August, 1984

INTRODUCTION

THE CIRCLES OF GOD

FROM the beginning humankind has engaged in a never-ceasing struggle to identify, cope with, and manipulate the powers and forces which have shaped and influenced the course of history and nature, the forces upon which life was, or was thought to be, dependent. The effort to identify or sway the powers which transcended life was in some measure an attempt to give life meaning, to achieve some mastery over it, or at least to reconcile oneself to fate.

For those of us "who live and move and have our being under the auspices of modern science" — to paraphrase the Apostle Paul according to Acts 17:28[3] — it is difficult indeed to appreciate the awe and reverence our pre-scientific ancestors had both for the forces of nature and for the power of God or the gods, as the case might have been, which ruled over them. Our progenitors were as convinced of the existence of God or the gods as they were of their own existence. They were equally certain that the divine powers directly intervened in the events of history and nature as well as in their personal lives. Depending upon their theologies, their destinies were thought to have been guided by providence or by the self-interested and capricious "will of the gods". Even in the West, as late as the sixteenth century, when one would have thought that Christian theology had effectively prevailed on the popular mind to understand that the world was sustained in contingent relationship to God who is father-like, faithful and benevolent, William Shakespeare (1564–1616) could continue to reflect the age-old fatalism in all its poignancy. In *King Lear* Gloucester in despair says to his old guide, "As flies to wanton boys, are we to the gods; they kill us for their sport".[4] Divine power and the powers of nature and society intermingled to determine one's fate.

Since it has always been and still is immensely difficult to differentiate God from nature and the power of God from the powers of nature, it should not surprise us that any attempt to trace the rise of science in relationship to theology will note mutual interaction between theological thought (thought about God) and natural scientific thought (thought about the natural world) from the beginning. Insofar as both theological thought, as expressed in varying enunciations of faith, and scientific thought, as worked out in different formulations of nature, are integral parts of the culture in which they arise, it is, of course, inevitable that they will impinge upon one another. Investigation shows, however, that rather than relation between the two disciplines being casual or incidental, they have, I shall argue, often intermingled and been mutually modifying.[5]

More than any other factor save perhaps the Christian faith itself, modern natural science which developed in conjunction with the Christian faith has made Western civilisation what it is. The fact that natural science and particularly physics were eventually to proclaim their absolute independence from the faith, and the theology by which faith is defined, in no way detracts from the primary interrelationship of the two "sciences". Rather, the eventual divorce simply indicates that the importance of those factors between theology and natural science, which were quite indispensable to the rise of modern science in the first place, was not recognised by those who inherited the results.

Beginning with ancient Greece where early science can be seen to have developed to its fullest, we find thought about God or the gods both intermingling with and exerting influence upon the thought about the world. The Greeks, of course, had inherited the rudiments of their scientific thought, specifically mathematics and astronomy, or "astrology" as it should properly be called (since it was the study of the stars for cultic purposes), from the Babylonians and perhaps from the Egyptians as well.

There seems little doubt that for the Babylonians and the

Egyptians interest in nature was religiously motivated. The material world was simply the medium through which the divine could be known, and worshipped or placated as the case might be. Though in the hands of the Greeks nature began to be objectified to the point that the rudiments of science could begin to develop, in Greece too religious presuppositions so dominated culture that science both arose within a religious milieu and continued to be affected by religious concepts throughout its history.

In Homeric Greece the "divine" and the "natural" were interwoven to the point that differentiation was all but impossible. What we would attribute to the results of "natural forces" for them was the "will of the gods". Fate or fortune was determined by Olympian powers whose own destinies were intermingled with earthly events.

However, with the Ionian philosophers at least, those who receive the credit for introducing the rudiments of science from ancient Babylon into somewhat less ancient Greece, a sufficient hiatus was developed between the "realm of the gods" and the world of nature so that nature could be seen as important enough and stable enough to begin to be examined for its own sake. Though we may regard the "atomic theory" of Leucippus and Democritus, for instance, as a "lucky guess" which is related to the particle theories of modern science by name only, the real importance of the effort to see nature as nature was not in its results. Rather the theory represents an early effort, perhaps the earliest, to understand nature in secular terms. It illustrates the fact that innovations in science, even those which are merely the result of thought rather than of experiment, come about only in an atmosphere which is relatively free of false and oppressive religious domination.

We, who are the beneficiaries of the humanising influences of the Renaissance which revived many of the positive values of Greek civilisation in late mediaeval Europe and helped to free European culture from some of its more oppressive religious components, are prone to think of ancient Greece as generally humanistic and secular. Nothing, however, could be further from the truth. The relative freedom from the influence of religion upon their "scientific thinking" which the Ionians enjoyed was short-lived.

For Pythagoras of Samos (c.582–c.507 B.C.) who is generally known as the greatest mathematician in ancient Greece and whose thought was foundational for the astronomy and philosophy of both Plato (c.427–c.347 B.C.) and Aristotle (384–322 B.C.) and thus for the kind of Greek philosophical thought that we in the West have learned to think most important, religion and science, mathematics and worship so entwined God, numbers, and forms that the components were basically indistinguishable. The heavenly circles described by the astronomical bodies, for instance, were not only manifestations of the divine, they were divine. To contemplate the heavens and calculate their ratios in numbers was both to know God and to worship him.

The fascinating but dangerous and eventually science-debilitating legacy was passed on to Plato and from him to Aristotle. It was Aristotle more than any other, when his philosophy was incorporated into theology by Thomas Aquinas (1225–74) in the thirteenth century, who was responsible for rekindling interest in science in the West. At the same time, Aristotle was also responsible for both the rigid thought structures and the ideas of nature's caprice which had to be thrown off before modern science could begin.

The Pythagorean divine heavenly circles defined for Plato godliness, reasonableness, and the soul of the universe in which humanity participated. The eternal heavens were the seat and reflection of perfection. The earth, by contrast, was the place of destruction and decay. The Circles of God thus became the basis of Greek astronomy. They were to remain the foundation of the study of the heavens even through Copernicus. Further, this principle of *circularity* and *regularity* of the heavenly bodies, in differentiation from the irregular, rectilinear motion of earthly ones was determinative for Plato's philosophy as well. In contrast to the *non-reality* of the

material world Plato stressed the *reality* of the transcendent. The realm of the idea was the realm of the soul
and the rational; that of the material was unreal and
irrational. Hence, the godly circles not only influenced
science but philosophical thought and its implicit religious ingredients as well. Some of these encompass
and shackle us still.

As said, it was the writings of Aristotle which, because of
their systematic ordering of plants and animals and their
attempt to explain natural phenomena in terms of physics,
gave impetus to the investigation of nature in the West in
the late Middle Ages. However, as far as astronomy was
concerned, Aristotle was as adamant in maintaining the
divine circles which inhibited science and in dividing the
ethereal *heavenly realm* from the *earthly material sphere* as
was his mentor, Plato.

It is true, of course, that Aristotle set up an ordered
cosmos in which he attempted to account for both the
heavenly and the earthly realms with admirable thoroughness. The fact that he was wrong on almost every count,
however, that in order to explain the inexplicable he
mingled physics with interventionary deities and made the
whole depend on *living and divine principles* rather than
upon natural processes, as Stanley Jaki has shown, did
more perhaps to prevent science from developing in
ancient Greece than any other single factor.[6] When
Aristotle's religiously-determined physics and metaphysics, along with his deductive logic, was amalgamated
with Christian theology by Thomas Aquinas at the end of
the Middle Ages, Aristotelian astronomy with its godlike
circles of the heavens received a second divine sanction and
continued even with Copernicus to prevent astronomy and
with it the rest of science from proper development. I say
"a second divine sanction" because, as already mentioned,
our usual idea that Greece was an open society without the
burden of any prescribed orthodoxy is far from true. Even
Socrates (c.469–399 B.C.) had accused the Ionians not of
false physics but of being atheists because they studied
things in themselves rather than trying to ascertain the

divine causes behind them. Since it was Plato who first prescribed the death penalty for unrepentant impiety, there was danger for science or at least for the scientists in Plutarch's report that Aristarchus, who a century after Plato had the temerity to set up the first heliocentric system, deserved to be accused not of false astronomy but of *impiety*![7]

However, though Socrates was forced to drink the hemlock by the elders of Athens for misleading its youth, no such fate, as far as we know, was meted out to any of the Greek "cosmologists". Such punishment was unfortunately enforced by the mediaeval Church which after conflating bad theology with bad astronomy moved against those who were so brazen as to defy its Aristotelian-inspired theology and cosmology. Accordingly Cecco d'Ascoli (1267–1327) and Giordano Bruno (1548–1600) were punished with the stake and Galileo Galilei (1564–1642) was beset with house arrest from 1633 to the end of his life.[8]

In ancient Greece, as the later Pythagoreans became more observant, they multiplied the heavenly circles and moved some off centre in order to try to account for the *apparent* irregular, i.e., non-circular, movement of the heavenly bodies. The more accurate observations became and the more sophisticated the mathematical calculations, the more intricate and complicated the system of divine circles was forced to become. A veritable wheel-on-wheel geocentric universe resulted as the irregular motion of the heavenly bodies was accounted for by placing the bodies on the edges of circles or spheres (the Greeks never differentiated between them) which were in turn centred on the edges of yet other circles or spheres. These were then centred on the circumferences of the main circles (deferents) drawn *approximately* concentric to the sphere of the earth. Intricate and ingenious movements were prescribed in order to "save the appearances", i.e., account for the apparent irregular movements of the planets in terms of regular and circular movement.

Insofar as mathematics, specifically geometry and trigonometry, could be used to calculate the ratios between the putative spheres to measure the distance from the earth, the moon, and the sun and to calculate the circumference of the circular earth, the Greeks performed brilliantly. Ptolemy (c.90–c.168 A.D.), who was an astronomer and geographer in addition to being a consummate mathematician, summed up Greek science with his *Syntaxis* which the Arabs named the *Almagest*. The work, which displays the genius of the Greek mathematical achievement as it applied to the most accurate astronomical observational data then available, explains the mathematics and the heavenly movements, gives the movements geometrical illustration, accompanies the illustrations with appropriate mathematical notations and furnishes the whole with tables of astronomical data. Though we now know that the *Almagest* was not entirely accurate, it was accurate enough to persuade the world of its authenticity. Hence its pattern of circles and the measurements and ratios it offered to explain their sizes, relationships and distances from one another were so persuasive that except for momentary doubts, the heavens were seen in accordance with the Ptolemaic patterns for the next 1400 years.

The doubts were first voiced by Christian cosmologists both on the basis of biblical cosmology and more seriously on the grounds of *creatio ex nihilo* (creation out of nothing). The heavenly circles of Greek cosmology were seen to be at variance with the biblical accounts wherein the world was sometimes alluded to as flat, sometimes square and sometimes having the form of a tabernacle, as well as sometimes round. In the light of *creatio ex nihilo*, the Greek concept of the *eternal nature* of the heavens began to be doubted. Water on earth was compared with the "waters above the firmament" in the Genesis narrative of creation. Fire on earth was compared with the fire of the heavenly bodies. In the sixth century the Christian Alexandrian Johannes Philoponos (c.490–c.566) looked through eyes focused by the biblical doctrine of creation and saw that the movements of the stars were something less than perfectly concentric and symmetrical. However, his vision was lost to a culture under the impact of Augustinian Neoplatonism which for the next thousand years was more interested in the self than in the world. As a result, even among the Christian cosmologists of the Middle Ages, wherever "authentic" cosmology arose largely on the basis of Pliny the Elder (c.23–79) or Boethius (c.480–524), the heavenly circles reasserted themselves.

The circles burst upon the scene anew and with consummate conviction when in the eleventh and twelfth centuries the Arabs brought first the writings of Aristotle and then the *Almagest* itself to the West. In the thirteenth century Thomas Aquinas built upon the Arab legacy and made Aristotle the foundation of his theology. With that, the circles, along with the whole geocentric cosmology which was supported by Aristotle's physics and metaphysics, became basic to both orthodox religion and orthodox astronomy. Although Thomas himself opposed Aristotle's doctrine of the eternity of the heavens because of the biblical doctrine of *creatio ex nihilo*, the heavenly circles remained. They were retained in the "scientific" writings of both Robert Grosseteste (c.1170–1253) and Roger Bacon (c.1214–c.1294) who otherwise challenged Aristotelian thought. In the late Middle Ages their survival was reinforced by the mystical Neoplatonism of Pseudo-Dionysius (fl. 6th cent. A.D.) who was cited again and again by Thomas and whose mystical cosmology was basic to the equally mystical conception of the world portrayed in both poetry and prose by Dante Alighieri (1265–1321). Nicholas of Cusa (c.1401–64) first used the circles to unify understanding of God, the heavens, and the earth and even imputed them to God himself so that the heavenly circles were held to represent nothing less than the perfection of divinity. The perfection, unity, and harmony of all things were just what Renaissance Hermeticism, that mystical mixture of Neoplatonism, Neopythagoreanism and pantheistic astrology disguised as Egyptian magic, was all about. The sun, representing God, was placed in the centre of the world. It was "the lantern", "the king on his central throne" ruling the planets which circle around the heavens and through which it brings forth generation on earth, rules its history, and influences the souls of humankind.

And then came Nicolaus Copernicus (1473–1543), a mathematical genius. Copernicus first studied mathematics at Cracow. He continued his studies in astronomy in Bologna in the effervescent atmosphere of Neoplatonic and Neopythagorean Renaissance Italy. Copernicus was familiar enough with Hermeticism to use its terminology to explain the position of the sun in the centre of the world. He was so convinced by the necessity of the harmony of the form and the regularity of the motion of the heavens that his objections to the Ptolemaic system stemmed largely from its deficiency in this respect. At the same time he remained so certain of the validity of the Renaissance quest for the truth in antiquity that he defended the Ptolemaic measurements even while he modified them and took Aristotelian physics into his own "heliocentric" system as far as the system would allow.

I have set "heliocentric" off with quotation marks because, in spite of the fact that Copernicus intended and even claimed to put the sun in the centre of the world — "in the centre of all rests the sun"[9] — he actually placed the sun off centre. Thus, the heliocentric diagram of concentric circles with which Copernicus illustrated his own system actually portrays the heliocentric system of Aristarchus of Samos rather than his own scheme.[10] In order to maintain the godlike circles, explain the apparent irregularities of planetary motion in terms of regularity, and achieve a greater harmony than that of Ptolemy, Copernicus simply imposed Ptolemy's epicycles upon Aristarchus' circular deferents and made the deferents themselves into eccentrics. The scheme, genial as it was and aesthetically pleasing as it seemed at first glance, failed simply because Copernicus, like the Greeks, insisted that the harmony of circularity and regular motion be maintained at all costs. The result was a *tour de force* of geometrical and mathematical elegance which, unfortunately, was at least as complicated, was less accurate, and in its own time was less convincing, than the Ptolemaic system which it sought to replace.

It was not until Johannes Kepler (1571–1630) saved the Copernican heliocentrism from oblivion by proving its basic tenet — "that the heavens move in eternal and perfect circles" — quite wrong that the "heliocentric" system proved tenable. In spite of its failure, however, the Copernican hypothesis is an excellent illustration of how science is actually done. Hypotheses are often advanced for wrong reasons. They may be supported by false evidence. Yet, if they are at least partially true, they may become the basis for further scientific development in spite of their inadequacies.

Thus in a backhanded sort of way the *Circles of God*, false as they were, had a positive effect upon science. Because the beauty, harmony and regularity they were thought to display represented eternity and even divinity itself, they enticed the human mind to contemplate the heavens. Out of such contemplation the rudiments of science arose. However, because the circles were false and the "scientists" continued to insist that they were true, in the end they had a debilitating influence on astronomy in particular and on science in general. The Copernican theory was "saved" only when Kepler proved it false by squashing its circles into the ellipses which, according to our present knowledge, represent the true shape of the orbits of the planets around the sun.

NOTES

1. Cf. T. F. Torrance, *Reality and Evangelical Theology* (Philadelphia: Westminster, 1982), pp. 140ff. and T. F. Torrance, *Theological Science* (London: Oxford, 1969), pp. 47f., 131, 133, 206f., 215, for an explanation of "epistemological inversion" in relationship to theological thinking.
2. Albert Einstein, *Out of My Later Years* (New York: Philosophical Library, 1950), p. 59.
3. "Sometimes attributed to Epimenides", *The Oxford Annotated Bible*, Revised Standard Version (New York: Oxford University, 1962).

4. William Shakespeare, *King Lear*, Act IV, Scene 1.

5. Cf. H. P. Nebelsick, *Theology and Science in Mutual Modification* (Belfast: Christian Journals, New York, Oxford University Press 1981) for an introduction to the subject.

6. Cf. Stanley Jaki, *The Relevance of Physics* (Chicago: University of Chicago, 1970), pp. 412ff. for a penetrating discussion of "Physics and Theology".

7. Plutarch, *De Facie Quae in Orbe Lunae Apparet (The Face on the Moon, Plutarch's Moralia*, Vol. XII, Loeb Classical Library (London: Heinemann, 1957), 6.923 A. Cf. Plato, *Laws, The Dialogues of Plato*, trans. Benjamin Jowett, 4 vols. (New York: Scribner, 1874), Book X, 907–908.

8. Cecco d'Ascoli, popular name for Francesco degli Stabili, was Professor of Astrology in Bologna and exposed his "heretical" views when he directed his vernacular poem, "L'Acerba", against Dante's astrological theories; Bruno mixed Copernican cosmology with a hermetic brand of pantheism and was most likely executed because of his heretical theology which included Copernicanism as a basic tenet rather than for his heretical cosmology as such; Galileo was accused because he both held and taught the Copernican theory as truth. The proposition that "the sun was immovable in the centre of the world and earth revolved around it" was formally declared to be heretical only in 1616 at the time of Galileo's first inquest. As a consequence Copernicus' *De Revolutionibus* was placed on the *Index Librorum Prohibitorum (The Index of Forbidden Books)*.

9. Nicolaus Copernicus, *On the Revolution of the Heavenly Spheres*, Great Books of the Western World, Vol. 16 (Chicago: *Encyclopaedia Britannica*, 1952), Book I.10, p. 526.

10. *Ibid.*

CHAPTER 1

GREEK THEOLOGY AND
GREEK SCIENCE

THERE would seem to be an overwhelming agreement
that of the ancient cultures, it was among the Greeks
that learning, philosophy and science, as then understood,
reached their pinnacle. However, the catalogue of Babylonian astronomical achievements alone, which preceded
the Greek scientific development and to which we will refer
inter alia in the following pages, indicates that the Greeks
were not as innovative as once was thought. In spite of the
fact that we possess no exact records of the transmission of
Babylonian "science" to the Greeks, it is safe to conjecture
that a good deal of the early Greek knowledge of astronomy
and mathematics initially came from the Babylonians,
whose achievements in those fields have been traced as far
back as the second millennium B.C. Much of that "science"
or at least the impetus from it eventually found its way to
Greece. Before it arrived, however, its reception was
prepared by Greek theological ideas.

Homeric Divinities and Natural Forces

Already the myths of Homer (fl. 9th cent. B.C.) reflect an
outlook in which nature is regarded both as an essential
whole and as differentiated into particular forces represented by different divinities. This is the precedent for
Aristotle's foredoomed identification of the divine and the
natural. Nature as a whole was understood as having
emanated from the great god and as represented by him.
Each of the manifestations of nature, however, was
considered the preserve of a different deity. Zeus, the
supreme deity, and the god of order, was flanked by Hera,

his wife. Hera, queen of the gods, was the protector of women and marriage, while Aphrodite, goddess of sexual love and beauty, was primarily responsible for male-female relationships. Leto was the goddess of fertility. Apollo, who stands next to Zeus, was initially the averter of evil. Later he was identified with Helios, the sun god. Artemis, Apollo's twin sister, was the goddess of the moon, wild animals, and hunting. Hermes was the messenger god, the god of commerce, eloquence, and cunning. More importantly for our thesis, he was the god of science. Almost as important was Hephaestus, the son of Zeus and Hera. As the god of fire and the forge he was allied with technology. Athena, too, the goddess of wisdom and skills, had to do with technical prowess as did Ares who, with Athena, was responsible for warfare. Related to them was Poseidon, the god of the sea and of horses, who displayed the power of both nature and beast.

Homer's depiction of the gods and goddesses as presiding and ruling over the particular forces for which they were responsible presents a fate-filled world in which the gods of the pantheon struggled to enforce their own particular wills upon the hapless creatures of earth. Reality was thus determined by the gods and life on earth was a matter of fortune or disaster depending upon the powers the gods exercised in relation to the "natural forces" to which persons and nations were subject. In the *Iliad*, for instance, the struggle of the gods and goddesses put both Greeks and Trojans at the mercy of supermundane but designated forces. Courageous and cunning as was Ulysses in the *Odyssey*, his destiny was finally determined by Athena's magic. This divine determination of reality continued to be emphasised in Greek dramas in which fame and fortune as well as destruction and death were finally controlled by one *deus ex machina* (god of the machine) or other. The divinity in question would emerge from the scenery or by cleverly conceived rope and pulley cranes be lowered to the stage. The god of the machine would rescue the hero, defeat the adversary, or throw the situation into chaos depending upon the "will of the gods".

Seen from our point of view, the gods and goddesses were the personifications of nature's fields of force. As understood from the Greek perspective, however, the drama was simply the earthly and hence less important manifestation of the eternal struggle of divine powers to whom all reality was subject. The plays, which attempted to instill understanding and thus effect a reconciliation with fate, were based upon the sincere conviction that the destiny of people and nations was subject to powers which were present, potent, mysterious and largely unpredictable. They were "god-like" and recognition of them, the ability to call them by name, helped both to explain them and to reconcile oneself with them. In a certain sense, at least, familiarity also served to tame them.

This same attempt to classify the powers of nature by mythically identifying them would seem to be the point of Hesiod's (fl. 8th cent. B.C.) systematisation of Greek mythology, his *Theogony*. Hesiod began his developmental scheme by first considering the origin of the universe (*cosmogony*). He then recounted the dynasties of Zeus and Cronos (*theogony* proper). Finally he recorded the lists of women who were married to gods of one type or another (*heroögony*). The whole arrangement was an effort both to show the origin of existence and to explain that life's inexorable arrangements were built into the nature of things. Ontology determined reality and if there was no escaping its inevitable consequences, one could at least look fate in the eye and accept its results.

Eduard Zeller's (1814–1908) exhaustive study of the development of Greek thought reinforces the above thesis by describing the general faith of the Greeks portrayed by the poems of Homer and Hesiod as a religion of nature through which the unseen powers and laws of nature first come to consciousness. Zeller goes on, however, to indicate that, though in its early stages Greek religion and Greek philosophical (including "scientific") thought were quite confused, the religious situation was fluid enough to allow the beginnings of scientific thought to develop.[1]

Pre-Socratic "Science"

The amalgamation of Greek religion and Greek thought about nature in the eighth and seventh centuries B.C. begins to sort itself out with the pre-Socratic philosophers who came upon the scene in the sixth century B.C. By then interest in nature *as nature* had grown to the point that there was a sufficient degree of a separation between "divine forces" and "natural phenomena" to allow the latter to be considered with some measure of independence from the former. Thus, even though the first problem Greek science tried to solve, that of *unity* and *diversity*, was based directly on theology (as Zeus, the all-powerful one, gave reality its *unity*, so the inclusion of the lesser deities, whose power stretched out to the uttermost regions of the world, accounted for the *diversity* of reality) among the pre-Socratics, theology was slowly being separated from the physical world and put into the realm of metaphysics. The inexorable will of the gods was still present ; it was not so oppressive, however, as to stifle speculation and novelty.

Zeller certainly overstates his case, especially with regard to the Pythagoreans, when he insists that with the Ionians, the Pythagoreans and the Eleatics there was enough of a divergence between philosophical and religious teachings so that, until Anaxagoras (c.500–428 B.C.), who marks the transition from pre-Socratic to Socratic philosophy, religion is moved either totally into the background or plays only a minor role in philosophical ("scientific") thought.[2] Nevertheless it is true that for a time the perfidious activity of the gods was ignored enough so that thought could direct itself to nature as such. Nature while still held to under divine control was thus freed from the direct influence of capricious intervening deities to the degree that allowed the pre-Socratic "scientists" (natural philosophers) to begin to see nature as having substantiality in itself rather than as being simply a secondary manifestation of the gods. Nature as nature, freed from whimsical control, could then be understood as having an identity of its own and with that natural science, at least in a preliminary way, could begin to develop.

The oldest Greek philosophers were in fact realists. To quote Zeller:

> The perception of nature [*Naturanschauung*] is the place from which the oldest philosophy begins. Even when supersensual principles are advanced, it must be realized that it is the consideration of that which is sensibly given, not the observation of the spiritual life, that led to them.[3]

That being the case, it was when the Greek mind turned from the forces of nature to the "stuff" of it, from the "causes" of events to the material of which nature was composed, that the Greeks may be said to have taken their first steps in the direction of science. The transition from the poets, Homer and Hesiod, to the sixth-century "Ionian philosophers" — Thales, Anaximander, and Anaximenes — was characterised by a shift from the "personal" (or perhaps the "personified") to concentration on the "corporeal", as Zeller expresses it, or what Stanley Jaki refers to as "the impersonal world of matter, motion and space".[4] Although the Ionians still saw reality as a struggle of opposing entities, the entities were nevertheless "of nature" and the beginnings of science arose in the attempt to identify them.

For Thales (c.624–c.548 B.C.) the basic material stuff was *water*. For Anaximander (c.611–c.547 B.C.) it was the *apeiron*, the "non-limited" which was the basic substance of the four elements. The elements in turn were "pairs of opposites, hot-cold, wet-dry".[5] For Anaximenes (c.550–c.480 B.C.), who followed Anaximander, everything was composed of *air*. Different densities determined *fire*, *water*, and *earth* in turn.[6]

More important for the eventual development of science, which by nature seeks the unity of simplest forms in an orderly universe, was the thought of Anaxagoras. Anaxagoras, who by the way is credited with making

Athens the seat of philosophy, and with being the teacher of Pericles (495–429 B.C.), was eventually charged with impiety and was exiled because he denied the deity of the heavenly bodies.[7] Hence his case is an illustration of the continuing influence of religion even among the Ionians. Nevertheless, his scientific thought, which both secularised the heavens and described reality as composed of an aggregation of distinct, indestructible units or "seeds", each with its own unique quality, was to point the way to the future. The units combined and separated to compose the different materials of the world under the influence of the universal mind. Permanence took precedence over change. And it was "the conviction that in the change of appearances there must be something permanent on which the change takes place", as Werner Heisenberg (1901–76) rightly acknowledged, which "leads to the doctrine of a basic material stuff".[8]

Although this conceptuality was definitely more favourable to the development of science than that which obtained under the intervention of capricious deities, it also had its drawbacks. As Thomas F. Torrance has shown, because the Ionians conceived of the cosmos as being self-subsistent, they were caught in an "ineluctable necessity" which meant that science had to be done not by examining nature but by an *a priori* rational deductive process.[9] This is nowhere better illustrated than in the case of the "atomists" Leucippus (fl. c.489 B.C.) and his pupil Democritus (c.460–c.357 B.C.) who converted Anaxagoras' "units" or "seeds" into the invisible and indestructible "atoms" which were basic to all reality and formed compounds purely on the basis of their own inner necessity. The atoms were considered to be colourless, odourless and tasteless, of the same matter and possessing no characteristics whatever except difference in size, weight, and shape. The totality of nature was supposed to be composed of different arrangements and movements of atoms and, most important, as far as showing how far the Ionian philosophers had left the Homeric deities behind, the compositions came about *without the necessity of any*

divine intervention whatever. Atoms which were lighter
formed the heavenly bodies. Heavier atoms formed the
earth. The new science could be understood in analogy to
the older art.

> In something of the same way that tragedy and
> comedy can be written down with the same letters of
> the alphabet, so it is possible that very different kinds
> of occurrences can come about in the world through
> the same atoms insofar as they take on different
> arrangements and follow different movements.[10]

Thus, within the space of three generations, which in
the course of history is an incredibly short length of time,
the pre-Socratic realists had moved the conceptuality of the
world from that resembling a theatre, where the acts of
creation and destruction were played by capricious deities
in the guise of natural forces, to an understanding of reality
as consisting of a basic material stuff. The stuff was divided
into atoms and these formed different aspects of nature
according to the aggregates of material that resulted when
the atoms came together under their own power. By
replacing erratic control of the deities over nature with
inexorable necessity in nature itself, the pre-Socratics no
doubt overemphasised the point. Theirs was a materialistic
world which, like that of Pierre Laplace (1749–1827) some
2500 years later, was so predictable that it tended to be
rigidly mechanistic.

Nevertheless, the Ionian attempt to understand the
material world as being independent of divine forces was a
precedent for the way experimental science was eventually
to develop. They were far advanced compared to the more
celebrated philosophers who were to succeed them.
Because the Ionians refused to consider the science-
debilitating concept of the constant intervention of the
gods in the construction of material reality, Socrates was
to condemn them as "atheists". Aristotle, Socrates' philosopher "grandson", spoke in the same vein when he
reprimanded the Ionians for thinking that there was only

one permanent element in the universe, a basic material stuff which was conserved in every change with nothing being generated or lost in the process.[11] The idea, which we may view as a precedent for the concept of the conservation of energy, was too "materialistic" for Aristotle for whom the material was but an accident of divine first and final causes by which reality was defined.

Forward-looking as were their concepts, the inability of the Ionians to develop a concept of the material forces which served to attract their atoms into compounds or to hold them together, allowed the pre-Ionian idea of the permanence of the divine over and within the material realm to reassert itself. Hence four centuries after Aristotle, Plutarch (A.D. c.46–c.120) could accurately describe the Greeks as having moved from understanding the world as made up of the manifestations of personified forces to the concept of reality as consisting of a random assortment of atoms. He thus identified that disastrous dichotomy which was a part of Greek thought from the beginning. When systematised by Plato and Aristotle, this bifurcation of reality resulted in the dualism between the ideal and the natural, the form and the content, which has continued to plague hellenistically based thought ever since. For the poets, according to Plutarch, it was "'Zeus the beginning, Zeus in the midst, and from Zeus comes all being'".[12] Plutarch went on to point out that the younger generation of physicists and philosophers, or the natural philosophers, reverse the procedure "and ascribe everything to bodies and their behaviour, to clashes, transmutations and combinations". Both parties, he concluded, are deficient in their reasoning, "the one ignores or omits the intermediary and the agent, the other the source and the means".[13]

Although Plutarch's rebuke of the atomists' materialism is to be taken seriously, if, as Zeller reminds us, we remember that for the Greeks the gods were parts and powers of the world, not transcendent over it,[14] Plutarch's reference to non-material reality cannot really be thought of as a reference to God who is independent of nature.

Rather, the "God" to whom Plutarch refers is that "divinity" within and behind reality in which reality is based and coheres. Hence Plutarch was contrasting the "materialism" of the Ionians to the *numbers* and *shapes* of the Pythagoreans, the *ideas* of Plato or the *forms* and *causes* of Aristotle. Thus, even in the wane of the philosophical age of Greece, Plutarch too continued to be caught in the ideal-material dualism which was endemic to Greek thought from the beginning.

Pythagorean Cultic Cosmology

As said at the outset of this chapter, impressive as Greek science eventually became, it would be quite wrong to think of it as having developed completely on its own. Though evidence is scarce, there would seem to be enough coincidence between the cosmology and mathematics of the early seventh and sixth century B.C. "scientists" and that of the Babylonians to indicate a rather high degree of dependence at least in the initial stages of Greek "science".

Thales of Miletus, mentioned above as one of the earliest of the Ionian "philosopher-scientists", is thought to have learned both the rudiments of mathematics and his knowledge of the heavens from the Babylonians prior to his having introduced both algebra and a pre-Euclidean geometry to Greece. An associate of Thales, Anaximander, like the Babylonians, was aware that the earth was a sphere. Likewise, Pythagoras of Samos, that most renowned of Greek mathematicians, is thought to have learned the basis of his astronomy from his "travels" which took him outside of Greece to "the East" and perhaps to Egypt as well.[15] Pythagoras' cosmology included the identification of the morning and evening stars, the recognition of the obliquity of the ecliptic and, most important perhaps, the supposition that the earth was a sphere freely floating in space. All of this was known to the Babylonians and Egyptians prior to his time.

Beginning with Pythagoras who was an Ionian, but established his community at Croton in the south of Italy, the development of science and cosmology became largely a Greek, or more accurately, an Hellenistic programme. In direct contrast to the earlier Ionians who, as said, were able to concentrate on the material world because they had freed their "scientific thought", at least to a certain degree, from their religious beliefs, Pythagoreanism was a "religion" before it was a "science" and it continued its religious interests through its science. Here, too, Pythagoras may well have followed the Babylonians whose cosmology and mathematics were deeply rooted in their religion and practised by a designated priesthood. The near universal practice of contemplating the heavens, which were thought to control human destiny, was refined by the Babylonians to the place where the rising and setting of the stars, the periodicities of the planets and the prediction of solar and lunar eclipses were known to be matters of routine. As a direct result a highly accurate calendar based upon the movement of the moon and the sun was constructed as early as the reign of Hammurabi in 1700 B.C.

Such knowledge, of course, gave the Babylonian priest-scientists tremendous power. To be able to "divine the stars" was to hold sway over the heavens and human affairs. To know the heavenly movements was not only to be able to set aside holy days in their proper sequence throughout the year but to discern the times and the seasons was to have power over agriculture. To be able to predict the periodicities of the planets was both to know the ways of the divine heavens and apparently to direct them. And, most awe-inspiring, to be able to foresee the eclipses of the moon and especially the sun was to be in league with the gods and cause terror at the darkening of the sky and, after fervent prayer and sacrifice, to be the channel through whom grace and mercy were again displayed even as the moon or sun again showed their benevolent faces when the eclipses had passed.

Pythagorean cultic practices eventually led to a body of data about the world which, when separated off from religion, formed much of the foundation for Greek mathematics and cosmology. Originally, however, the Pythagorean interest in the heavens and the movement of the stars, like that of the Babylonians, was directed primarily to discovering the divine principle displayed by the phenomena observed. That which was real and important was not what was seen. Rather, reality, whether of the heavens or of the earth, consisted of an unseen essence which showed itself in the manifestations of nature. For the Pythagoreans the divine essence, the essence which at one and the same time constituted the *real* and was the basis of the content of the secret knowledge of the Pythagorean cult, was *number*. As number was the *reality* of reality, so it united the whole of existence into a mystical unity.

Number united the heavenly bodies with one another and joined these with the earth and its elements. Number was the essence of medicine and music, the former to cure the body, the latter to cure the soul. It was the substance of both unity and diversity. The cultic quest driven forward by the search for the secrets of the inherent diversity and harmony of the whole of reality necessarily united God, the soul and nature into a single whole. When nature began to be seen as a stable correlate to the numbers programme, rudimentary science arose. It arose, however, as an accident, as a side effect of the quest for the unities and disunities revealed in the hidden numbers and ratios by which God, nature and the self were correlated. To know nature and the numbers behind its manifestations was to know God. "Science" was for the sake of religion.

The Pythagoreans practised their cult by contemplating the heavens. They attempted to probe behind the movements of the heavenly bodies and the relations between them because these were the manifest movements of divinity which reached into the self. To uncover the secrets of the stars was to know the mysteries of one's own existence. To be able to trace the heavenly movements was to know the universe in which all souls were caught up and with which they could identify insofar as they had knowledge of it. To investigate the heavens, therefore, was to participate in cultic cosmology. It was to contemplate and be absorbed into the highest reality, the reality of the divine, which showed itself in the heavenly harmonies and revealed itself in appropriate number-ratios and shapes.

To study the stars, then, was for the Pythagoreans to reach into the soul of the universe and to aspire to the heart of God. To see the mystic patterns and hear reflected there the music hummed by the heavenly bodies — the moon, sun, and planets — which were tuned according to the intervals between them, was to experience unity and be in harmony with the whole of reality.

To formulate the ratios of the heavenly movements by the use of number was to encode divinity itself. By number, the heavenly mysteries were reduced to terms of human understanding and thus the heavens were brought to earth. In this way the formulas which reflected the relationships of the heavenly bodies, and which in the first instance comprised the content of the cultic mysteries, were at the same time references to universal reality and could be understood outside the cult. The doctrines of faith that referred to the "secrets of the universe" thus slowly became public property. Although the novices of the cult were sworn to strictest secrecy about the interrelation-ships between the numbers themselves and the initiates were allowed to divulge those dogmas only with utmost perspicacity, those ratios which expressed the relative positions of the heavenly bodies began to be understood as having astronomical meaning rather than simply cultic significance.

In that the celestial circles could be plotted, quantified and known with some degree of exactitude, their ratios could be calculated. Since the heavens not only came around, they came around again and again at set times, with set intervals and with "exact" precision, their patterns could be designated mathematically. Thus, when the Pythagoreans charted the stars by number, their religion flowed into mathematics and the stage was set for the beginnings of what we now take to be authentic astronomy.

The earth was a spherical body floating in space and around it, in orbits set at regular intervals, floated the moon, the sun, and the five planets. This "kosmos", a word which Pythagoras is thought to have invented and which the later Pythagoreans designated as "the realm of regulated motion", was surrounded by the sphere of the stars.[16] According to Plato's report, the intervals between the orbits of the heavenly bodies were designated with numbers selected from the two geometrical progressions — 2, 3, 4, 8 and 1, 3, 9, 27 — respectively. The moon was assigned the number 1; the sun, 2; Venus, 3; Mercury, 4; Mars, 8; Jupiter, 9; and Saturn, 27.[17] The series 1, 2, 3, 4, 8, 9, 27 seemed both a reasonable enough reflection of the distances of the different bodies from earth and equally important, if not more so, the series satisfied the demand that the numerical intervals between the heavenly bodies reflect the kind of mathematical harmony which the ratios represented. Number thus prescribed reality.

As the heavenly movements reflected the harmony of numbers, so the intervals between the bodies produced appropriate tones. According to the report of Pliny the Elder (c. A.D. 23–79) regarding Pythagorean cosmology, the tones assigned to the earth-moon interval was a whole tone; to moon-Mercury, a semitone; to Mercury-Venus, a semitone; to Venus-sun, a tone and a half; to sun-Mars, a tone; to Mars-Jupiter, half a tone; to Jupiter-Saturn, half a tone; and to Saturn-the zodiac [fixed stars], a tone and a half. Not surprisingly as the numbers assigned to the celestial bodies corresponded to known progressions, so the tones corresponded to the Pythagorean scale: C, D, Eb, E, G, A, Bb, B, D.[18] Numbers and music, themselves divine, transferred the divinity of the heavens to earth where the souls, caught up in cultic contemplation, became convinced that they too were being absorbed into divinity itself.

With Plato the correlation between numbers and the motions of the divine heavens became the basis for rationality. Plato, whose writings reveal so much a debt to the Pythagoreans that, as far as mathematics and cos-

mology are concerned, it may be quite legitimate to say,
"No Pythagoras, no Plato", could testify that the "never-
ceasing and rational life" shown by the circularity of the
heavenly motions was a creation and reflection of divinity
itself.[19] Thus it is hardly surprising to note that Plato is at
one with the Pythagoreans in pointing out the efficacy of
the study of the stars. To study the heavens was to
contemplate "the principles which are prior to these
[which] God only knows, and he of men whom God
loves".[20] The aim of the exercise was not only to become
holy, it was to become wise as well. To be absorbed in this
contemplation was to be a lover of wisdom (a *philosophos*),
"a philosopher", a term which the Pythagoreans introduced into the language.

Thus, as we will elucidate more fully below in the
discussion of Greek mathematics, important as numbers
eventually became for science because of the influence of
the Pythagoreans, for the early Pythagoreans at least,
numbers were not primarily *counters* as they are for us.
Rather than being the means of calculating the relationships between the things of reality, *they were reality*.
Numbers were the form of the secret divine principles of
which reality was made and which the appearances of
reality only reflected. Geometric forms and mathematical
formulas were manifestations of God and were seen in the
world as the pattern behind things and the proportion
between them. Numbers were *being*. The triangle was the
basic form and space was a series of figures made up of
triangular planes. The ratios of the heavens and the earthly
elements re-presented different geometric configurations.
The structures of the universe, even those of the earthly
realm, were numbers and/or geometric forms in disguise.

In direct contrast to the "materialism" of Thales,
Anaximander and Anaxagoras, who in setting religion
aside were able to think about the material substance of
nature, the Pythagorean interest in the basic elements —
earth, water, fire, and air — was not primarily to identify
them as the non-reducible essences of the material world.
Rather, they were but the corporeal representations of the

essential forms of which the whole of reality was constructed. They were, we may say, "number-substances".
The cube was represented by *earth*, the icosahedron by
water, the octahedron by *air*, and the tetrahedron by
fire.[21]

So thoroughgoing was the Pythagoreans' passion with
numbers that, as indicated, for them even medicine and
music were matters of numerology. Poisons which, if taken
in large doses, were certain to be fatal, were, if mixed and
administered according to proportional prescriptions,
proper purgatives for ailing bodies. Earthly music, the
sounds of which were produced by the vibrations of a
plucked string of a certain length — the longer the string,
the slower the vibration and the lower the tone; the shorter
the string, the faster the vibration and the higher the tone
— was a matter of interrelated number ratios. Tones which
could be produced on earth were hummed by the heavenly
bodies as they moved in their eternal orbits. Thus as the
Psalmist could proclaim, "The heavens reflect the glory of
God and the earth is his handiwork", the Pythagoreans
could declare that the reflection was made through number
and resounded in heavenly melodies.

At first glance at least, it would seem that Pythagorean
cultic cosmology was so shot through with religious
presuppositions that it would be of little use in the
development of an accurate understanding of the nature of
either the heavens or the earth. And yet, the fact that both
mathematics and music connected the heavens with the
earth eventually led to proportional comparison between
the two spheres. Thus mathematics could be used for
quantification and the heavenly distances compared with
earthly measurements. Although it was no doubt religious
fervour rather than interest in the heavenly bodies as such
which was the primary cause of the heavenward gaze of
the Pythagoreans, when the objects of the heavens and
the numbers assigned to them gained an independence of
their own, something of science began to germinate and
eventually to grow out of the cult. In the process of
contemplating the heavens in order to learn their eternal

secrets for the benefit of faith, the Pythagoreans also acquired information about the heavenly bodies and their motions which, to a certain degree of approximation, reflected the actualities of the universe.

Anaximenes set the stage for Greek cosmology in general by explaining stellar motion on the basis of the stars being affixed to the surface of a crystal hemisphere which, like a "hat turning round the head", made a daily rotation above the flat earth.[22] Though the concept of the rotating heavens was later to become a dogma of Greek cosmology, Philolaus (fl. c.470 B.C.), a pupil of Pythagoras, continued to reflect the teaching of his master by insisting not only that the earth floated in space, as Pythagoras had taught, but that as it floated it revolved in a circle once each day and night around a central fire. The fire was considered to be the "hearth of the universe" or, as Aristotle reports, "the Watch-tower of Zeus".[23]

The central fire was thought to lie off the side of the earth and the earth was thought to move around it at a close distance. In a similar way in which we now know the moon moves around the earth, Philolaus believed that the side of the earth on which Greece was located always pointed away from the fire. Since it was the earth that circled the fire, like someone riding a bicycle around a tight circular track at great speed to whom the rest of the landscape seems to turn around, so from the point of view of one standing on the earth opposite the central fire, the whole heaven appeared to turn once daily from east to west in a direction opposite to that of the moving earth. When combined with the observation that the sun and the moon and the other heavenly bodies arose and set once in the course of a day and a night, the arrangement offered the advantage that all heavenly motion occurred in the same direction. The scheme allowed the Pythagoreans of the fifth century B.C. to identify the sun, the moon, and the planets as bodies that made their way through the heavens in circular paths and with regular periodicities. They calculated that the moon took $29\frac{1}{2}$ days to travel around the central fire. Above it the sun took a year to complete its orbit through the zodiac.

The periodicities of the planets (the wandering stars) were apparently still considered too erratic for exact notation, however.

According to Aristotle, some of the Pythagoreans at least postulated another planet, a counter-earth (*antichthon*) which was variously supposed to have protected the earth from the central fire or perhaps to have balanced it. As Aristotle also reports, however, the *antichthon* may simply have been a mathematical convenience because, as he said, when the Pythagoreans "find a gap in the numerical ratio of things, they fill them up in order to complete the system". Aristotle went on to explain that since ten was a perfect number comprising the whole nature of numbers, they maintain that there must be ten bodies moving in the universe and if only nine are visible, they make up the *antichthon*, the tenth.[24]

At any rate, the evidence would seem to indicate that, in addition to the posited *antichthon* which Philolaus may well have created to complete the Pythagorean number system, the Pythagorean cosmology, which became basic for all future Greek astronomy, comprised nine bodies or spheres. These were the earth, the moon, the sun, the five planets, and the sphere of the fixed stars.[25]

The religious or metaphysical emphases, which characterised the Pythagorean study of the heavens and gave rise to a bifurcation in their thought between the real ethereal realm and the less than real material realm, were passed on from the Pythagoreans to Plato and from him to Aristotle. There the battle between the speculation of the mind and the observation of the eye continued. As far as Plato was concerned, those who thought sight was the pathway to the deepest insight were naïve in the extreme — even "bird-brained" perhaps, for "the race of birds was created out of innocent light-minded men who, although their thoughts were directed toward heaven, imagined, in their simplicity, that the clearest demonstration of the things above was to be obtained by sight".[26]

Platonic Ethereality

In the light of Pythagorean thought, it is no coincidence that when Plato displayed his "scientific ideas", which were apparently not worthy of Socrates or at any rate were so completely out of character with Socrates' interests, he turned the dialogue over to Timaeus, the Pythagorean. Most of Plato's ideas about astronomy came from the Pythagoreans in the first place. Like them he was concerned to stress the spherical notion of the world as well as the division of the universe into different realms. The divine heavens were ungenerated, eternal, immutable and characterised by circular motion. The material, generated world consisted of the elements of fire, water, earth, and air which God fashioned by form and order. It was subject to rectilinear motion, measurable by rectilinear figures composed of triangles and prone to decay. Hence, for Plato, as initially for Pythagoras and his followers, interest in the heavenly sphere was in their motion which revealed the characteristics of "the soul of the world".[27]

> Now when the creator had framed the soul according to his will, he formed within her the corporeal universe, and brought the two together, and united them centre to centre. The soul, interfused everywhere from the centre to the circumference of heaven, of which also she is the external development, herself turning in herself, began a divine beginning of never-ceasing and rational life, enduring throughout all time.[28]

Thus, and this was of the utmost importance for Plato and his impact on astronomy, the heavenly bodies themselves were held to be reflective of the soul, of reason, of harmony, and of reality.

> The body of heaven is visible, but the soul invisible, and partakes of reason and harmony, and being made

by the best of intelligible and everlasting beings, is the best of things created.[29]

The soul, then, functions within the perfect circularity of the movements of the heavenly bodies themselves. Rationality and knowledge depended upon the movement of "the other" (Plato's designation of the sublunar region) imitating "the same" (his name for the immutable heavenly sphere). Reason spanned both realms.

> And when reason, which works with equal truth both in the circle of the other and of the same, — in the sphere of the self-moved in voiceless silence moving, — when reason, I say, is in the neighbourhood of sense, and the circle of the other also moving truly imparts the intimations of sense to the whole soul, then arise fixed and true opinions and beliefs. But when reason is in the sphere of the rational, and the circle of the same moving smoothly indicates this, then intelligence and knowledge are of necessity perfected.[30]

And woe be to those who don't believe it for, ". . . if anyone affirms that in which these are found to be other than the soul, he will say the very opposite of the truth".[31]

The stars, then, were not cosmic bodies of earthly stuff as they were for the impious Anaxagoras, but for Plato and those influenced by him — the Aristotelians and the Neoplatonists of various kinds who propagated their beliefs right up through the Middle Ages — they were of the stuff of divinity. In his cosmogony Plato explains that the fact that the heavens were divine was the result of creation itself. The heavens were created first — they were the "first species", "the heavenly race of the gods", the heavenly bodies or "the divine".

> Of the divine, he made the greater part out of fire [i.e., the stars], that they might be the brightest and fairest to the sight, and he made them after the likeness of the

universe in the form of a circle, and gave them to know
and follow the best, distributing them over the whole
circumference of the heaven, which was to be a true
cosmos or glory spangled with them.[32]

When he created time which is as eternal as the heavens,
the creator created

> . . . the sun and the moon and five other stars, which
> are called the planets, to distinguish and preserve the
> numbers of time, and when God made the bodies of
> these several stars he gave them orbits in the circle of
> the other. There were seven orbits, as the stars were
> seven: first, there was the moon in the orbit nearest the
> earth, and then the sun in the next nearest orbit
> beyond the earth, and the morning star [Venus] and
> then the star sacred to Hermes [Mercury], which
> revolve in their orbits as swiftly as the sun . . .[33]

Plato attributed his failure to designate the orbits of the
planets to their troublesome nature. However complicated
the orbits of the "wanderers" might be, Plato was
convinced that their bodies were fastened by vital chains
and that they had come into being as *living creatures*. Since
they were vital, they learned their appointed tasks
"according to the motions of *the other*, which is oblique,
and passes through and is overruled by the motion of *the
same*". Therefore, though some of the bodies revolved in
larger orbits than others, those in the lesser orbits revolved
faster and those in the larger ones more slowly;[34] their
periodicities were regular.

> And yet there is no difficulty in seeing that the perfect
> number of time completes the perfect year when all
> the eight revolutions, having their relative degrees of
> swiftness, are accomplished together and again meet
> at their original point of departure, measured by the
> circle of the same moving equally. Thus, and to this
> end, came into existence such of the stars as moved

and returned through the heaven, in order that the created heaven might be as like as possible to the perfect and intelligible animal, and imitate the eternal nature.[35]

Two motions are involved. First, there is the motion of the outer stars which "being divine and eternal animals" have the motion of *the same* (i.e., of eternity which is spherical) or perfect circular motion. Second, there is the motion of "the other stars", i.e., the planets which were created after the "likeness" of the first stars but which "revolve and also wander".[36] The earth is an exception to motion; it is compacted around the pole or axis "which is extended through the universe".[37] The outer stars both circle and revolve; the earth *stands still* in the middle of the universe. The movement of the planets is complicated indeed. They are "the others" and their orbits defy calculation. "Vain would be the labour of telling about all the figures of them moving as in a dance, and their meetings with one another, and the return of their orbits on themselves."[38] This includes their progression and their retrogression, their variations in luminosity, their appearances and their disappearances which, and very importantly, send "terrors and intimations of things about to happen to those who can calculate them".[39]

The whole complicated motion is eventually traced back to the eternal motion which is the motion of "the same". However, since motion never exists in equal proportions, it is as impossible, according to Plato, to think that anything could exist without a mover as it is to conceive of there being "a mover" without "something that will be moved".[40] Indeed, it is motion which is essential to the world. It holds the world in its spherical form. "The revolution of the universe in which are comprehended all natures, being circular and having a tendency to unite with itself, compresses all things and will not allow any place to be left void."[41]

Further, and of extreme importance for Plato's concept of the world and for his influence upon religion, the *souls* of human beings, those "most religious of animals",[42] who were created a mixture of mortal and the immortal, were distributed among the stars. "Having placed them as in a chariot, he [the creator] showed them the nature of the universe and the decrees of destiny appointed for them."[43]

Thus in spite of Plato's denigration of sight as the means by which one could obtain knowledge of the way the heavens were made, in the end he admitted that the sense of sight is of the highest value for studying the heavens. Their study in fact afforded insight into the ways of nature, of ourselves and of God.

> The sight in my opinion is the source of the greatest benefit to us, for had the eyes never seen the stars, and the sun, and the heaven, none of the words which we have spoken about the universe would ever have been uttered. But now the sight of day and night, and the revolution of the months and years, have given us the invention of number, and a conception of time, and the power of inquiring about the nature of the whole; and from this source we have derived philosophy ... that we might behold the courses of intelligence in the heaven, and apply them to the courses of our own intelligence which are akin to them, the unperturbed to the perturbed; and that we, learning them and being partakers of the true computations of nature, might imitate the absolutely unerring courses of God and regulate our own vagaries.[44]

Thus the course of Greek astronomy was set. The heavenly movements declared *the ways of God* toward which humankind was to aspire.

In addition to the long narrative on "science" in the *Timaeus*, Plato has another reference to astronomical motion which sums up his concept of the universe and may even have been the main precedent for the cosmological concepts of Eudoxus, Callippus, Aristotle, and finally Descartes. In the *Republic*, Plato describes the movement of the heavenly bodies as due to "necessity" or the spindle on which the "whorls" of the world were created. They were eight in number, fitted together like circular boxes into one another and with edges turned upwards like so many hats with upturned brims. The largest, the lip of which formed the fixed stars, was spangled. The seven inner whorls, five for the planets, one for the sun, and one for the moon, varied in size, brightness, colour, and velocity depending upon which body they represented. All were perceived to be moved by the spindle which is "driven home" in the eighth (the celestial) whorl. But whereas "the whole" (the celestial sphere) revolves in one direction, the seven circles (of the sun, the moon and the planets) move slowly in "the other". Each of the seven moved at different velocities. Likewise, as if to document his direct dependence on the Pythagoreans, Plato reported that "on the upper surface of each circle is a siren, who goes around with them, hymning a single sound and note. The eight together form one harmony."[45]

Plato's concentric "whorls" by means of which he explained the mechanics of heavenly motion may very well have been the inspiration for Eudoxus' "homocentric spheres". These were to be improved upon by Callippus and then adopted by Aristotle. Though we have no evidence that René Descartes (1596–1650) read Plato's *Republic*, his "vortices" by which he supposed motion was imparted to the planets could have been patterned after Plato's whorls as well.

Homocentric Spheres

Eudoxus of Cnidus (c.406–c.355 B.C.), a member of Plato's Academy, like his master Plato, was certain that the real motions of the heavens were simple, uniform and circular, reflecting the movement of the celestial sphere. Since, however, the movement of the planets, the sun, and the moon *appeared* to be irregular, the problem facing Eudoxus was to translate *known* regular motion into the *apparent* irregular movement of the heavenly bodies. His solution was a geocentric system of homocentric spheres which continued to influence the way astronomers observed the heavens until Ptolemy and beyond.

The problem must be appreciated for its complexity. A simple set of eight transparent spheres surrounding the earth on the equators of which the heavenly bodies were thought to be attached — one sphere for the stars, one for each of the five planets and one each for the sun and the moon — could in no way account for the irregular movements of the bodies involved. The outer stars appeared to follow perfectly circular orbits and hence caused no difficulty. However, close observation showed that even the moon and the sun varied in velocity and that they seemed at times closer and at times further away. They also changed their angle in the skies with relationship to any set place on earth. The planets, however, those "wandering stars", appeared not only to move in looping paths in their general progress against the motion of the stellar sphere but sometimes they simply seemed to stop, then to regress, and after a time to proceed again in their proper directions.

Eudoxus, who was a brilliant mathematician, provided a *geometrical solution*. Inside the stellar sphere he fitted each of the heavenly bodies with a series of spheres, the one stacked inside the other like the layers of a very large and simple onion. The whole was centred on the earth. On the surface and at the equators of specific spheres were attached the particular heavenly bodies. Like the outer stellar sphere, each of the spheres assigned to the planets and to the sun and the moon rotated with uniform velocity around its two poles but the spheres turned in divergent directions to compensate for the observed movements of the bodies involved. The spheres of the five planets, the sun, and the moon were each moved in diverse but circular motion by other spheres which surrounded them and these by others still. The sun and the moon each needed three spheres; each of the planets needed four. Every one of the spheres, therefore, had its own independent, idiosyncratic yet regular movement. In this way the coordination of the total of twenty-seven was thought to serve as a geometrical explanation for the transmission of celestial regularity into *what appeared to be* the irregular motion of the heavenly bodies.[46] The spheres within spheres arrangement thus "saved" both the *regularity of motion* and the *irregularity of appearance*.

As a geometric device Eudoxus' nest of twenty-seven spheres was both ingenious and elegant. It was, in fact, hardly improved upon until Kepler explained the orbits of the planets as ellipses. Nevertheless, the arrangement was less than satisfactory. It accounted for the so-called "stations" and "retrogressions" in the planetary orbits only imprecisely. Since the spheres were rigid, the system was not successful at all in explaining the various distances of the moon and the sun from the earth. Nor could it account for the fact that the planets seemed to vary in size and luminosity, sometimes appearing larger and sometimes smaller, sometimes brighter and sometimes dimmer, a direct result of their varied distances from earth.

Since no better idea was apparently available at the time, Callippus of Cyzicus (c.370–c.300 B.C.) attempted to improve upon it and accounted for the heavenly movements more precisely by adding more spheres to the system. He added one each for Mars, Venus, and Mercury, two more for the sun and two more for the moon, making a total of thirty-four.[47] Aristotle, whom J. L. E. Dreyer (1852–1926) calls "the last great speculative philosopher who figures in the history of ancient astronomy",[48] inherited the system of homocentric spheres from Callippus and "improved" or at least complicated the system still further.

Aristotelian Geocentricity

Although Aristotle moved in the direction of scientific cosmology by attempting to correlate theory with observation, he remained completely beholden to Plato's dogma of the necessity of circular motion for all heavenly bodies. Thus, in spite of his good intentions, he did nothing but continue to pave the path to error and mis-representation. Contrary to his desire to correlate theory with actuality and thus be "scientific", Aristotle's basic conception of the cosmos was governed as much by metaphysical conceptualities as was that of Plato and the Pythagoreans. In fact his *pretension* at correlating hypo-theses with observation made his system more dangerous than that of Plato because his conclusions feigned "scien-tific procedures" and hence could pass as *physics* rather than as metaphysics. It was for this reason that, when his system was combined with his deductive logic, his ideas seemed so natural and indubitable that alternative sugges-tions hardly got a hearing.

Having adopted the Pythagorean-Platonic conceptions of the heavens, Aristotle began his description of the universe with motion. Circular and divine motion *is proper* to the celestial world, the higher nature. Rectilinear motion *is proper* to the sub-lunar world, the lower nature.[49] Circular motion, which characterised the heavens, has no beginning or end. Aristotle assigned it to the gods. It supported the universe. Following from this he considered the heavens, the "upper region", which were described by circular motion to be indestructible and ungenerated, eternal and unchanging.[50] Thus, Aristotle argued, "there is no need . . . to give credence to the ancient mythological explanation" that the heavens were held up by some kind of Atlas or, as later thinkers thought, that the heavenly bodies were "earthlike and had weight" so that "we must say with Empedocles that it has been kept up all this time by the cosmic whirl".[51] Plato's concept of some kind of a cosmic soul which caused the heavenly motions was "equally inadmissible".[52] Rather, that which continues the heavenly motions from eternity to eternity must be "restless, a stranger to leisure and reason". It is the "first motion" and the first motion, which moved the first body and imparts that motion to all others, must be given by divinity itself, *the unmoved mover*.[53]

From motion Aristotle derived his concept of "form". Because perfect circular motion is imparted to the heavens, "the shape of the heaven must be spherical".[54] As the circle is "the primary plane figure", the sphere is the primary solid, "for it alone is bounded by a single surface, rectangular solids by several".[55] It is the only body which in revolving continually occupies the same space.[56] Thus, circularity of motion and sphericity of shape were the *sine qua non* of heavenly movement and form. It was exactly this "obvious" but mistaken differentiation between circular "perfect" motion, which was assigned to the heavens, and the rectilinear "irregular" motion, which was assigned to the earthly sphere, that was to prevent astronomy, and with it most of science, from properly becoming *science* for the next two thousand years.

> A rectilinear body revolving in a circle will never occupy the same space, but owing to the change in position of the corners there will at one time be no body where there was body before, and there will be body again where now there is none. It would be the same if it were of some other shape whose radii were unequal, that of a lentil or an egg for example. All will involve the existence of place and void outside the revolution, because the whole does not occupy the same space throughout.[57]

Thus there was an exact correlation between the perfect movement of the heavens in circles and the spherical shape of the bodies involved. Egg-shaped motion, i.e. ellipses, which participated in imperfection and which some two thousand years later proved to be the actual pattern of the planetary orbits, was specifically ruled out. For Aristotle, as for Plato and the Pythagoreans before him, perfection defined by circularity and perfection defined by sphericity were of a piece. Circular motion was the simplest of motions. The sphere was the simplest form. Thus "Ockham's razor" — the simplest explanation is the best explanation — which was the criterion of reality, beauty, and rationality for Plato and the Pythagoreans was also adopted by Aristotle as integral to the nature of things.

Motion, shape, and simplicity define the perfect harmony which reflected eternity itself and became the measure of everything else.

> . . . the revolution of the heaven is the measure of all motions, because it alone is continuous and unvarying and eternal, the measure in every class of things is the smallest member, and the shortest motion is the quickest, therefore the motion of the heaven must clearly be the quickest of all motions. But the shortest path of those which return upon their starting-point is represented by the circumference of a circle and the quickest motion is that along the shortest path. If therefore the heaven (a) revolves in a circle and (b) moves faster than anything else, it must be spherical.[58]

The sphericity of all heavenly bodies, therefore, was proved not only by the fact that their shape must be harmonious with their motion, but also on the ground that the bodies must resemble one another. As evidence that Aristotle did depend on observation to a certain degree, or at least used its results when they supported his hypotheses, he reported that the moon's crescent shape or "gibbousness" during the greater part of its waxing and waning and the crescent shape of the sun during eclipses gave "the evidence of sight" that these two bodies are spherical. If, then, "one of the heavenly bodies is spherical the others will clearly be spherical also".[59]

By combining a large proportion of metaphysics with a small amount of physics, Aristotle, like Eudoxus and Callippus, constructed a geocentric universe of concentric spheres centred on the earth. In Aristotle, the number is fifty-five, the one nesting inside of the other. The outside surface of the second sphere is positioned close to but not touching the inner surface of the first. The inside surface of the first rubs in *frictionless contact* with the outer surface of the second and down through the universe from the *primum mobile* and the sphere of the stars to the sphere of the moon. It was Eudoxus' "onion world" but more complicated. The layers were clear and crystalline and, for Aristotle, they were of ethereal material, eternal and immutable. The layers slip and move within one another, influencing but not determining one another's direction, so that each had its own particular movement which was proper to itself; but, at the same time, each sphere also obeyed the direction given by the combined movements of the spheres outward from it. While the spheres were simple and eternal, the earth, by contrast, consisted of the four elements — earth, water, fire, and air. It was time-bound and subject to generation and change.

Hence, and very important for Aristotle's thought, the movement that resulted and which was demonstrated by the heavenly bodies was not a direct consequence of the mechanics of the system. Rather, each of the heavenly bodies, each "god", had its own soul. Instead of being moved only by the influence of the prime mover, each of the heavenly bodies moved according *to its own intelligence*. In *desire* and *love* each of the bodies strove to emulate the prime mover's eternal movement which was the measure of perfection both physical and spiritual. Thus, in order to explain primary circular motion, on the one hand, and apparent irregular motion, on the other, alongside the dependable and deterministic motion imported by the prime mover, Aristotle introduced the capriciousness of individual and non-predictable motion of the individual planets. It is exactly this dichotomy between inexorable determinism and capricious independability that lies at the very basis of Aristotle's system and makes it unsuited as a basis for science and eventually for theology as well. It is also this inconsistency that in the long run tore the system apart.

Hence, rather than explain the movements of the heavenly bodies on the basis of either physics or mathematics, in the end Aristotle assigned to each of the heavenly bodies a mind of its own. As in Plato, there was coordination of course, because each of the bodies desired to conform to the will of the whole. Irregular, then, as the movements of the moon and the sun were and erratic as the planets appeared to be, they all came back to their appointed places in due season. Predictability was possible only within large parameters.

Nature as a whole, like the movements of the planets, was harmonious only in general. Even the "circular movements" of the heavens were not traceable. Rather, the individual heavenly bodies moved themselves as do animals. Their direction was finally determined not by movement impressed upon them from the outside, but by virtue of an inherent vital principle, by *the increase of desire* rather than by mechanical impact. Each desired to participate in the harmony of perfection of that which is above it while each at the same time affected that which was directly below.

It is of vast importance for Aristotle's conception of reality to realise that the relationship that obtains in the ethereal realm, where that which is above influences that which is below and that which is below desires to participate in that which is above, is also reflected in the intercourse between ethereal reality and the world of material elements where human beings are found. Both material events and history are ruled by the stars. Individual persons desire divinity even while they are being directed by particular heavenly bodies. Divinity is pervasive. From the circumference to the centre, from the celestial sphere to the lowest sphere of earth, there is the influence of the divine. By the same token, from the lowest to the highest, from the centre to the circumference, from the elements of the material world to human beings, who are a combination of the divine and the material, there are ennobling aspirations toward that which is above.[60]

Thus Aristotle's universe of homocentric spheres, although built upon those of Eudoxus and Callippus, is primarily the result of metaphysics rather than of physics or even of mathematics. In the end it was more theology than it was physics; or to put it accurately, for Aristotle, cosmology and theology were not only correlated, they were one and the same. Astronomy was a part of theology. Astronomy, "that branch of mathematical science which is most akin to philosophy ... has for its object a substance which is sensible but eternal".[61] For Aristotle, then, as for the Pythagoreans, to know the spherical, eternal, and circular moving heavens was to know God.

With Aristotle the correlation between "science" and theology, which goes back to the Babylonians and was continued by the Pythagoreans and Plato, reaches its final and fateful Greek form. Based as it was on the geocentric, spherical concept of the universe, where all movements were uniform and circular, it summed up what, up to that time, people had learned to believe, think, and see. So thoroughgoing was the system that, as we shall see, though it was challenged by the partial heliocentric model of Heraclides and the totally heliocentric system of Aristarchus, it remained too persuasive to be displaced. When the scheme was completed with eccentrics and epicycles and given mathematical notation by Ptolemy, it was to rule cosmology and to influence theology deeply for the next 1400 years.

Before the Aristotelian system reached Ptolemy, however, the spheres-within-the-spheres system which descended from the highest heavens to the earth, was challenged by the geometers who, try as they might, simply could not make the thoroughgoing homocentric universe work. Aristotle, like Eudoxus and Callippus before him, was too sophisticated to accept the simplistic earth-centred system consisting of seven concentric spheres or circles (one each for the moon, Mercury, Venus, the sun, Mars, Jupiter, Saturn and the surrounding all, i.e., the stellar heavens). Instead he adopted the scheme of multiple spheres for each planet. He was also dissatisfied with the explanation of the movements of the planets on the basis of mechanical motion alone. It was for theological reasons that he introduced into his system the concept of *emulation* in accordance with which each of the bodies was held to be alive, had its own vital principle and desired to emulate that which was superior to it in progressive steps up to the divine prime mover. Theology thus determined cosmology. And though the introduction of divine will gave explanation to the idiomatic movements of the heavenly bodies, it also destroyed the Pythagorean, and for cosmology necessary, condition that explanations be mathematically explicable and that harmony and simplicity be applicable not only to the *whole* but to the *parts* in relation to the whole as well.

Circularity, of course, which defined both harmony and simplicity and hence God himself, was the *sine qua non* of all Greek cosmology and had to be maintained at all costs. Therefore, even the divinely oriented heavenly bodies, because they desired to emulate perfect circular motion, moved themselves in accordance with the motion of the prime mover. Nevertheless Aristotle's employment of the fifty-five astral deities, which he used to keep his spheres in some kind of coordinated movement, along with his animation of the spheres and bodies, indicate a regression into Platonic-inspired mythology and away from the strict geometric explanations of Eudoxus and Callippus. Ingenious as the system was, however, as long as circular homocentric motion was maintained, there was no way to explain why the heavenly bodies sometimes appear to be closer and sometimes farther away, sometimes brighter and sometimes dimmer. It is hardly surprising, therefore, that the mathematicians again took over.

Circles, Epicycles and Eccentrics

Heraclides of Pontus (c.390–c.322 B.C.), contemporary with Aristotle and also a member of Plato's Academy, was evidently more interested in explaining the planetary motions on the basis of observation and geometry than on the basis of theology. Heraclides advanced on the idea of Hicetas of Syracuse (date unknown) that the apparent rotation of the heavens was due to the rotation of the earth. Since, as mentioned above, earlier Pythagoreans, specifically Philolaus, had advocated that the apparent movement of the heavens was due to observing the stars from the earth as it orbited the central fire, the idea of movement of the earth was not entirely new. Rather than having the earth orbit around a central fire, however, Heraclides suggested that the earth rotated around its own central axis in the centre of the universe. According to Aëtius' (date unknown) report, Heraclides explained, "Let the earth move ... like a wheel fitted with an axis, from west to east round its own centre".[62] With that the rotating earth became a possibility for cosmology.

Thus, like Philolaus, Heraclides pictured the stellar sphere as being fixed. The stellar sphere only appeared to rotate because those who observed it stand on the surface of the spinning spherical earth in the centre of the world and watch the "stationary" stars go by. The rotating earth had the same advantage as Philolaus' orbiting one in that it allowed all the heavenly motions to proceed in the same general direction. At the same time it avoided the idea of the central fire which the Pythagoreans had long since abandoned along with the "antichthon", that "tenth world" for which there was no physical evidence.

Philolaus' "central fire" with its orbiting earth may have had some continuing relevance, however, in inspiring Heraclides to think of placing the sun in the centre of the orbits of Mercury and Venus and thereby to invent the first *partial heliocentric system*. He placed the sun with the two planets as satellites well beyond the orbit of the moon so that the orbits of Mercury and Venus would not interfere with that of the moon. The moon and the sun, the latter trailing its orbiting planets, then continued to orbit the earth in the usual way. The five other known planets (the outer or superior planets) also orbited around the earth at greater distances. This partial heliocentric model was so successful in helping to explain the irregularities of the planets — that Achilles' heel of all astronomy until Kepler — that the renowned astronomer Tycho Brahe (1546–1601) used it as a basis for his own largely heliocentric system some fifty years after Copernicus had allowed his *De Revolutionibus Orbium Caelestium* (1543) to be published. Tycho, who found Copernicus' system far from satisfactory, placed all the planets in orbits around the sun and had the sun, with the planets, circle the earth.

Ingenious as was Heraclides' partial heliocentric system, it had two obvious faults as far as the immediate future of astronomy was concerned. First, it was only partially satisfactory in explaining the irregularities and idiosyncrasies of the planetary movements. Secondly, in opposition to main-stream astronomy, it had the disadvantage of displacing the earth from its "proper position" as the centre of all the movements of the universe.

Half a century after Heraclides had promulgated his partial sun-centred system, Aristarchus of Samos (c.320–c.250 B.C.) invented his *total heliocentric* one. By ignoring the mainstay of the geocentric system, i.e., the stationary earth in the centre of the world, Aristarchus advanced on Heraclides' partial heliocentric system by placing all of the planets, including the earth, in concentric orbits about the sun. The moon continued in orbit about the earth. The system was simple, elegant, and complete. It even retained the usual spherical nature of the universe along with an insistence on the thorough-going circularity of all heavenly motions. In the end it was the continued insistence on circularity, that *absolute* of Greek astronomy which was the touchstone of both God and rationality, that perhaps more than anything else spelled the downfall of Aristarchus' sun-centred system. For all its elegance, as Copernicus was to discover some 1800 years later when he revived Aristarchus' heliocentric universe, there was no way the apparent irregularities of planetary motion could be explained by putting the planets in simple, circular orbits around the sun. Rather, a whole series of deferents, epicycles, and eccentrics had to be added for the system to approximate to the evidence of observation.

The main critique of Aristarchus' system in its own time, however, was apparently the unbelievable amount of space his world demanded. The earth in orbit around the sun entailed its moving under different parts of the stellar sphere at different times of the year. Since to the naked eye the angle of observation directed to any one of the fixed stars remained constant, i.e., there was no parallactic motion caused by the supposed movement of the earth from which the stars were observed, the distance to the fixed stars would have needed to have been thousands of times greater than that generally accepted. If in the observation of particular stars on the dates of January 1 and again on July 1, for instance, when the earth would have been at diametrically opposite positions in its orbit, the angle did not undergo observable change, the universe would have had to assume what at the time were considered gigantic proportions.

Aristarchus recognised the difficulty and set out a formula to try to deal with it: "The circle in which . . . the earth [is supposed] to revolve bears such a proportion to the distance of the fixed stars as the centre of a sphere bears to its surface".[63] The formula would seem to make the best sense if translated: "The ratio which the size of the earth bears to the size of its orbit about the sun is equal to that which the size of that orbit bears to the size of the sphere of the fixed stars." Modest though this estimate was, it seemed to relegate the earth to being but a speck floating in what in comparison was an unfathomably huge sea of space. The formula signified a universe the size of which, without doubt, was well beyond even the wildest imaginations of the time.[64]

Even four centuries later, Ptolemy could object to the system on the grounds of physics. In that the forces of gravity and inertia were unknown, were the earth, which according to Aristotle's physics was the heaviest of the elements, placed in orbit like the other "ethereal" heavenly bodies, it would "simply fall out of the heavens". Further, since the earth was held to be of greater weight than any other objects, and in consideration of the fact that, according to Aristotelian physics, the heavier a body, the faster it fell, were it to revolve on its axis or rotate in orbit around the sun, it would simply leave the "animals and lesser weights hanging in the air" as it moved out from under them. In addition, as explained in more detail below, clouds as well as things thrown in the air would be left behind as the earth outstripped them in its eastward motion. Clouds would always appear to move to the west.

Projectiles would be thrown in an eastwardly direction and flying bodies moving in an eastward direction would have all they could do just to maintain position over the rotating earth. Little wonder that, from the point of view of Aristotelian physics, which was part and parcel of his system, Ptolemy could pronounce the heliocentric system with its moving earth "ridiculous" and "absurd".[65]

In addition to Ptolemy the only other references to the Aristarchian heliocentric system were by Archimedes, Plutarch, and the doxographers.[66] Thus, the theory died an undeserved death and remained moribund until it was revived by Copernicus.

A century after Aristarchus, Apollonius of Perga (c.262–c.190 B.C.) ignored Aristarchus' heliocentric concepts as well as Eudoxus' and Callippus' complicated set of homocentric spheres which Aristotle had adopted and made *de rigueur*. Apollonius filled the heavens with circles centred on the circumference of circles which were centred on the earth. Taking as his basis the geocentric system so trenchantly defended by both Plato and Aristotle and maintaining the dogma of circular movement, Apollonius explained that the reason the planets at times appeared to move forward and at times to move backward was that each one was located on the circumference of a small sphere, *an epicycle*, which in turn was located on the circumference of the larger sphere, *the deferent*, which itself was centred on the earth. As the larger sphere turned around the earth, the smaller epicyclic sphere rotated independently on the circumference of the larger sphere and carried the planet around on its own circumference. Each planet, that is, moved in its own small circle or orbit. The centre of each epicycle, like the hub of a wheel of which the planet's movement formed the rim, moved along on the rim of a much larger wheel — the deferent. The hub of the larger wheel was located on the earth. This combination of movements described the planets' apparent irregular motion.[67]

Still later Hipparchus (fl. 146–127 B.C.), who has been called "the greatest astronomical observer in antiquity", and whose notations became basic for Ptolemy, made the system of deferents and epicycles conform more rigorously to observation by adding *eccentrics* to the arrangement. The eccentrics resulted from placing the centre of the deferents, to which the epicycles of each of the planets were supposedly attached, off to the side of the earth. Thus, though the planets' movements continued to be made up by a combination of perfect circles, the eccentric pattern of the main deferents, combined with the circular motion of the epicycles, allowed the planets to display apparent deviations from the circular as far as observation was concerned. The apparent forward, stationary, retrograde, and looping motions of the planets were explained by the rotation of each planet on its epicycle. The observed changes of size and variations in luminosity were explained by the eccentric pattern of the deferents which allowed the planets to vary in distance from the earth. Correspondingly, the changes in orbital velocity of the sun and moon were explained simply by placing the centre of their supposed circular orbits slightly off the centre of the earth, i.e., making their orbits eccentrics as well, so that when the bodies were farther away, they *appeared* to move more slowly; when closer they *appeared* to move more quickly.[68] The combination of epicycles, eccentrics, and deferents served to protect circularity, the *sine qua non* of perfection and hence, according to Plato and Aristotle, the divinity of the heavens. At the same time, the system allowed a much closer relationship between theory and observation than had previously been the case. The combination of eccentrics, deferents, and epicycles was so effective that it was incorporated both by Ptolemy and also by Copernicus into their systems.

The *geocentric system* was, with deviations, well over half a millennium in development. It represented *the best* in Greek science and, as we shall see, in Greek philosophy as well. The system was to be brought to completion by Ptolemy of Alexandria, who "perfected" it by the addition of *equants*, points which were placed somewhat off the centre of the main orbits of each of the heavenly bodies and

38	CIRCLES OF GOD

in relation to which the *apparent irregularity* of the body's motion could be calculated as being *regular*. Then, by assiduously following the observational notations of Hipparchus and adding those which he himself had made from twenty-seven years of close observation, Ptolemy so successfully elaborated the system with astronomical tables and mathematical formulae that, wrong though it was as a description of the physical world, it held sway for some 1400 years.

NOTES

1. Eduard Zeller, *Die Philosophie der Griechen in ihrer geschichtlichen Entwicklung*, I. Teil, 1. Abt. (Hildesheim: Olms, 1963), pp. 55, 66.
2. *Ibid.*, pp. 86f.
3. *Ibid.*, pp. 236f.
4. Jaki, *The Relevance of Physics*, p. 6.
5. Kathleen Freeman, *The Pre-Socratic Philosophers* (Oxford: Blackwell, 1946), p. 56. Cf. Frederick Copleston, *A History of Philosophy:* Vol. I, *Greece and Rome*, Part I (New York: Doubleday, 1962), p. 41. Jaki apparently translates the *apeiron* as "air", hence his statement, "Anaximander derived everything from air". Jaki, *Relevance of Physics*, p. 6.
6. Freeman, *Pre-Socratic Philosophers*, p. 65.
7. *Ibid.*, p. 263.
8. Werner Heisenberg, *Wandlungen in den Grundlagen der Naturwissenchaften* (Stuttgart: Hirzel, 1973), p. 77.
9. Thomas F. Torrance, *Divine and Contingent Order* (New York: Oxford, 1981), p. 31.
10. Heisenberg, *Wandlungen*, p. 146.
11. Aristotle, *Metaphysics* I, Loeb Classical Library (London: Heinemann, 1933), I. iii, 983b.
12. Plutarch, *The Obsolescence of Oracles* in *Plutarch's Moralia*, 14 vols. (London: Heinemann, 1936), V. 436D. Plutarch is quoting from the *Orphic Fragments*, vi. 10 (21a, 2).
13. *Ibid.*, V. 436E.
14. Cf. above, pp. 1ff.
15. J. L. E. Dreyer, *A History of Astronomy from Thales to Kepler* (New York: Dover, 1953), pp. 35f.
16. Diogenes Laertius, *Lives of Eminent Philosophers*, Vol. II, Loeb Classical Library (London: Heinemann, 1925), VIII. 48. Cf. Dreyer, *History of Astronomy*, p. 37. For the Pythagoreans the heaven, *ouranos*, was a technical term signifying the place of generation and change. It included the earth, the moon, the sublunar sphere. In contrast, the cosmos, *kosmos*, a term Pythagoras

himself was thought to have invented, was the place of regulated motion and embraced the moon, the stars, the sun, and the five planets. The fixed stars occupied the *olympos*, the place of the elements in all purity. Outside this was the "outer fire" which balanced the inner one and the whole was surrounded by the *to apeiron*, the infinite air, from which the whole world draws its breath.

17. Plato, *Timaeus* in *The Dialogues of Plato*, trans. B. Jowett, 4 vols. (New York: Scribner, 1874), 35–36. Cf. Dreyer, *History of Astronomy*, pp. 62, 178f.

18. Pliny, *Natural History*, Vol. I, Loeb Classical Library (London: Heinemann, 1938), Book II, xx. 84; Dreyer, *History of Astronomy*, p. 179.

19. Plato, *Timaeus*, 36–37.

20. *Ibid.*, 53.

21. Described by Plato, *ibid.*, 55–56.

22. *Aëtii Placita* II, 14. 3 in Hermann Diels, *Doxographi Graeci* (Berlin, Reimer, 1879), p. 344. Cf. Dreyer, *History of Astronomy*, p. 16.

23. Aristotle, *On the Heavens*, Loeb Classical Library (London: Heinemann, 1939), II. xiii, 293b.

24. Aristotle, *Metaphysics*, I. v, 986a.

25. Dreyer, *History of Astronomy*, pp. 45–47. In the light of succeeding cosmologies, it is important to note, with Dreyer, that the central fire was by no means considered to be the only or even the chief source of light and heat in the universe. Rather than the sun being a source of its own heat and light, it acts more as a lens which borrows light from both the central fire and that surrounding the sphere of the visible universe, the ethereal fire or "the fire from above", sifting it first through its own body and then scattering it on all sides. The moon, then, which was held to be a body like the earth with plants and animals and with a day fifteen times as long as our own, had its main source of light in the sun which it reflects to earth.

26. Plato, *Timaeus*, 91.

27. *Ibid.*, 48–50, 52–57.

28. *Ibid.*, 36.

29. *Ibid.*, 36–37.

30. *Ibid.*, 37.

31. *Ibid.*

32. *Ibid.*, 40.

33. *Ibid.*, 38.

34. *Ibid.*, Italics added.

35. *Ibid.*, 39.

36. *Ibid.*, 40.

37. *Ibid.*

38. *Ibid.*

39. *Ibid.*

40. *Ibid.*, 57.
41. *Ibid.*, 58.
42. *Ibid.*, 41–42.
43. *Ibid.*, 41.
44. *Ibid.*, 47.
45. Plato, *The Republic*, in *The Dialogues of Plato*, trans. B. Jowett, 4 vols. (New York: Scribner, 1874), II, Book X, 616–617.
46. Dreyer, *History of Astronomy*, p. 90.
47. *Ibid.*, pp. 104–107.
48. *Ibid.*, p. 108.
49. Aristotle, *On the Heavens*, I. ii–I. iii, 269a–269b.
50. *Ibid.*, II. i, 284a.
51. *Ibid.*
52. *Ibid.*
53. *Ibid.*
54. *Ibid.*, II, iv, 286b.
55. *Ibid.*
56. *Ibid.*, II. iv, 287a. Dreyer points out that "this is an unfortunate argument, since the same may be said of any solid of revolution", *History of Astronomy*, p. 109. Aristotle is quite correct if the revolution is around a multiple number of possible axes.
57. Aristotle, *On the Heavens*, II. iv, 287a.
58. *Ibid.*
59. *Ibid.*, II. xi, 291b.
60. Aristotle, *Metaphysics (Books X–XIV)*, Loeb Classical Library (London: Heinemann, 1962), XII. viii, ix, 1074b.
61. *Ibid.*, XII. viii, 1073b.
62. *Aëtii Placita* III, 13.3, in *Doxographi Graeci*, p. 378. Cf. Hermann Diels, *Die Fragmente der Vorsokratiker*, Sixth Edition, 2 vols. (Berlin: Weidmann, 1951–1952), 51, 5 Ekphantos, p. 442; and Dreyer, *History of Astronomy*, p. 51.
63. Cf. T. L. Heath, *The Works of Archimedes* (Cambridge: University Press, 1897), p. 222. Heath's translation of the formula is a rather opaque, "The ratio which the earth bears to what we describe as 'the universe' is the same as the ratio which the sphere containing the circle in which he supposed the earth to revolve bears to the sphere of the fixed stars. The radius of the earth's orbit was equal to the ratio of this to the radius of the fixed stars." Cf. also Jaki, *Relevance of Physics*, p. 192.
64. Even in the fifteenth century the "immense space necessity" was still considered absurd and fantastic. It was just this idea of immense space which the Copernican theory necessitated that formed one of the main objections to it. Cf. Arthur Koestler, *The Sleepwalkers* (London: Hutchinson, 1968), p. 218 and Thomas S. Kuhn, *The Copernican Revolution* (Cambridge: Harvard, 1979), pp. 220f.

65. Ptolemy, *The Almagest*, Great Books of the Western World, Vol. 16 (Chicago: Encyclopaedia Britannica, 1952) Book I.6, pp. 11f. Cf. below, pp. 71ff.
66. Cf. Dreyer, *History of Astronomy*, pp. 137ff.
67. Cf. Kuhn, *Copernican Revolution*, pp. 55ff. for his discussion of homocentric spheres, epicycles and deferents.
68. Cf. *ibid.*, pp. 72–74 for Kuhn's discussion on Hipparchus' "eccentrics".

CHAPTER 2

MEASURING THE UNIVERSE

G REEK "science", which began and continued as a mixture of theological ideas and thought about nature, was to make a singularly important contribution to the understanding of the world with the development of mathematics. The earlier Ionian "atomic theory" — proposed by Leucippus and Democritus — which saw material reality as composed of parts, became productive for science when it was complemented by Pythagorean mathematics by which the parts could be enumerated, combined, or divided as necessary. Although Pythagorean mathematics was a by-product, a "spin-off" of Pythagorean cultic practice, it, like Pythagorean cosmology, eventually took on a life of its own and became basic to the whole of scientific thought.

Greek Mathematics

As said above, mathematics, like astronomy, arose in Babylon before it developed in Greece. In Babylon, as later in Greece, it was the religious interest in the heavens that led to the study of the stars and to the quantification of their movements and distances by means of mathematics. From the second millennium B.C. onward, Babylonian mathematics, based on the sexagesimal system, was notable for its sophistication. The Babylonians utilised the zero and developed equations which involved both simple addition and subtraction as well as squares. Their linear and quadratic equations featured unknown quantities; their second-order equations when squared, produced equations of the fourth order. They discovered and used the theorem for right-angled triangles and calculated the relation of right-angled triangles to the circle. They knew the approximation of square roots and computed the value of π as $3\frac{1}{8}$ to represent the ratio of the circumference of a circle to its diameter. Thus, Thales most probably learned the rudiments of mathematics from the Babylonians, and Pythagoras, who imported the rudiments of his cosmology "from the East" and whose Pythagorean theorem was identical with the Babylonian formula, most likely learned the basis of his number system from "the East" as well.[1]

For the Pythagoreans, however, as mentioned above, numbers were not only integers for counting and a means for calculating astronomical ratios, but were of the essence of reality and the focus of their faith. Numbers were not simply symbols for measuring reality; they were reality. Thus, Aristotle was quite right when he claimed that, for the Pythagoreans, nature itself consisted of the elements of number.[2] Though these predecessors of Descartes may have over-stressed their argument as well as the role of numbers, when they related their numbers to theories of nature, their emphasis gave rise to a system of quantification without which modern experimental science could not have come into being.

As the atomists posited a single substance, unit, or seed as the basis of reality, so the Pythagoreans supposed that the foundation of all things was a single number. Like a picture on a television screen, and strangely similar to Einstein's conception of space as a "continuous series of points, or lines",[3] for the Pythagoreans lines consisted of successive points, surfaces of successive lines, bodies of interrelated surfaces, elements of cohering bodies, and the world of manifold elements, all of which were manifestations of number.

If Aristotle is right, which seems likely, the Pythagoreans arranged their numbers, which they thought of as having spatiality and which they represented by dots (one dot equals 1, two dots equal 2, three dots equal 3, etc.), in such a way as to form and represent the geometrical shapes of which space was made up. They illustrated this by arranging the dots inside a *gnomon*, a right-angled Greek "carpenter's square". Two lines of two dots each set within the frame of the *gnomon* formed a square, as did three lines of three, four lines of four, five lines of five, etc. Thus, the numbers 4, 9, 16, and 25 were square numbers. By the same token, twelve dots when arranged in two parallel lines of six or three lines of four within the area bounded by the carpenter's square produced a rectangle and the number 12 was designated as a rectangular number. Three dots with the first set above but equidistant from the other two produced the most basic triangle. The basic three-dot triangle could, of course, be expanded so that triangles of five, ten, fifteen, or twenty-one dots resulted. The numbers involved comprised the triangular numbers. If the triangle were "made solid" with dots placed equidistant from one another: one on the first line, two on the second, three on the third, and four on the fourth, the result was a pyramid of ten dots, and 10 was the sacred number.

Even the "Pythagorean theorem" — the square of the hypotenuse of a right-angled triangle is equal to the sum of the squares of the other two sides — can be illustrated by constructing square figures of dots adjacent to but in proportion with each of the other sides and the hypotenuse of the triangle involved. Surprisingly enough or not surprising at all, if one remembers the limitation of all thought, this most famous of Pythagorean formulas also contains within it the basic contradiction of the Pythagorean system. All was well if the triangle under consideration were a 3, 4, 5 triangle or multiples thereof, so that the square of 3 which is 9 plus the square of 4 which is 16 equals 25 which is the square of the hypotenuse, 5. However, were the other two sides of the triangle of equal length, 4 and 4, for instance, the length of the hypotenuse would not be a whole number but a fraction. Thus, when the Pythagoreans discovered that the diagonal of a square figure of unit sides could not be measured in the same units, the "irrationality" which resulted was such a threat both to the system and to the Pythagorean cult that members were sworn to secrecy about it. The matter was considered so serious that the "heretic" Hippasus (dates unknown), who apparently made a point of proclaiming the fallibility of the system, is reported to have been drowned because he betrayed the orthodoxy of the order. However, neither this nor, as Jaki reports, the discovery of irrational numbers as exemplified by the square root of 2 ($\sqrt{2}$) was enough to deter the Pythagorean spirit.[4] As is often the case in science, or in any system of thought for that matter, irrationality and inconsistency were overlooked and fascination with and adherence to the system continued.

Fascination verging on fanaticism is reflected by Archytas (c.430–c.360 B.C.), who speaks like a later disciple of Descartes when he says that only mathematicians, those "who have gained an exact knowledge of the universe" and are concerned with "the two related primitive forms of being" (numbers and form), are capable of true apprehension of reality. They alone have handed down to us a "clear insight into the speed of the stars, about their rising and setting, and about geometry, numbers (arithmetic), sphericity and, not least of all, about music as well".[5]

The Pythagorean obsession with numbers, although primarily a matter of cultic inquiry, can also be explained, at least partially, on the basis of the inner rationality afforded by the number system. Although the system may not have been perfect, it was as near to perfection as the earthly realm of generation and change apparently allowed. One could form a series of the so-called square numbers simply by adding a series of odd numbers to each preceding number. The addition of 3 to the square number 1 equals the square number 4. Likewise, 4 plus the next odd number 5 would equal the square number 9 and so on ($1+3=4$, $4+5=9$, $9+7=16$, $16+9=25$, $25+11=36$, etc.). The Pythagorean discovery that there was a direct relationship between the length of a string and the tone the string produced when it was plucked no doubt added to their conception of the basic "number-harmony" of all reality. Once established, intervals of the musical octave were as regular as a 3, 4, 5 triangle: 2(2:1, octave) + 4 = 6(3:2, fifth) + 6 = 12(4:3, fourth).[6]

Though it can be argued that mathematics (even that related to the vibrations of a string in music referred to above) is only a system of conventions, the propositions of which apply properly only within itself and not outside itself,[7] the Pythagoreans, like all natural scientists, were highly impressed by the correlations that seemed evident between their numbers system and nature. The geometric structure of crystals—in which, as we now know, the atoms and molecules are arranged in identical patterns while the plane surfaces are oriented in such a way that they are harmonious with their internal structures — lent support to the Pythagorean system to a degree that, in the elementary stages of the study of nature, at least, could be most convincing. Specifically, crystals of quartz form a perfect pyramid of five sides or a double pyramid of eight. Those of beryl are in the shape of a perfect hexagon. Garnet, as every gem cutter knows, has crystals which form a twelve-sided dodecahedron, a hexagon with six angles and six sides. The whole is a pyramid on which the sloping faces intersect the vertical and lateral axis forming triangular surfaces which meet at a common vortex and are set on a polygonal base.

For the Pythagoreans, then, mathematics embraced the heavens and the earth, divinity, and creation. For them, as for Leopold Kronecker (1823–91), pioneer in the field of algebraic numbers, "God is responsible for making the numbers. Everything else is of human creation."[8] Little wonder that Aristotle could complain that, for the Pythagoreans, the whole universe consisted of numbers. Aristotle was quite wrong, however, in pressing his complaint to the extent of arguing that, like the other philosophers of nature (specifically the Ionians), the Pythagoreans presupposed that the sensible world comprised all reality. Nevertheless, this criticism does indicate that by the time of Aristotle the Pythagoreans as illustrated by Eudoxus and Callippus had taken the sensible world seriously. For them nature had to be understood and be explained in a system of mathematical notations that accounted for its appearances.[9]

Fortunately, however, Aristotle's complaint against the Pythagoreans did not end the Greek fascination for mathematics. While Eudoxus and Callippus worked out their homocentric spherical systems in order to find a geometrical solution to the movements of the heavens by way of mathematics, only to have their systems distorted by Aristotle's fifty-five intervening deities, those who after Aristotle contributed so much to the development of astronomy did so by working out strictly geometrical solutions. This is true for Heraclides' partial heliocentric system, Aristarchus' complete heliocentric model, Apollonius' use of epicycles, Hipparchus' addition of eccentrics and for Ptolemy, the greatest of the mathematicians, who used equants to explain regular motion, noted the ratios of the heavenly bodies in mathematical terms and added astronomical tables to substantiate his system. All were primarily mathematicians.

Most of the mathematicians attempted to correlate numbers with reality. However, one of the most noted among them, Euclid (fl. c.300 B.C.) developed a plain geometry which dealt only with numbers and shapes. A generation after Aristotle, Euclid took over the Pythagorean theorem and developed mathematics into a science of its own. He began by defining terms such as "point" and "line", and then set out his five unproved and unprovable postulates to produce his system of "plane geometry" with such *simplicity*, *elegance*, and *thoroughness* that, until the nineteenth century, all space was thought to be subject to his formulae. The system formed the basis for the highly accurate astronomical measurements and ratios of both Hipparchus and Ptolemy and it described the world of space as it usually appears to us, in spite of the fact that the parallel postulate has been open to question for the last 150 years.[10] So impressive was the system that Einstein was quite right in saying:

> Here for the first time the world witnessed the miracle of a logical system which proceeded from step to step

with such precision that every single one of its propositions was absolutely indubitable — I refer to Euclid's geometry.[11]

The fact, however, that even after Euclid, Greek science in and of itself developed only in a rudimentary way, would not seem to substantiate Einstein's further statement, "This admirable triumph of reasoning gave the human intellect the necessary confidence in itself for its subsequent achievements."[12] Such confidence did not really arise until the seventeenth century by which time *theology*, not mathematics, had given the confidence necessary to apply mathematics to nature in quite unequivocal terms.

The Dimensions of the World

As indicated, the Greeks, in all probability, learned to observe, admire and study the heavens from the Babylonians and most likely copied the beginnings of mathematics from them as well. In Babylon, however, as indeed in ancient Egypt and Crete, "science" was so encumbered by a general mythology which included a mélange of religion, astrology, philosophy, sociology, and politics that it was unable to break free and develop clear systematic thought on its own.[13]

With the scientific advance which the Ionian "atheists" made when they took over the rudiments of science from earlier Middle Eastern cultures but ignored both the Babylonian and Homeric penchant for a cosmos controlled by capricious deities, the world could be understood as consisting of self-subsistent matter which was subject to quantitative description. As thought regarding nature progressed, all reality was considered to be open to measurement in distinctive units. The "breakthrough" came about by conceiving the universe as a single system of which the earth was representative. The earth could then be postulated as a unit of measure and the sizes of the heavenly bodies and the distances between them could be quantified accordingly. Earthly and heavenly bodies were thus related to one another, both in kind and in measurement. When earthly and heavenly reality began to be seen as a unitary structure, the Pythagorean concept of number and the thought of the Ionian "materialists" combined to form a heuristic system which eventually led to the discovery of some quite valid ideas of the world. Of more subtle, but certainly of equal importance, was that the success at measuring the universe inspired one of the basic beliefs which undergirds all science — the faith that the world can be known in terms available to us.[14]

As in the development of science in general, the procedure for measuring the universe rests on what we now consider to be extremely naïve beginnings. The Ionians, unsuperstitious as they were, were still "flat-earth people". They pictured the cosmos as a huge sphere, a giant globular fishbowl which was half filled with the waters of the seas. The earth, shaped in the form of a gigantic disk, floated on the waters. In all probability the disk represented the then known dry land which reached from the Indian Ocean in the east to the Straits of Gibraltar in the west. Anaximander, engaged in unfounded speculation rather than scientific calculation, guessed that the thickness of the disk was equal to one-third its diameter.[15] He showed his scientific ingenuity, however, by using the diameter of the disk as a unit of measure in his attempts to calculate the size of the sun and moon. Although neither his identification of the moon and the sun nor his computation as to their size was close to being accurate, he considered that the sun and the moon were huge rings inside of which burned eternal fire and calculated the diameter of the moon ring to be nineteen times as large as the earth's disk and the rim of the sun to be twenty-seven times as large as that of the earth[16] — he nevertheless moved in the direction of genuine scientific method. In reckoning the sun to be larger than the earth, his speculations represented a first step in going beyond immediate "sensory impression" as far as cosmological dimensions were concerned. From the point of view of simple observation, however, the estimate of the size of the sun at high noon and of a full moon in the month of June would seem to have some correlation to the difference in the size of the two bodies as they usually appear to us.

Also, inaccurate as his calculations were, Anaximander's sixth-century B.C. use of "*terrestria*" (earthly dimensions) to compute the size of heavenly bodies was of immense significance for the development of scientific method. His arrangement recognised both that the heavens and the earth were parts of an interrelated system which was subject to uniform measurement and that all measurements were to be referred back to a *single specified unit*. Thus, though his calculations were less than accurate, Anaximander's method was of value in itself. His measurements were, at any rate, far better than the naked-eye view of Heraclides of Pontus, who, in contrast to all his other achievements in astronomy, made the mistake of estimating the size of the sun according to simple sense perception, "the breadth of a human foot" (25–30 centimetres or 10–12 inches in diameter).[17] Empedocles (c.495–c.435 B.C.) was also inaccurate. He calculated the moon to be twice as far from the sun as from the earth and the distance of the moon from the earth to be one-third the radius of the stellar sphere which surrounded the world.[18] Nevertheless, in attempting to grasp the size and distance of heavenly bodies in terms of the earth's measurement, he, like Anaximander, took a proper step in the direction of the development of science by relating both size and distance to known quantities. The attempt to conceive and measure the "unknown" in analogy to the "known" is basic to all physical science and indeed is a test applicable to all thought.

Pythagoras' supposition that the earth was a sphere which, as claimed above, he probably learned from the Babylonians, was substantiated by his followers when they noted the disk-like shadow of the earth passing over the surface of the moon during lunar eclipses.[19] Examination of meteorites convinced them that heavenly bodies were of earthly stuff. Reversing the analogy, the Pythagoreans concluded that the earth was a sphere among other material spheres and its measurability applied to the measurability of the whole.

Since the days of Thales in the late seventh and early sixth centuries B.C. trigonometry, by which linear distance is computed on the basis of angular measurement, had been employed to calculate the distance of ships from shore. The Pythagoreans, who showed their "scientific intuition" by borrowing an idea from one area and applying it to another, used the method first in their attempts to measure the earth and then in their efforts to reckon both the size of the heavenly bodies and the distance between them. The process resulted in respectably accurate calculations of the size of the earth as early as the beginning of the fourth century B.C. Aristotle, who had a good deal more respect for the mathematicians than for the atomists in spite of the fact that he disagreed with the mathematicians' conclusion that the essence of all reality consists of number, reports that the mathematicians had calculated the earth's circumference to be 400,000 stadia.[20] Since each stade is something over 150 metres (c. 500 ft.), the result is about 60,000 kilometres (c. 39,000 miles) or somewhat over 50 per cent larger than 40,000 kilometres (c. 25,000 miles) which represents the current figure.

Aristotle's further statement that "astronomical researches have now shown that the size of the sun is greater than that of the earth and that the stars are far farther away than the sun from the earth, just as the sun is farther than the moon from the earth",[21] indicates that by his time the size of the earth with respect to the sun at least, and the distance between the bodies of the cosmos, were beginning to be seen in perspective. When Aristotle goes on to report that the "bulk of the earth" is "a mere nothing when compared in size with the surrounding universe",[22] he gives evidence that quantitative relationships, those all-important factors in scientific thought, had begun to undergo modification so that the size of the cosmic bodies and the distance between them could be understood somewhat in terms of today's ratios. In comparison to the distance from the earth to the fixed stars, the distance between the earth and the sun began to be seen as comparatively small. The solar system or, as it was then understood, the "earth system" began to be perceived as relatively diminutive when seen in relation to the vastness of the universe which was bordered by the celestial sphere.

As yet, however, even the realisation of the vastness of the universe made no difference to the continued acceptance of geocentric theory whereby the earth was set in the centre of the universe with all the heavenly bodies orbiting round it. In fact, the rather accurate computations of the earth's size and the use of *earth-size* as the unit of measurement to calculate the size of the heavenly bodies and the distance between them, advantageous as it was for the development of the understanding of the universe, also had somewhat damaging side effects. With the earth as the standard of measurement, its centrality became more fixed than ever. Hence, not only did the fifth-century atomists' speculation about other worlds continue to seem foolish, but more ominously, Aristarchus of Samos' heliocentric theory which he developed in the first half of the third century B.C. seemed ridiculous simply because of the immensity of space necessitated by the system. Even if Aristarchus' genial heliocentric system had not been revived by Copernicus nearly two millennia after its discovery, the ingenuity he showed in calculating the distance from the earth to the sun and the moon during a lunar eclipse would have been enough to recommend him to posterity. The calculation is surprising both for its accuracy as far as the distance to the moon was concerned and the ingenuity of its method. However, when he expanded his calculations (explained below) to measure the distance from earth to sun and found it to be equal to the radius of the supposed orbit of the earth necessitated by his heliocentric system, the figure was too great to be believed.

Aristarchus, however, was not a complete failure. The acceptance of part of his theory militated against the acceptance of the rest. His use of the earth as a standard of measurement was accepted. His heliocentric speculations incorporating "cosmic measurement" in relation to which the earth appeared to have little size at all were rejected. Aristarchus' calculation of the moon's diameter as his computation of the distance from the earth to the moon fared much better than did his more profound heliocentric theory. He calculated the diameter of the moon to be one-third that of the earth, a figure which is at least respectable in relationship to today's figures which give the moon to earth ratio as *one to four*. His procedure for measuring the distance from the earth to the moon is perhaps more astounding for its method than for the accuracy of its result. We have record of the way it was done from Ptolemy who tells us that the method of calculation was also used by Hipparchus in the latter part of the second century B.C. It was consequently used by astronomers for some 1600 years as well.[23] The procedure involved the observation of the earth's shadow on the surface of the moon during a lunar eclipse. Measurement was made of the width of the shadow in relationship to the time the shadow took to cross the moon's surface. The figure that resulted was then calculated against that of the angular radius of the sun and against the angular radii of the parallaxes of the sun and the moon. The ratios which resulted gave the distance from the earth to the moon as forty earth diameters. Our measurements today calculate the ratio to be approximately *thirty to one*.[24]

Unfortunately, Aristarchus' estimate of the size of the sun, which he gave as only nineteen earth diameters, was a great deal less than the 110 earth diameters we now know it to be. His equations gave him an earth–sun distance of approximately 764 diameters of the earth. Although the figure is only about 6 per cent of that which we now consider to be accurate, it meant that the orbit of the earth in his heliocentric system would necessarily have been over 1500 earth diameters. When the distance from the sun to the orbit of Saturn, the outermost planet, was calculated, or that of the sun to the sphere of the fixed stars beyond, the

figures were even more astounding. They demanded that
the size of the universe be increased by some 400,000
times than that which at the time was accepted. Small as
the figures were in relationship to the size of the universe
as we know it, they were so outlandish at the time that
accepting them and the heliocentric theory which presupposed them was quite out of the question.[25]

If the measurements of Aristarchus are considered
surprising for their accuracy, those of Hipparchus, 150
years later, who, as said, adopted Aristarchus' method,
are simply astonishing at least as far as the moon was
concerned. According to Cleomedes (fl. c. A.D. 1), Hipparchus calculated the diameter of the moon to be 12/41 or
0.29 of the earth's diameter and its distance from the earth
to be 30.25 earth diameters, values which are nearly equal
to those we currently accept. Accuracy in one area does not
necessarily ensure it in another, however. Since, as Dreyer
informs us, no accurate method of calculating the sun's size
and its distance from the earth was possible until the
invention of the telescope, Hipparchus, like other astronomers, simply had to give estimates. There are various
reports of Hipparchus' conclusions. The one which
appears to be most reliable indicates that he estimated the
radius of the sun to be 12 1/3 times as great as that of the
earth and its distance from the earth to be 2550 earth-radii.
The figures amount to about 10 per cent of the values given
by current astronomy.[26]

As far as accurate measurement of the earth is concerned, it was Eratosthenes (c.275–c.195 B.C.), the librarian at the museum in Alexandria and the one who
is rightly known as the founder of geodesy, who accomplished the task with a stroke of genius. In addition to
being librarian to what is generally conceded to be the
greatest collection of manuscripts in the ancient world,
Eratosthenes is reputed to have been competent in the
fields of grammar, philosophy, mathematics, and astronomy. It is thus not surprising to note that he was fully
aware that the earth was a sphere. Measuring that sphere
was something else, however. Trigonometric formulae had

been in use since the Pythagoreans. Hence, Eratosthenes knew that the arc of a circle marked off by two radii was related directly to the measurement of the angle at which the two radii intersected each other at the centre of the circle. In applying that formula to the measurement of the earth, Eratosthenes demonstrated both his own innovative powers and the level to which Greek mathematics had progressed.

In that the earth was a sphere, the great circle of which formed its circumference, Eratosthenes speculated that, were he able to correlate the measurement of the angle between two radii of the earth drawn from the same meridian to its centre with the length of the arc of the earth's surface marked off by the same two radii, ascertaining the circumference of the earth and hence its diameter would be a matter of simple calculation. Further, and as a matter of application, Eratosthenes surmised that, were he able to measure the differentiation of the angle of the sun at its zenith in relation to the surface of the earth at two different points on the same meridian, the degree of differentiation would, for all intents and purposes, be equal to the angle formed by the intersection of the two radii at the centre of the earth. He knew that at noon on the longest day of the year, June 21, the sun at its zenith over the city of Syene (now Aswan), which lies on the Tropic of Cancer, was directly overhead. It could be observed to shine directly into a deep well casting no shadow whatever.

Hence, he projected two radii from the centre of the earth to its surface — the one joining the surface at Syene, the other at Alexandria, directly to the north. The angle of intersection of the radii was to be determined by the degree of angle south of the vertical with which the sun's rays struck the earth at Alexandria. To say it another way, the angle made by the intersection of the two radii at the centre of the earth could be ascertained by measuring the degree of differentiation between the angles at which the sun's rays would strike the earth at the two points where the radii joined the circumference of the great circle of the earth. The degree of the angle formed by the intersection of the radii, in turn, would stand in the same ratio to the 360 degrees of a circle as the length of the segment of the earth's circumference, that was marked off by the two radii, stood in relation to the earth's circumference as a whole.

In practical terms, the number of degrees which differentiated the angle of the sun as seen from Syene from the angle as observed from Alexandria would stand in the same ratio to the 360 degrees of a circle as the linear distance between Syene and Alexandria stood in relationship to the circumference of the earth.

Like all genial achievements, the scheme, seen in retrospect, is simplicity itself. On the day of the summer solstice when the sun cast no shadow in Syene, Eratosthenes erected a perfectly perpendicular stake on level ground at Alexandria which lay 5000 stadia (c. 800 kilometres) directly north. By measuring the length of the shadow cast by the stake at high noon and relating it to the height of the stake itself, Eratosthenes found that while the sun was directly overhead at Syene (at 0° of angle), it stood 7° (in round numbers) south of vertical at Alexandria.

Although we are not aware of Eratosthenes' exact procedure, it is most likely that he then simply followed Euclid, who had founded his School of Mathematics at Alexandria a generation earlier. He would, therefore, have used the Euclidean procedure and calculated the circumference of the earth by using the formula:

$$\frac{l}{c} = \frac{v°}{360}$$

where l = the length of the measured arc, c = the circumference, $v°$ = the measurement of the central angle, and 360 = the degrees in a circle. If so, then, $v°c = 360\ l$, or, substituting numerical values, $7c = 360(5000) = 1,800,000$, and $c = 257,000$ stades as the measurement of the earth's circumference. Utilising the formula:

$$d = (c/\pi)$$

(diameter equals circumference divided by π), he then would have divided c. 257,000 by c. 3·14 and obtained the result of c. 81,850 stadia or c. 13,100 kilometres (c. 8100 miles) as the earth's diameter.

In actuality, Eratosthenes' angle was slightly greater than 7° and the distance between the two cities somewhat greater than 800 kilometres (500 miles) so that he calculated the diameter of the earth to be c. 12,800 kilometres, about 110 kilometres (c. 70 miles) less than the figures we are now able to obtain with our best instruments. It was a truly astounding feat. The feat had psychological as well as scientific value. To know the earth as a sphere was one thing, but to know the exact size of that sphere was to move from the probability of hypothesis to the realm of certainty. Truth, as far as "science" is concerned, was becoming a matter of the reconciliation of observation with mathematics and *vice versa*.

Motion and the God of Motion

With foundations such as those referred to above, it would seem that Greek science should have been well on the way toward continuing development. The Greeks were able to appreciate the beauty and harmony of the cosmos and the position of the heavenly bodies. By relating astronomy to geodesy they calculated the exact size (within acceptable margins) of the earth. By relating size and distance of the celestial spheres to terrestrial measurements they could calculate the inherent mathematical relationships involved. Greek science which, as we have said, began with the consideration of motion and change of earthly substance[29] was finally to stumble and eventually to fall when the attention of science moved from considering the size and the positions of the heavenly bodies to concentration upon the cause of their motion. In spite of the fact that, already in the fifth century B.C. Leucippus, like Democritus somewhat later, attempted to explain both matter and motion in the cosmos in relationship to the location and motion of atoms — those smallest indestructible and unchangeable pieces of matter which caused alteration by pressing, pushing, and colliding with one another — it was obvious that such an explanation was inadequate to hold the stars in their places and the moon, the sun, and the planets in their supposed concentric orbits around the earth.

The problem of understanding celestial movement from any kind of earthly analogy must, of course, be appreciated for its difficulty. Not only was the movement of the sun and the moon and the planets seen to be the very essence of beauty and order, bespeaking transcendent patterns of deity itself, but in contrast to every observable motion on earth, where even a ball rolling down a smooth plane eventually comes to a standstill, the heavenly bodies continued to turn and turn eternally. Since eternity belonged to deity alone, the only conceivable and available power which could be considered responsible for such a feat was the mysterious power of divinity itself. Only through the constant power of the *divine world reason* (*nous*), the prime mover, could cosmic movement continue and continue to be assured.[30]

Here, as so often in human history, false physics and false theology interpenetrated and supported one another. Even Anaxagoras, who on the basis of a large meteorite which had fallen near Aegospotamoi helped "to ground the heavens", was not immune to substituting religious speculation for answers to physical problems. Contrary to previous speculations when meteorites were considered to be gifts of the gods — hence they reinforced the concept of divine celestial spheres — Anaxagoras interpreted the spheres in terms of the meteorite. He concluded that the sun, moon, and stars consisted of glowing stone-like masses which were subject to the same forces as things on earth.[31] However, when he was faced with the question of what overwhelming power was necessary to keep the stars in their places and the planets in their orbits — what in fact prevented them from falling to earth as had the meteorite — Anaxagoras, like his Greek predecessors and successors, relied on the only power of sufficient magnitude which appeared to be available, that of divinity itself. Anaxagoras posited a "world-building spirit", a *nous*, a single cause upon which the whole of reality was thought to rest and in view of which the different parts were systematised into a single unity. This *nous* which was responsible for the world's motion was a power which was necessarily "the finest and purest of all things".[32] It was responsible for but not bound to the material world and it took on different forms throughout the development of Greek thought and beyond, as *number* for the Pythagoreans and as the *good* in Plato. It was the *first cause* and *prime mover* in Aristotle. So impressive was the legacy that even for Newton some 2000 years later, this divine, purposive, intelligent, world-ruling and world-moving spiritual power remained responsible for the continuation of the celestial order.

Although Anaxagoras' answer was wrong, it was not to be improved upon until the seventeenth century A.D. Even then Newton's discovery of gravity did not free him entirely from the idea of divine intervention in the regularities of nature. In Anaxagoras' own time there were definite advantages to his conception of the *nous*. The appreciation of a *single*, divine, super-cosmic power symbolised by Zeus as responsible for world order and separate from the material realm, marked the victory of a philosophical concept of a divine reason over the older, amorphous, popular, mythological view of a plurality of deities each of whom was responsible for particular aspects of the world.

As early as the seventh century B.C., Archilochos (fl. c.650 B.C.), "a great poet in antiquity", who was probably born during the lifetime of Hesiod, is thought to have been the first of the Greeks to indicate a monotheistic tendency as reflected in his use of the phrase, ". . . he who rules the gods".[33] Philosophers from Xenophon (c.430–c.355 B.C.) through the later Pythagoreans followed Anaxagoras in proclaiming the idea of a single divinity presented by Zeus who delegated particular powers to lesser divinities.[34] Yet in popular Greek religion, the gods were many. Even worse, so far as science was concerned, instead of being regarded as constituents of the material world, the sun, the moon, and the stars were themselves considered to be divinities who determined the ways of the world. Hence

Anaxagoras' conception of a single *nous* responsible for both the existence of the material world and its motion, much as it implied the danger of inexorable necessity and determinism,[35] signalled a measured triumph, at least, of monotheism over polytheism. The idea of a single power above nature who was responsible for its order was thus established, at least in an elementary way. The fact that this power was *simple* allowed nature the kind of dependability which is necessary for any kind of scientific understanding or explanation. The fact that it was supremely powerful compromised the necessity of lesser powers.

Deities of Plato and Aristotle

The *Nous-Zeus* concept was taken over by Plato in the fourth century B.C. as *the good* and later by Plato's student, Aristotle, who transformed it into the *unmoved Mover*. However, as indicated in our discussion of cosmology, neither Plato nor Aristotle was able to think of monotheistic *world reason* as totally responsible for celestial properties or, as it turned out, for earthly events. In spite of Zeus, the supreme deity, Aristotle (who is most important for our purposes since his was the philosophy which upheld the mediaeval synthesis) followed his master, Plato, who followed his master, Socrates, who would have nothing to do with the "theological reductionism" of the nature philosophers (the *physikoi*) like Anaxagoras and those associated with him. Hence, even Anaxagoras' *nous*, his world-building spirit, was for Socrates, Plato, and Aristotle too simple. Faith in a single extra-terrestrial power was too naïve to explain either the complexity of the heavens or their influence upon earthly existence. As was obvious in Aristotle's cosmology, a plethora of powers was necessary to account for the multitude of necessary forces involved in the heavenly movements. In addition to the "prime Mover", Aristotle went back behind the pre-Socratic Ionian nature philosophers, who had separated the popular mythical conceptions of the gods and goddesses as world forces from their philosophy of nature,[36] and specified fifty-five lesser divinities to take care of the world. These "astral spirits" not only kept the stars in their proper places and moved planets in their eternal orbits, but they embraced both the substantial forms of the living world and the realm of the immortal spirits which were bound to human souls as well.

Socrates, it will be remembered, had rejected the *physikoi* on the basis of their "crass materialism". They had given no thought "to the *good* which must embrace and hold together all things".[37] Anaxagoras' "all-pervading mind", and "arranger and cause of all things", was not the kind of a mind or will concerned with the good, the true and the beautiful which, for Socrates, was the real substance of reality. So distrustful was Socrates of the materialistic phenomenological approach of the *physikoi*, who dealt with things as they found them rather than in terms of the "causes behind these things" that, as the *Phaedo* records, he renounced the direct investigation of realities as such. A passage, beautiful as an illustration of the understanding of "truth" based purely upon mental speculation as over against that which is verified by observation, illustrates the point:

> I decided that I must be careful not to suffer the misfortune which happens to people who look at the sun and watch it during an eclipse. For some of them ruin their eyes unless they look at its image in water or in something of the sort. I thought of that danger, and I was afraid my soul would be blinded if I looked at things with my eyes and tried to grasp them with any of my senses. So I thought I must have recourse to conceptions and examine in them the truth of realities.[38]

Plato, following his master, is equally outspoken in his opposition to the "scientists" of his day. He castigated the *physikoi* because they thought "that the divine entities, the sun, moon and stars were merely stones which care not at all for human affairs". Likewise, he chastised the popular astronomers for their godlessness and for propagating the pernicious inclination to see "as far as they can see, things happening by *necessity* and not by an intelligent will accomplishing good".[39]

Even Aristotle, the "scientist" of the three, was intent on the "spiritual" rather than the "material". There is no gainsaying Aristotle's scientific innovations. His method of classifying species, his teleological approach to biology and his attempt to explain the nature of the world in his *Physics*, indicate the direction science was to take. However, his insistence that *form* was the essence or substance of reality while *matter*, of which reality was composed, was secondary, a mere "accident", did not allow him to trust observation or experimentation in getting at the reality of things. Hence he was completely antagonistic to the kind of physics practised by the *physikoi* who sought to see things as composed of parts and take things apart in order to grasp them in their component elements.

Thus, like Johann Wolfgang von Goethe (1749–1832) two millennia later, Aristotle rejected the analytical approach. As Aristotle criticised the *physikoi*'s method of trying to understand reality partitively rather than seeing within reality that which was essential, i.e., the immaterial causes of things,[40] so too Goethe objected to Isaac Newton's experimental approach. It was irresponsible of Newton to think he could understand light as a whole by sitting in a dark chamber, letting in light by means of a slit in the window shutter and then refracting the beam into its different wave-lengths by means of a prism.[41] Goethe's memorable verses are a lasting eulogy to the romanticism of attempting to understand nature immediately as given, a protest against the scientific method.

> Friends, escape the darkened chamber
> Where they for you distort the light
> And with wretched lamentation
> In confusion stoop to concepts trite.

Superstitious idolisers
Have the years produced enough,
In the minds of your teachers
Caused phantoms, madness, fraudulent stuff.[42]

Plato, of course, had accused both the Ionians and the atomists of sheer atheism. For them, all religion was simply "a cooking up of words and a make-believe".[43] Though Plato was no doubt correct in his denunciation from his own perspective, the accusation is parallel to the censure passed on the early Christians who were also condemned as atheists because they believed only in one God in contrast to the many gods which made up the Roman pantheon. Hence, when one recalls both Plato's and Aristotle's "religious concepts", the judgement of the Ionians as "atheists" might be considered a compliment.

Aristotle's physics and theology are of especial interest because of the effect his concepts have had on the western world in general, and of their effect on the rise of science in particular. Here we face the paradoxical situation in which we must recognise that, though initially Aristotelian thought was basic to the development of science in the West, eventually it became responsible for holding that development in check. Aristotle's cosmology was at one and the same time theology. The universe was an harmonious and interrelated plenum wherein "the foremost and highest divinity" occupied the highest echelon in being.[44] Next to him was located the sphere of the stars which possessed divinity in themselves. These, in turn, were responsible for the ways of the cosmos and humankind. The cosmos itself was considered to consist of an *ether* which, like the rest of celestial reality, was thought to be divine, immortal, and unlimited in motion.[45] Both the heavenly bodies and the cosmic spheres possessed immortal souls. Inbuilt intelligences directed the movements of the stars which, being motivated by desire and love, attempted to imitate the Prime Mover, the eternal, unalterable inciter of primary motion which for Aristotle was God himself.[46] Little wonder that Aristotle's astronomy was part of his theology rather than of his physics.

It is over against this Aristotelian dogmatism that we can understand the profound insight of Francis Bacon (1561–1626) who, perhaps more than any other figure in seventeenth-century science, was the advocate of the experimental method, though he was singularly wanting in its application. Bacon insisted that philosophers like Democritus "who removed God and Mind from the structure of things", had more real insight into the processes of nature than Plato and Aristotle for the very simple reason that the natural philosophers did not mix final causes with their physics.[47] Hence, Francis Bacon, like Roger Bacon some four centuries earlier, saw that taken as a whole Aristotle's thought made experimental science quite impossible.[48]

The important point to note here, however, is that in opting for "the religious point of view" over the "secularism" of the Ionians in general and the *physikoi* in particular, Plato and especially Aristotle, the "renowned scientists" of the ancient world, really prevented science as we know it from developing in ancient Greece. As Francis Bacon so shrewdly perceived, not only did Aristotle's insistence upon the identity of deity with certain aspects of nature make natural science impossible, but in confusing aspects of deity with aspects of nature, Aristotle's philosophy made faith impossible as well.[49]

> When he [Aristotle] had made nature pregnant with final causes, laying it down that "Nature does nothing in vain, and always effects her will when freed from impediments", and many other things of the same kind, [he] had no further need of a God.[50]

By effectively substituting nature for God, Aristotle not only lost out on physics but, according to Bacon, he lost out on God as well.[51]

With Aristotle theology and "science" were of a piece. As Günter Howe (1908–68) has pointed out, here we see physics, philosophy, and a monotheistic faith merging together in the vast unity of Greek metaphysics. This faith

was at one and the same time both the source of fundamental astronomical knowledge and the foundation of a
belief in a world organiser responsible for the order and
movement of the planets. "The whole was a great but
dangerous inheritance which the Middle Ages took over
from the Greeks."[52] Herbert Butterfield underscores
Howe's judgement.

A universe constructed on the mechanics of Aristotle
had the door half-way open for spirits already: it was a
universe in which unseen hands had to be in constant
operation, and sublime Intelligences had to roll the
planetary spheres around. Alternatively, bodies had to
be endowed with souls and aspirations, with a
"disposition" to certain kinds of motion, so that
matter itself seemed to possess mystical qualities.[53]

Thus in spite of the fact that in the "Christian West"
Aristotle's writings inspired the kind of interest and
investigation that gave rise to modern science, his
theologically determined physics was a hindrance to the
development of science in his own time and right up
through the Middle Ages. In following his teachers, Plato
and Socrates, he rejected the earlier Greek scientists such
as the *atomists* or the *physikoi*, and turned back the
advances made by them. Thus he undermined the ground
for natural science in two ways. First, Aristotle's world was
so filled with divinities, sublime intelligences, souls and
aspirations that nature was unpredictable at best and
downright capricious at worst. Secondly, and quite
contradictorily, the concept of the "Unmoved Mover",
which he had inherited as the "Zeus-nous world-
organiser" from Anaxagoras, became in Aristotle the
source not only of efficient causation but also of all final
causes. Because of this, the world was understood to be so
tightly structured that the whole of reality was essentially
predestined and predetermined. The result was an
inexorable logico-deductive system in which function
followed being in such a way that the kind of open heuristic
thinking on which experimental science depends was

necessarily ruled out. Science was understood not as the study of nature by means of observation and experimentation, but as a way of observing and classifying phenomena which brought to light the original forms immanent in the world. Further, the purpose of the exercise was not even to recognise the original forms as such but really to recognise the meaning behind them.

In sum, it would seem proper to regard the thought of the pre-Socratics as an attempt to turn away from or at least ignore the kind of spirit-dominated, enchanted and therefore capricious world represented by the myths of Homer and Hesiod and to move toward a world of substance and numbers, a world which, because it was stable, allowed for predictability and intelligibility. In that for the Ionians thought itself was considered to stand in direct relationship to its object, they may have been too *naïvely realistic*, as Zeller points out. Since it was out of this "objective conception of the world" that the propositions of knowledge were derived, the Ionian programme had promise. On the other hand, the "naïve realism" of the pre-Socratics limited their scope. As for many of their post-Newtonian successors some two millennia later, for the *physikoi* all "reality" was held to be corporeal reality. Hence the Platonic Socrates had a right to complain that the *physikoi*'s view of reality may have been too circumscribed, though his own concept of a divinely and morally directed world which neglected material things was hardly a valid alternative.[54] In the end the Ionians' consistent denial of all that was not material and their inability to differentiate between "levels" in which "reality" manifests itself led them to understand even the *nous*, "the world-building mind", as a power of nature.[55]

Thus though the pre-Socratics did not recognise God as transcendent, as did the Jews and later the Christians, their attempts in that direction had a good deal more hope than those of Socrates, Plato, and even Aristotle in whom we find a return to the pre-pre-Socratic attitude which Plutarch described as "Zeus the beginning, Zeus in the midst, and from Zeus comes all things".[56]

The Socratic, Platonic, and Aristotelian emphases upon the divine, which at best were of an illustrative rather than of an explanatory character, went back to the Pythagorean identification of faith and physics. Pythagoreanism, of course, was a cult before it was a "science" at all. The rules of Pythagorean cultic life were largely inherited from Orphism: an injunction against speaking about the holy, the wearing of white garments, the observation of sexual purity, regulations about diet and, of particular importance, the discipline of silence, especially for novitiates in respect of the celestial secrets. It was of great importance for the development of science, however, that purification of the soul involved musical and mental activity. The contemplation of divine realities lying behind nature and reflected in it was held to be the way of holiness. In the course of time the study of the cosmos, especially of the heavens which represented divinity in all its perfection, led to cosmology. The patterns set out by the heavenly movements which reflected divinity were discerned as geometric forms which, when interpreted by number, were reduced to mathematical proportions. They constituted the rational or divine properties permeating and giving harmony to the universe in which the religiously oriented self became absorbed. However, the quantifying activity involved in that mathematical approach had the effect of opening the way for science.

The Pythagorean contribution to science was thus a spin-off of the quest for the holy. Although it was originally only of secondary import for the Pythagoreans themselves, it came to have primary importance both for exact science and for the way in which humankind has continually mingled faith with science, with the latter depending for its development upon the former. Thus it happened that the Pythagoreans, who supplied the basis for both Platonic and Aristotelian thought and hence for Greek science as a whole, through their search for the holy began to bring the celestial movements, which for them reflected divinity, down to earth. This had the effect of encouraging definitions of celestial realities in earthly terms. Since number had extension, even the form of the divine heavens could be set out in proportionalities recognisable in dimensions which applied to earthly realities as well. Numbers governed both realms. Music, too, played a mediating role. The music of the heavenly spheres could be approximated on earth by tuned strings of known length which when plucked vibrated at a calculable rate. Again there was a correspondence between the heavenly and the earthly.

According to Benjamin Farrington, people like Plutarch continued to reflect and mediate the early Pythagorean and Platonic approach in their claim that "the function of geometry . . . is to draw us away from the sensible and the perishable to the contemplation of the eternal".[57] Thus religion, not "science", dominated the traditional Greek desire to know reality. Nevertheless, the religious adoration of eternity displayed by "the circularity" of heavenly movements gave birth to geometrical formulae by which not only the eternal heavens but the sensible and corruptible earth could be measured and reduced to human understanding as well. As we shall see, the significance of this Pythagorean quest for heavenly harmonies was later to become evident with Kepler who began his study of the heavens in order to "hear" the music of the spheres. Thus, while in Pythagorean fashion his work in discovering the three laws of planetary motion began with mysticism, it ended in mathematics.[58]

The history of the term, *theoria* (theory), as Arthur Koestler points out, exemplifies this change from religious to scientific thinking.[59] The verb, *theorein*, originally meant "to behold" or "to contemplate". In the hands of the Pythagoreans it moved from the Orphic religious use of the term signifying "a state of fervent religious contemplation" toward a scientific use. With them we see the channelisation of "religious fervour" into intellectual fervour and "religious ecstasy" into the excitement of discovery. Thus *theoria* gradually changed its meaning into "theory" in the modern sense of hypothesis.[60]

Much as we are indebted to them, the Pythagoreans,

more than any others, show us that though religion may well be the impetus for scientific development, if the scientific aspects of thought remain captive to the religious ideology, which may have given them birth, science will hardly move beyond its rudimentary stages. In turn, religion is likely to remain caught in its own presuppositions and to remain insipid as well. Thus, while the later Pythagoreans stressed mathematics and geometry and made real advances in accounting for the movements of the heavenly bodies, Plato's continued insistence on reading primary reality as "divinity" resulted in the elevation of the realm of "ideas" over the realm of the sensible or material. In Aristotle the prime mover and perfect circles of astronomy were matched by the emphasis in his metaphysics on first and final causes. These interpenetrated the universe to such an extent that pre-existent forms were considered to be the real substance and continued to be the focus of thought while material reality was considered only of minor import. "Scientist" though he was, Aristotle's lack of trust in observation really prevented him from developing a consistent method by which nature could be understood. For him, to be sure, as for Immanuel Kant later, the reality which the senses perceived was a secondary form of existence.[61] Reality in the proper sense, however, that which was really real, could only be deduced by the mind from given principles. In addition, the fact that, for Aristotle, the world was immanent with capricious divinities who directed the life of the heavens and life on earth, contributed to a system in which the whole of reality was subject to the non-predictable artifice of intervening spirits.

As always, however, capriciousness and inexorability are two sides of the same coin. Hence, once harmony and beauty were "discerned", eternal purpose, interpreted as "the will of the gods", was understood with such certainty that nature was structured in pre-determined paths toward finality. An attitude of awe and subservience rather than of respect and questioning was the result. In the final analysis, destiny was held to be totally in "the hands of the gods" who inhabited the heavens and ruled the earth.

On the face of it Aristotelian philosophy could have moved in either direction, i.e. toward a completely unpredictable universe subject to deities directing things according to their own capricious wills, or to a universe in which the first cause predominated to such an extent that final causes were everywhere determinative. However, when the system was combined with Aristotelian deductive logic which moves inexorably from first to final cause, then for all intents and purposes, the end was determined from the beginning.

The proper understanding of reality was thus either a matter of deduction from known principle or of logical extrapolation from known reality. This kind of deductive rationalism along with the consciousness of the possibility of capricious divine interpenetration of nature made fundamental investigative procedures at one and the same time both superfluous and impossible. As long as Aristotle prevailed, therefore, experimental sciences were ruled out.

This critique is admittedly offered from within a very different perspective, one which, as we shall see below, has been focused by some thirteen hundred years of criticism of Aristotle. It is motivated in part at least by seeing Aristotle in the light of biblical thought, was begun by Johannes Philoponos in the sixth century and carried forward by Franciscan thinkers — Robert Grosseteste (c.1170–1253), Roger Bacon (c.1214–c.1294), John Duns Scotus (c.1266–1308), and William of Ockham (c.1284–c.1349) from the twelfth to the fourteenth centuries. It was continued in the Renaissance and was finalised by the Protestant Reformation and the rise of seventeenth-century science. However, in the latter part of the pre-Christian era and throughout the age of Ptolemy in the second century A.D. and beyond, while Aristotle's cosmology was questioned at different points, his influence in the "scientific world" was largely unchallenged. So persuasive was Aristotle that even John Calvin who did not regard himself as an Aristotelian, and indeed castigated

Aristotle's observations and conclusions, continued to think of him as "the greatest of philosophers".[62]

The Ptolemaic "Summa"

Ptolemy's Μαθηματικῆς σηντάξεως βιβλίον πρῶτον was with good reason called by the Arabs "al megiste". By prefixing their definite article, *al*, to the Greek, *megiste*, they coined the term *Almagest* (the greatest), the name by which the work has been known ever since. Originally the name was used to distinguish Ptolemy's writings known as *The Great Astronomer* from a collection known as *The Little Astronomer* but the work deserves the name on its own account. As Thomas Aquinas summed up mediaeval theology on the basis of Aristotle in his *Summa Theologica* at the end of the Middle Ages, so in an analogous way Ptolemy summed up Greek mathematics and astronomy in his *Almagest* at the end of the Hellenistic age. It is hardly an exaggeration, therefore, to call it a *Summa*.

Ptolemy was a Renaissance man before the Renaissance. Not only was he the greatest mathematician of antiquity, but as heir to Pythagorean philosophy, which included mathematics and geodesy as well as astronomy, he wrote a treatise on music called the *Harmonia* and was responsible for a primary work on geography. His *Guide to Geography*, in which he tabulated the locations of places on earth according to their latitude and longitude and mapped out the size of the "inhabited" world, was of such importance that right up to the Renaissance, Ptolemy was as well known as "the geographer" as he was as "the astronomer". The book remained a primary text on the subject even after Copernicus in his *De Revolutionibus Orbium Caelestium* called the *Almagest* into question. In addition, Ptolemy's *Optics* records one of history's first attempts to deal with the refraction of light through different media. It may be somewhat ironic that when the science of optics was transferred to the West by way of Alghazali, it became the basis for the development of the telescope. The telescope, in turn, allowed Galileo to gather the kind of astronomical information that, along with Kepler's calculations, finally set Ptolemy's geocentric system aside.

As some 1400 years later Copernicus introduced his system with a short summary called the *Commentariolus*, so Ptolemy summarised his system in his *Hypothesis on the Planets*. In this writing he listed the principal theories of the *Almagest* including an explanation of the motion of the heavenly bodies, notations of the annual sidereal phenomena and, perhaps just to be practical, a chronological table which correlated the reigns of the Assyrian, Persian, Greek, and Roman kings. The table served the purpose of fixing the dates of historical events that were recorded as having happened in a certain year in the reign of a certain king.[63]

Since, as R. C. Taliaferro points out, the works of Eudoxus, Callippus, Heraclides, Aristarchus, Apollonius, and Hipparchus have for the most part been lost, the *Almagest* "is the only completely comprehensive treatise of Greek astronomy to come down to us".[64] Aristarchus' work *On the Sizes and Distances of the Sun and Moon* which, as we discussed above, describes the method of measuring the sizes of those bodies and their distances from the earth, has survived as well but its treatment is quite limited. Thus, with the exception of the writings of Plato and Aristotle and brief allusions to the partial heliocentric theory of Heraclides and the complete heliocentric theory of Aristarchus, information about which has survived only in scattered fragments, almost all we know of Greek astronomy is preserved for us by the *Almagest*.

However, in contradistinction to Kepler whose discovery of elliptical orbits finally broke the restraints of circularity upon astronomy and whose writings give us full details not only of the modes of discovery but also of his doubts, his rêveries and the workings of his mind, Ptolemy remained something of a secretive Pythagorean. Hence, while the *Almagest* is remarkable for detail in regard to the geometry and mathematics incorporated in the formulation of his geocentric theory, the calculations regarding the sizes and distances displayed by the heavenly bodies and the notations on the various tables of angles and stars, Ptolemy indicates nothing at all of the methods he used in his observations and discoveries. He is straightforward, however, in pointing out the general assumptions behind the geocentric theory. These, based primarily on the philosophy and physics of Aristotle, are worked out by incorporating the modifications to the Aristotelian system that had been discovered by later Pythagorean astronomers and by the use of the evidence gained from the observations of Hipparchus as well as his own.

In order to explain his mathematics Ptolemy introduced and developed the theorems for spherical trigonometry necessary for his astronomical theories. He then moved into the details of his system which showed the angles of the horizons in different latitudes to the ecliptic and explained the movements of each of the heavenly bodies according to a geometry which included the use of deferents, epicycles, eccentrics, and equants. Following that, he traced the movements of the sun, explained the phases and eclipses of the moon, the precession of the equinoxes and supplied the whole with elaborate notations and tables. Most important for our purposes, Ptolemy offered an account of the continued and "science-preventing" Platonic and Aristotelian insistence on the divine nature of the heavens. This conception, so fateful for the development of both astronomy and science, involved the necessity of both circularity and sphericity, attributed to each of the planets its own particular will, differentiated between mathematics and physics, and divided the world between the super-lunar and sub-lunar spheres.

In the preface to the *Almagest*, Ptolemy pays homage to Aristotle for dividing theoretical thought "into three immediate genera: the physical, the mathematical, and the theological".[65] The kind of science which seeks after God is theological. It answers the question of simplicity, "the first cause of the first movement of the universe". It finds "God invisible and unchanging".[66] Physical science, on the other hand, "traces through the material and ever-moving quality" and has to do with the "essence" (οὐσία) of what is to be "found in corruptible things and below the lunar sphere".[67] Mathematical science which "shows up quality with respect to forms and local motions, seeking figure, number, and magnitude, and also place, time, and similar things", has to do with the essence of things which fall between "theology", on the one hand, and "physics", on the other.[68] It deals with that which is "an accident" in all mortal and immortal beings, a feature which changes with the things that change "according to their inseparable form, and preserving unchangeable the changelessness of form in things eternal and of an ethereal nature".[69] Further, since things theological are "in no way phenomenal and attainable" and things physical are composed of matter which is "unstable and obscure",[70] trustworthy knowledge of "the divine and heavenly" can only be given by the "theoretical discipline" (θεωρία) of mathematical science "both arithmetic and geometric".[71] Thus, mathematical theory "would most readily prepare the way to the theological, since it alone could take good aim at that unchangeable and separate act, so close to that act are the properties having to do with translations and arrangements of movements, belonging to those heavenly beings which are sensible and both moving and moved, but eternal and impassible".[72]

Like a true Pythagorean, then, Ptolemy was certain that mathematics was universally relevant and that it mediated between the divine and the physical. By mathematics one could know not only sameness, good order and true proportion but the "simple directness contemplated in divine things, making its followers lovers of that divine beauty, and making habitual in them, and as it were natural, a like condition of the soul".[73]

As far as physics was concerned, however, Ptolemy remained a true Aristotelian. His differentiation between the corruptible and the incorruptible was correlated with that between *straight* and *circular* movement. The heavy and the light, the passive and the active, were sorted out

according to whether they were directed *to the centre* or
away from the centre.[74] In true Aristotelian fashion he
explained that the heavens move spherically. The earth,
too, was defined as being of a spherical nature. However, in
contradistinction to the sphericity of the heavens which
Ptolemy "proved" on metaphysical grounds (they were
held to be necessarily spherical because sphericity is an
inescapable correlate of circular motion), the evidence he
gave for the spherical nature of the earth was from
observation. Stars rise and set at different times for
different peoples at different locations on the earth. Certain
stars are visible at some locations and not at others: "the
more we advance toward the north pole, the more the
southern stars are hidden and the northern stars appear".[75]
Again, when anyone sails toward mountains, for instance,
they appear to rise little by little from the seas, whereas
from a distance they appear to be submerged because of the
curvature of the surface of the water.[76]

When it comes to "proving" that the earth is "in the
middle of the heavens", Ptolemy again marshalled his
arguments from astronomy. Only if the earth were in the
centre of the universe would the equinoxes come about
when once in spring and once in autumn the sun crosses the
equator and makes day and night of equal length in all parts
of the earth and when the shadows of the *gnomons*
(sundials) cast a shadow at sunrise on a straight line with
the shadow at sunset. Only if the earth were exactly in the
midst of the celestial spheres could the horizon always
appear to cut the zodiac in half. Further, the fact that "the
earth has the ratio of a point to the heavens" (a formula
which Ptolemy apparently picked up from Aristarchus)
explained the observation that the angular distances of the
stars were identical no matter what the latitude from which
they were measured. Thus, wherever sundials were placed
on the earth, the circling and locations of the shadows were
exactly the same as they would have been had the instruments been placed at the centre of the earth.[77]

In attempting to prove "that the earth does not in any
way move locally", Ptolemy called upon both observation

and Aristotle. His arguments were so persuasive that they remained the prime reasons for the deep doubts which greeted the Copernican system 1400 years later. They were, in fact, the basis for the condemnation of Galileo and the reason why Galileo was forced to admit the Aristotelian-Ptolemaic fiction that "the earth did not move".

Ptolemy's argument for the stationary earth is at first a repetition of the evidence he had garnered to "prove" the earth's centrality in the midst of the heavens with a ratio of a point to the heavenly sphere. For his physics, however, he reiterated the teaching of Aristotle who had divided all local *motions* into those which were "natural" and those which were "violent", all *bodies* into those which were "single" and those which were "compound", and the *universe* between the "super-" and "sub-lunar" spheres. "Compound bodies" were those which were a part of the universe lying below the lunar sphere and which, therefore, were subject to generation and corruption. Their *natural motion* was of unimpeded and unpropelled fall. By contrast, *violent motion*, which again concerned only bodies of the sub-lunar realm, consisted of motion that was propelled or interrupted. The only motion that was *natural* to the heavenly bodies was, in true Pythagorean, Platonic, and Aristotelian fashion, regular, uniform, and circular.[78]

The fact that, as according to Aristotle, the proper motion of bodies below the lunar sphere was that *they fell toward the centre* explained for Ptolemy why bodies placed above the earth always fell toward the centre of the earth perpendicular to the plane tangent of the earth's spherical surface. It also explained the reason why the earth held together. All its parts tended to fall toward its centre and pressed against all sides equally at the same angle. Thus, too, Ptolemy was convinced there was no "up" and "down". "Down" is simply the direction "from our feet to the earth's centre". "Up" is the direction from above our heads "to the enveloping surface of the universe". Since heavy objects fall "down" and "toward the centre", were not the earth to occupy the centre toward which all heavy objects fall, animals and other weights would be left hanging in the air and the earth itself would "fall out of the heavens".[79]

As the earth is in the centre of the universe, so, too, it is stationary. Ptolemy knew the arguments of those such as Heraclides and Aristarchus who perceived that rather than the earth being immobile in the centre of the world, the heavens were immobile and the earth turned on its axis from west to east once each day. It is true, Ptolemy admitted, that though this thesis might indeed conform to the appearances of the stars, such a notion was absured if one were to consider what would happen in the immediate proximity of a spinning earth. Since the hypothesis made no differentiation between the movement of light and heavy bodies and presupposed that the earth moved with great swiftness to make so great a revolution in so short a time, all kinds of things should happen that were contrary to experience. Everything that was not attached to the earth would surely be seen to have a movement contrary to it. The earth would spin under the clouds and these would never be seen to move toward the east. Rather, the spinning earth would simply outstrip them. So, too, the spinning earth would outstrip a stone thrown into the air. Airborne bodies would simply be "left behind and move toward the west" as the earth revolved to the east under them. Even if it were admitted that the air was carried along with the earth in the same direction at the same speed as the earth was moving, it was a fact that the movement, the slowness or swiftness, of flying bodies or projectiles was not observed to "follow at all from the earth's movement".[80]

In agreement with astronomical observations, however, Ptolemy willingly admitted "that there are two different prime motions in the heavens".[81] There is a general movement of everything from east to west uniformly in circles which are both parallel to each other and are clearly described about the poles of the regularly revolving celestial sphere. In modification of Aristotle's concentric universe, however, Ptolemy recognised certain local motions in the opposite direction of the general motion and around other centres. In addition to moving generally in paths "sensibly similar" to those of the stars, "the sun and moon and planets make certain complex movements unequal to each other, but all contrary to the general movement".[82] Thus, while the planets move generally to the east, they move irregularly toward the north and south poles, that is, "without any uniform magnitudes being observed in this deviation, *so that it seems to befall them through* impulsions".[83] These "impulsions" correlate with the "individual wills" which Aristotle assigned to each of the heavenly spheres. Nevertheless, since the planets always resumed their regular places among the stars after certain periods of time, even this irregular motion was seen to be confined within a prescribed distance and governed by rule. Thus, even though Ptolemy's system had its deficiences, its demonstration of *order* in place of *disorder* and its coordination of geometry, measurement, and appearance showed it to be a "scientific system" in the best sense in spite of its inadequacies.

The system had, of course, to explain the complicated movements of the planets. To do so Ptolemy adopted the deferents and epicycles of Apollonius whereby the deferents were centred on the pole of the ecliptic and moved continually at right angles to the horizon. The second movement, Ptolemy explained, consisted of many parts. It is the motion which Plato in his *Timaeus* had described as the motion of "the other" as differentiated from the motion of "the same".[84] This motion in the opposite direction of the ecliptic is that which is described by the epicycles attached to the deferents. Though revolving around their own centres, the epicycles were carried around by the first revolution which centred on the earth so that all of the planets were kept in positions on the circle of the ecliptic.

Ptolemy's introduction of the plane and spherical trigonometry which he used to explain astronomical theories, and his calculations for the determination of the inclination of the ecliptic and the equator, display his mathematical genius. He worked out the correlations of the arcs on the ecliptic and the equator to the oblique sphere in relationship to the position of the horizons and the shadows cast by sundials at different latitudes.[85] He ended his introduction to mathematics by explaining the way the circles which result from his calculation differ in inclination from one another. He then moved on to explain that the movements of the sun and the moon, which were basic to the understanding of the heavens in general, had to be provided with deferents, epicycles, and eccentrics in order that their irregularities could be accounted for. "Without a prior understanding of them", Ptolemy claimed, "none of the appearances having to do with the stars can be discovered."[86]

Ptolemy's explanation of the "apparent irregularity" of the sun in which he states his "hypothesis concerning regular and circular movement" shows his adherence to three prime presuppositions of Greek cosmology: *circularity*, *regularity*, and *immutability*, which were eventually to give the lie to his system as well as to that of Copernicus. Copernicus, as we shall see, insisted upon the principles with even more tenacity than Ptolemy. Ptolemy explained as follows:

> Since the next thing is to explain the apparent irregularity of the sun, it is first necessary to assume in general that the motions of the planets in the direction contrary to the movement of the heavens are *all regular and circular by nature*, like the movement of the universe in the other direction. That is, the straight lines, conceived as revolving the stars or their circles, cut off in equal times on absolutely all circumferences equal angles at the centres of each; and their apparent irregularities result from the positions and arrangements of the circles on their spheres through which they produce these movements, but *no departure from their unchangeableness has really occurred* in their nature in regard to the supposed disorder of their appearances.[87]

In reality, as Copernicus was to point out, the much vaunted "regularity" and "circularity" were not really maintained by Ptolemy. In order to make the geometry of the system correlate with the appearance of the heavenly bodies, "two primary simple hypotheses" were necessary. These were that of the *eccentricity of the primary circles* or *deferents* which centred on the earth and that of the *epicycles* attached to the edge of the deferents. These "other circles" which were "not concentric with the cosmos" were multiple so that epicycles bore epicycles which finally carried the planets.[88] Though Ptolemy was certain that either the hypothesis of multiple epicycles on concentric deferents or the use of eccentrics with fewer epicycles would suffice to allow the planets to appear to pass "in equal periods of time, through unequal arcs of the ecliptic circle which is concentric with the cosmos",[89] in reality, as already explained, he actually used both eccentrics and multiple epicycles and invented the *equants* to explain the regular motion as well. The equants were points near the centre of each deferent from which the regular motion of each body, though not observable from earth, could be calculated.

The complexity of the system is best illustrated by Mercury whose orbit is so complicated that the precession of its orbit was not properly understood until Einstein developed the Theory of General Relativity. Ptolemy attempted to explain the complexity by providing Mercury with an eccentric deferent, multiple epicycles and an equant which itself moved around in a small circle around a point near to but somewhat off centre of the deferent.

The fact that the Ptolemaic system, as Copernicus was to see, severely compromised the primary principle of spherical mechanics — circularity and regularity — did not in the least lessen the force of Ptolemy's assent to this basic tenet of Greek theological cosmology. Rather, his compromises of principle allowed him to call upon the observations of Hipparchus as well as those he made on his own at Canopus (located about twenty-five kilometres to the east of and on the same latitude as Alexandria), observations which he made between the years 127–151 A.D., and to fill the heavens with circular geometry which

appeared to "save the appearances" with such felicity that
the system was not really to be improved upon until
Copernicus, if then.[90] His explanations moved back and
forth across the history of astronomy from the Babylonians
to his own time. The geocentric system which he worked
out on the basis of Aristotelian theology, physics, and
cosmology as modified by Apollonius and Hipparchus was
so carefully constructed that to doubt its validity was to
doubt the very foundation of Greek learning. He annotated
the whole with Greek mathematics and supplied it with the
necessary astronomical tables to produce a cosmological
summa that must be admired not only for its accuracy and
detail but for its integrity. Although he was misled both by
"circularity" and "geocentricity", his work was a model of
scientific procedure. He set out the principles he intended
to follow, argued for their validity and, even though in
many cases they were wrong, for the most part he carried
them out according to his explicit intention. In so doing he
was able to satisfy not only the immediate observational
demands of experience and the necessities of mathematics
but the physics and theology which Aristotle had taught
the popular mind as well.[91] By employing geometry to
explain the configuration of the earth-centred system and
mathematics to calculate the planetary distances, Ptolemy
produced a solution that, because of its elegance, left little
question as to its accuracy.

In sum, Ptolemy, like Aristotle, placed the earth as a
sphere in the middle of the cosmos. In order to describe
irregular movement, he displaced Aristotle's series of
concentric crystal spheres on the surfaces of which were
affixed the moon, the sun, and the seven known planets,
and which together orbited majestically around the earth,
with separate circular deferents for each of the heavenly
bodies. Following the lead of Apollonius and Hipparchus,
Ptolemy allowed each of the deferents to move eccentri-
cally, and supplied each planet with epicycles which were
connected to their particular deferents and to which each of
the planets was attached. The combined movements of the
deferents and epicycles accounted for both the regular and

the apparent irregular motion of each planet in its orbit around the earth. In addition, Ptolemy provided the system with his own innovation of equants which, as explained above, were the postulated positions placed somewhat off the centre of each of the deferents and likewise somewhat off the centre of the earth. From these "regular motion" for each of the planets was supposed to be measurable. All this was necessary to explain that any apparent "irregularity" of the particular body in question could be accounted for in terms of motion that was perfectly regular. As befitted the holy harmony of the heavens, all actual movements of the celestial spheres were thus shown to be the result of circular motion.

Ptolemy, then, gave the geocentric system which was surrounded by the revolving sphere of fixed stars a complete and detailed mathematical explanation so that observation and calculation not only coincided but the pattern determined what was observed. The system as a whole, which was measured by reference to the size of the earth, not only summed up all the relevant cosmological and mathematical data, but satisfied the demands of religious concepts, ideas of perfection, and principles of rationality, even as it explained away the anomalies of observation. The result was that any possible doubt about the harmony of the heavens was considered a fault to the eye and mind of the observer rather than a critique of the system. Ptolemy's universe was beautiful to contemplate, satisfying to both sense and soul, and substantiated by scientific explanations.

This harmonious and, for a millennium and a half, scientifically satisfying concept showed people the universe as they had learned to experience it. The fact that it was wrong did not in the least prevent it from being "the truth" in its own time and remaining "the truth" for nearly 1500 years. *Truth* was a matter of seeing and interpreting reality as people had been taught. The system remained "the truth", however, largely because of its coincidence with Greek and especially Aristotelian thought, not least Aristotelian theological thought. Thus, wrong as it turned out to be, there is no slighting the grandeur of the Ptolemaic system. It is thus quite understandable, as Howe reports, that when Greek science which accompanied the works of Aristotle came into the Christian West at the end of the Middle Ages, the Occident saw with wonder and shock what tremendous accomplishments the human mind was able to bring about "without the light of divine revelation".[92] When in the thirteenth century Thomas Aquinas integrated the thought of Aristotle with Christian theology and produced the mediaeval synthesis, the system was given divine and ecclesiastical sanction. Having become the acknowledged and even mandatory representation of reality, the Ptolemaic system not only determined the cosmology of the West well into the sixteenth century but, when the Thomistic synthesis was accepted, it became an obligatory part of theology as well. So persuasive was the argument for the necessity of circular motion that even when geocentricity was set aside by Copernicus, circularity, which had never been doubted, continued to persist. However, it was precisely this circular and regular motion, that motion which, it was held, alone revealed the glory, majesty, and perfection of God, which proved to be the Achilles' heel of both the Ptolemaic and the Copernican astronomical systems.

NOTES

1. For Jaki's discussion of mathematics, cf. "The World As a Pattern of Numbers," *Relevance of Physics*, pp. 95–137.
2. Aristotle, *Metaphysics* I, I. iv–v, 985b–986a.
3. Albert Einstein, *The Meaning of Relativity* (London: Chapman and Hall, 1980), p. 3.
4. Jaki, *Relevance of Physics*, p. 7; cf. *ibid.*, pp. 98f.
5. Diels, *Fragmente*, 47, B, 1., Archytas, p. 432.
6. Cf. Koestler, *Sleepwalkers*, p. 30.
7. Cf. Albert Einstein on this, "Geometry and Experience", *Sidelights on Relativity* (London: Methuen, 1922), p. 28. Cf., *ibid.*, p. 34.
8. David Bergamini and others, *Die Mathematik* (Nederland: Time-Life, 1965), p. 173.
9. Aristotle, *Physics* I, Loeb Classical Library (London: Heinemann, 1929), III. iv–viii, 203a–208a. Cf. Aristotle, *Metaphysics* I, I. vii–viii, 988b–989b.

10. The discovery that Euclid's "Fifth Postulate", that one and only one line can be drawn parallel through a point adjacent to a given line, could not be proven led, in fact, to the construction of the non-Euclidian geometries of Nikolai Lobachewski (1826), Janos Bolyai (1872), and, most important for modern cosmology, Bernhard Riemann (1854).
11. Albert Einstein, *Essays in Science* (New York: Philosophical Library, 1955? c.1934), p. 13.
12. *Ibid.*
13. Günter Howe, *Mensch und Physik* (Berlin: Eckart, 1963), pp. 14ff.
14. According to Einstein, "the eternal mystery of the world is its comprehensibility". Einstein, *Out of My Later Years*, p. 61.
15. Diels, *Fragmente* 12, A 10, Anaximandros, p. 83.
16. *Ibid.*, 12, A 18, Anaximandros, p. 86.
17. *Ibid.*, 22, B 3, Herakleitos, p. 151.
18. Diels, *Fragmente* 31, A 61, Empedokles. Cf. Dreyer, *History of Astronomy*, p. 25. Anaxagoras, who postulated the composition of the sun on the basis of the meteorite which fell at Aegospotamoi in 467 B.C., deducing that it was a red-hot stone, was equally bold in supposing the sun to be greater in size than the Peloponnesus (ὑπερέχειν δὲ τον ἥλιον μεγέθει τὸν Πελοπόννησον), Diels, *Fragmente*, 59, A 42. Cf. Dreyer, *op. cit.*, p. 31. As Jaki points out, however, "there are no indications that he had ever compared this magnitude to the size and distance of other parts and objects of the skies", *Relevance of Physics*, p. 553, Chapter V, fn. 5. For Jaki's discussion, cf. *ibid.*, "Frontiers of the Cosmos", pp. 188–235.
19. Cf. Kuhn, "Ancient Competitors of the Two-Sphere Universe", *Copernican Revolution*, pp. 41–44.
20. Aristotle, *On the Heavens*, II. xiv, 298a. According to Jaki, Aristotle is here dependent on Eudoxus and Archytas, *Relevance of Physics*, pp. 189f.
21. Aristotle, *Meteorologica*, Loeb Classical Library (London: Heinemann, 1952), I. viii, 345b.
22. *Ibid.*, I. iii, 340a. Cf. Jaki, *Relevance of Physics*, pp. 192f.
23. So Dreyer, *History of Astronomy*, p. 183. The acceptance of earth-size as cosmic measure is a typical example of the scientific process which is paradigmatic for all thought processes wherein the focusing in on one "advance" entails the focusing out of another equally important possible development.
24. *Ibid.* For an explanation and diagram of Aristarchus' method, cf. Kuhn, *Copernican Revolution*, pp. 274–278.
25. Dreyer, *History of Astronomy*, p. 183; cf., *ibid.*, pp. 123–148. Cf. also Kuhn's explanation, *Copernican Revolution*, pp. 276f. and p. 160 for the size of the Copernican universe.
26. Dreyer, *History of Astronomy*, p. 184.
27. *Ibid.*, pp. 174ff.

28. *Ibid.*, pp. 174–176. For Kuhn's explanation and diagram, cf. *Copernican Revolution*, pp. 273f.
29. Cf. above, p. 4ff.
30. 28. Howe, *Mensch und Physik*, p. 16.
31. The nickeliferous iron beads found in the pre-dynastic graves at Geizeh, Egypt, which are dated prior to 3100 B.C. and iron fragments at Ur in Mesopotamia which pre-date iron smelting would seem to be evidence of much earlier meteorites.
32. Zeller, *Philosophie*, p. 359.
33. Archilochus is thought to have lived shortly after the Odyssey was written. The authorship of the phrase, a part of a lyric poem quoted by A. Snodgrass, is in some dispute. A. Snodgrass, *Archaic Greece* (London: Dent, 1980), p. 172; cf. *ibid.*, pp. 169–174. I am indebted for this reference to my son, Louis Nebelsick, and his reading in Archaeology at the University of Edinburgh.
34. Cf. Zeller, *Philosophie*, p. 480.
35. Cf. above, p. 6f.
36. Cf. Zeller, *Philosophie*, pp. 228ff.
37. Plato, *Phaedo*, Loeb Classical Library (London: Heinemann, 1914), 99C; cf. *ibid.*, 96–101. Italics added.
38. *Ibid.*, 99D–E.
39. Plato, *Laws*, Book 12, 967. Italics added.
40. Aristotle, *On the Heavens*, III. iii–viii, 302b–307b. Cf. Stanley L. Jaki, *Science and Creation* (Edinburgh: Scottish Academic Press, 1974), p. 104 where Jaki points out that Aristotle's success in biology with its emphasis on goals was, when translated into the "first cause" in the inanimate world, responsible for his failure in physics.
41. Cf. Isaac Newton, *Opticks* (based on the Fourth Edition [London, 1730]) (New York: Dover, 1952) for Newton's description of the innumerable and intricately described experiments with light.
42. Translated from Johann Wolfgang von Goethe, "Zahme Xenien VI", *Poetische Werke*, 19 vols. (Berlin: Aufbau, 1965–1973), I, pp. 706f. In the same volume, "Katzenpastete" begins with the warning, "Beware of the investigation of nature," *ibid.*, p. 414.
43. Plato, *Laws*, Book 10, 886.
44. Aristotle, *On the Heavens*, I. ix, 279a.
45. *Ibid.*, I. ix, 279a–b.
46. Aristotle, *Metaphysics*, XII. vii–ix, 1072b–1074b. For Jaki's incisive insights cf. *Relevance of Physics*, p. 414.
47. Francis Bacon, *On the Dignity and Advancement of Learning*, *The Works of Francis Bacon*, ed. J. Spedding, R. L. Ellis, D. D. Heath, 7 vols. (London: Longman, 1857–1858), IV, Book 3, chap. 4, p. 363.
48. Cf. below, pp. 135ff.
49. Cf. below, pp. 109ff, for earlier challenges to Aristotle going back to Philoponos in the sixth century.

50. Bacon, *Advancement of Learning*, Book 3, chap. 4, p. 365.

51. *Ibid.*

52. Howe, *Mensch und Physik*, p. 17. Howe, mistakenly, it seems to me, includes Anaxagoras along with Plato and Aristotle in this movement. As I have pointed out, however, Anaxagoras' monotheism was of a quite different sort from that of Plato and Aristotle.

53. Herbert Butterfield, *The Origins of Modern Science 1300–1800* (London: Bell, 1973), p. 7.

54. Cf. above, p. 61.

55. Zeller, *Philosophie*, pp. 236ff.

56. Cf. above, pp. 1ff.

57. Benjamin Farrington, *Greek Science* (Harmondsworth: Penguin Books, 1953), p. 45. Farrington gives no reference.

58. Kepler improved the Pythagorean and Euclidian number system and founded the beginnings of calculus which he used in his calculations of planetary motion.

59. Koestler, *Sleepwalkers*, p. 37.

60. *Ibid.*

61. Kant divided the world between the *phenomena*, things as they appear and about which knowledge can be gained, and *noumena*, things in themselves which are not subject to knowledge. Cf. Immanuel Kant, *Prolegomena to any Future Metaphysic*, trans. J. Mahaffy and J. Bernard (London: Macmillan, 1889), pp. 77ff.; also Nebelsick, *Theology and Science*, pp. 63–71.

62. John Calvin, *Commentaries on The First Book of Moses called Genesis*, 2 vols. (Edinburgh: Office of Calvin Translations, 1847), "Epistle Dedicatory", I, xlix.

63. R. C. Taliaferro, "Biographical Note," to Ptolemy, *Almagest*, p. ix.

64. *Ibid.*, "Introduction", p. 1.

65. Ptolemy, *Almagest*, "Preface", I, 1, p. 5.

66. *Ibid.*

67. *Ibid.*

68. *Ibid.*

69. *Ibid.*

70. *Ibid.*

71. *Ibid.*, p. 6.

72. *Ibid.*

73. *Ibid.*

74. *Ibid.*

75. *Ibid.*, I. 4, p. 9.

76. *Ibid.*

77. *Ibid.*, I. 6, p. 10.

78. *Ibid.*, I. 7, p. 11. The argument was so impressive that even Galileo preserved it in his *Two New Sciences* in which he founded the science of dynamics. He devoted the "third day" to discussing *natural motion* and the "fourth day" to *violent motion*. Cf. Galileo,

Dialogues Concerning Two New Sciences New York: Dover, 1954).
Newton finally dissolved the distinction.

79. Ptolemy, *Almagest*, I. 7, p. 11.
80. *Ibid.*, p. 12.
81. *Ibid.*, I. 8, p. 12.
82. *Ibid.*, p. 13.
83. *Ibid.* Italics added.
84. Cf. above, pp. 18ff.
85. Ptolemy, *Almagest*, I. 9–12, pp. 14–26.
86. *Ibid.*, III, "Introductory Paragraph", p. 77.
87. *Ibid.*, III. 3, p. 86.
88. *Ibid.*, p. 87.
89. *Ibid.*
90. Ptolemy records his observations between 17 Pachom, Hadrian 9, and 11 Thoth, Antonine 14, according to the current dates and the reigning monarchs. Taliaferro, "Introduction", *Almagest*, p. 1. As we shall see, the Copernican system was less accurate than the Ptolemaic one. Cf. below, pp. 228ff, especially 232ff.
91. Ptolemy's *He Mathematike Syntaxis (The Mathematical Collection)* known as the *Syntaxis*, the classic exposition of the theory in thirteen volumes, is one of Greece's most prestigious scientific efforts. In the course of time the work became known as *Ho Megas Astronomos (The Great Astronomer)* to distinguish it from *The Little Astronomer*, a collection of works by other Greek mathematicians and astronomers. Cf. De Lacy O'Leary, *How Greek Science Passed to the Arabs* (London: Routledge, 1951), p. 157.
92. Howe, *Mensch und Physik*, p. 25.

CHAPTER 3

SCIENCE ENCOUNTERS THE
CHRISTIAN FAITH

THE history of science, especially the history of
cosmology, is often written as if the impetus to the
scientific developments in the West during the Middle
Ages and the Renaissance was due solely to the transfer
of Hellenistic learning to the West by the Arabs. The
pioneering efforts of the Greeks, which began with the pre-
Socratics and the early Pythagoreans, were recognised by
Plato, developed by Aristotle and the later Pythagoreans,
culminated in Ptolemy, and were transmitted by way of
Syria to the East. From there, after having been translated
into Arabic by Nestorian Christians, who knew both Greek
and Arabic, Greek learning was brought to the West by the
Arabs through North Africa and the Iberian peninsula. In
western Europe, Arab learning then became the basis for
the Renaissance, the Reformation, and the rise of modern
science.

While there is no gainsaying the Arab contribution to the
West, and we will give the Arabs their due below, it would
be quite incorrect, as Dreyer has shown, to think the world
was dependent for its cosmological ideas upon Arab
sources alone.[1] In the same way that theological ideas and
cosmological ideas overlapped and influenced one another
from the earliest ages of Greek recorded learning onward,
so they are found intermingled in the doctrines of the early
post-Apostolic Christian writers as well. When Christianity moved to the West, cosmology moved with it. As
Christianity developed from the post-Apostolic period
through the Middle Ages and into the Renaissance, the
cosmological concepts of the Jewish and Christian Scrip-

88

tures vied with and were interlaced with those which had been developed by the pre-Christian Greeks.

Since the Christian faith, like the Jewish faith upon which it was built, was primarily interested in the worship of God and the life of humankind, the early Christian thinkers were less interested in the structure of the world as such than in trying to understand these structures in relation to their faith. As Plato and Aristotle understood the reality of the world according to theological prescriptions, so the early Christian writers were influenced by the doctrines of their faith in their understanding of the world. More often than not their allusions to cosmology were qualified by and hidden within their soteriological concerns.

Accommodation and Critique

Following Dreyer in this regard, we find that the earliest specifically Christian writing in the immediate post-Apostolic period to refer to cosmology was that of Clement of Rome (fl. A.D. 96). In his *Epistle to the Corinthians*, Clement began his cosmological discussions by referring to the "Father and Maker of the whole World", thereby stressing that what was of utmost importance for the Christian writers was the *createdness* of both heaven and earth. The whole of creation and its order was to be appreciated as a blessing of God. "The heavens are moved by his direction and obey him in peace."[2] Likewise, day and night follow the course assigned to them. "The sun, the moon and the dancing stars [$\dot{\alpha}\sigma\tau\epsilon\rho\omega\nu \tau\epsilon \chi\rho\rho\sigma\acute{\iota}$], according to his appointment circle in harmony within the bounds assigned to them without any swerving aside."[3]

Clement also made an allusion to the "Antipodes", people who were supposed to dwell on the side of the earth opposite to the inhabited Mediterranean basin. In that the term "antipodes" refers literally to "those with the feet opposite", Clement apparently took for granted that the earth was a sphere. The place where "Antipodes" were supposed to have lived could not be approached by people from the side of the known world nor could the inhabitants of the "antipodes" (the term is used for both the location and its inhabitants) cross over to the known world. There was real question, therefore, as to whether or not those who lived at the antipodes could have stemmed from Adam. For Clement, however, there was no question as to God's sovereignty over the whole of creation, both that known and that which was beyond human knowledge. His assertion that "the ocean which is impassable for men, and the worlds beyond it, are directed by the same ordinances of the Master", has implications for both theology and science.[4] The statement may be taken as an early example of a theological doctrine which is basic to understanding the world as a *universe* rather than as a series of different natural systems. The modern concept of *isotropy* which posits a basic uniformity throughout the universe is founded upon the same kind of homogeneity which Clement attributed to the earth on the basis of his Christian theology.

Clement's discussion of the antipodes, which was carried on by Christian thinkers right up through the twelfth century, was like the rest of cosmology less a concern for the existence of the people or places involved than for the theological issues that were at stake. He was aware of the patterns of the heavens reported by classical Hellenistic astronomy as well as the geography of the earth as accepted in the Hellenistic world. He used such knowledge, however, not to further investigation into nature but to substantiate his claim that "the great Creator and Master of the universe ordered [all things] to be in peace and concord".[5]

A century later, Clement of Alexandria (c.150–c.212), who was not only from the same city as Ptolemy but was either contemporary with him or was slightly younger, seems to have been thoroughly conversant with the Ptolemaic system of the universe. He utilised the system, however, not to explain the order of the heavens, which he apparently took for granted, but as a basis for an allegorical interpretation of reality that emphasised the relationship between cosmology and the tabernacle of Moses with its furniture. "The seven circuits around the Temple" and the decorations on the priests' robes were held to have cosmic significance.[6] The covering of the altar was coloured according to the four earthly elements of Greek science: "For purple is from *water*, linen from the *earth*, blue being dark, is like the *air*, as scarlet is like *fire*."[7] The five loaves of the shewbread symbolised the five senses by which one is to look around and appreciate the universe.[8] The four pillars before the temple, like the four covenants, correlated with the four letters of the name of God in both Hebrew, *Jave* (as Clement spelled it), and Greek, Θεός. The high priest's robe was adorned with five stones and two carbuncles representing the seven planets. On the other hand, the stones could as well have referred to the seven stages of salvation.[9] Likewise, the carbuncle which represented Saturn stood for "moist", "earthy", and "heavy", while the one which represented the moon referred to the "aerial". The golden figures (the cherubim), each of which had wings, represented either the two celestial bears, the Ursus Major and the Ursus Minor, or the two hemispheres of heaven.[10] The ark stood for that eighth and most exalted region beyond the heavenly bodies which was the sphere of the thought of God or the world of God.[11] Most important was the lamp which was placed to the south of the altar of incense and which, interestingly enough, represented, for Clement, a kind of heliocentric universe.

By it were shown the motions of the seven planets, that perform their revolutions toward the south. For three branches rose on either side of the lamp, and lights on them; since also the sun, like the lamp, set in the midst of all the planets, dispenses with a kind of divine music the light to those above and to those below.[12]

Origen (c.185–c.254), who was the allegorist *par excellence* among the post-Apostolic writers, introduced the subject of the "heavenly waters" into the cosmological-theological discussion. His own interpretation of the waters is pure allegory. He took the Genesis account of the separation of the waters above the firmament from those below it as a reference to the admonition that we should separate our spirits from the darkness of the abyss, the dwelling place of the adversary and his angels.[13] Later Fathers, as we shall see, used the Genesis account of the heavenly waters as an indication that one of the elements of the "sub-lunar" sphere was integral to the heavens. This had the effect of uniting the heavens and the earth into a single order of creation and moved directly against Aristotelian physics which divided the earth into the sub-lunar and super-lunar realms. The sub-lunar earthly sphere was the place of the four corruptible, changeable substances — earth, water, air, and fire. The super-lunar heavenly sphere consisted of a fifth, ethereal, divine, eternal, immutable, incorruptible essence. For Christians, who stressed the sovereignty of God over the whole of creation, the "waters" were evidence that the heavens, like the earth, consisted, partially at least, of corruptible, non-eternal substance.

A shift from the acknowledgement of cosmology and the use of its concepts for theological explanations toward "anti-science" may be seen in Lactantius (c.240–c.320). Lactantius wrote his *Divine Institutes* at about the same time Constantine the Great (c.288–337) recognised Christianity as a legitimate religion in the empire (A.D. 313).[14] In the third book of the *Institutes* which he entitled, "On False Philosophy", Lactantius showed familiarity with the cosmology of "the philosophers" but took the opportunity to ridicule their ideas. He knew that the philosophers believed the sun and moon always rose and set in the same directions, that there were stars which wandered into decline or set. He knew too that the philosophers were supposed to have ascribed the motion of the stars to the "whirling of the world" because they could not find any other mechanism which was responsible for the heavenly movements.

Although Lactantius mistakenly thought that the

philosophers believed the world was round "like a pillar",[15] he knew that they fabricated "aerial orbs" which they adorned with "portent-like images which they said were stars".[16] In contradistinction to Clement of Rome, Lactantius thought it absurd to think that the earth was spherical or that the antipodes existed. It was nonsense to believe that there were people "whose footprints are higher than their heads" or that there were places where "rain and snow and hail fall upwards upon the earth". Hence, he considered that the philosophers who "make fields and cities and seas and mountains 'hanging'" were ridiculous.[17] Interestingly enough, Lactantius considered that Aristotle's idea of heavy bodies seeking the centre of the world, where the earth was supposed to be, was just as erroneous as the notion that the heavens could be lower than the earth.[18] Lactantius then represents a case, not of ignorance of "science", but of disagreement and distrust. Thus, rather early on in the history of the Church, we find evidence of a stream of thought that moved in the direction of "anti-science".

Some forty years later, however, Basil the Great (c.329–379) who, as Father George Dragas has reminded us, had studied at the Philosophical Academy in Athens,[19] showed that "philosophical wisdom" and theology were not necessarily mutually exclusive. In the nine homilies of his *Hexaemeron*, the whole of which he entitled "Creation of the Heavens and the Earth", he made explicit that the doctrines of faith have definite ramifications for scientific thought. By introducing the first of the homilies with Genesis 1:1, "In the beginning God created the heavens and the earth", Basil set out to show the relevance of the doctrine of creation for the way the world was to be understood. Specifically he intended to break with both the Platonic and the Aristotelian concepts of the eternity of the world as well as to revoke the latter's division of the world into two spheres: the divine and eternal super-lunar sphere and the temporal and corruptible sub-lunar sphere.[20]

Since God created the world, the world could not have

co-existed from eternity with God. Further, as over against Aristotle's contention that circularity was coterminous with eternity, Basil pointed out that, although it was possible to imagine a circle without a beginning, if one were to draw it, one must begin at a single point. Thus, circles like the world have *beginning* and *end*.[21] He compared fire and water on earth to that of the heavens to show that there is a basic unity of all creation. The heavens which, according to Isaiah 51:6 (Septuagint version), were established by God "as of smoke" were composed of the same genre of created elements of which the earth was made.[22] By using biblical evidences to support his contention that the heavenly bodies consist of a number of elements rather than of the ethereal "fifth element", as Aristotle believed, Basil cleverly played Aristotle's physics off against his cosmology. According to Aristotle's physics, the natural motion of *complex* bodies was rectilinear while that of the *simple* bodies of the heavens, those composed of the ethereal element, was circular. Basil insisted, however, that it was perfectly legitimate to understand the heavenly bodies as being complex and that it was equally valid to think that such complex bodies, the stars for instance, moved in circles as indeed Aristotle himself had insisted.[23]

The heavenly waters, that touchstone of the created nature of the heavens, caused Basil a problem but it was not insuperable. There was no doubt in Basil's mind that there were waters above the firmament as attested by the biblical account of creation. However, since the firmament appeared to be curved, the heavenly waters were likely to pour off a dome-like surface and fall to earth. With admirable ingenuity Basil suggested that the firmament, which appears hemispherical on the underside, may, like a building enclosing a dome-shaped bath, have a flat roof.[24] In any case, the heavenly waters were quite necessary because their vapours helped to cool the universe which otherwise might well be burned to ashes by the heat of the sun.[25]

Although the argument for the presence of and the description of the waters may seem somewhat far-fetched to us, it indicates both the seriousness with which the early Christian theologians treated the biblical account of creation and the way they used the account to break with the unacceptable idea of the division of the world into an eternal and immutable heavenly sphere and a corruptible earthly realm. In this way the words of Genesis,

> Let there be a firmament in the midst of the waters, and let it separate the waters from the waters. And God made the firmament and separated the waters which were below the firmament from the waters which were above the firmament. (Gen. 1:6–7)

became the means by which the early Christian cosmologists could claim to demonstrate the createdness of the whole world and its contingent relationship to God who, at one and the same time, transcended it and yet sustained it and remained responsible for it.

Hence, in contrast to Lactantius, Basil expressed himself as one who was both informed and largely appreciative of the cosmology which the Greeks had developed. He knew that there were stars about the south pole of the earth which were invisible to one living in Alexandria.[26] He was aware that the change of the seasons depended on the movement of the sun through the northern and southern halves of the zodiac.[27] In addition, Basil recognised that the "great lights", that is the sun and the moon, were immense in size and that the earth was lighted by them. In comparison to these the stars gave only feeble light.[28]

In Basil, then, we see a breakthrough in the relationship of theology and science. His "science" continued to be speculative to a large extent. Yet his *Hexaemeron* was written to show specifically that God is the Lord of all creation which includes both the heavens and the earth. The heavenly waters and the fires of heaven as well as the finite nature of circles are cases in point. As all have a beginning, so eventually all must end. Even Basil's thrones, or dominions, or principalities, or powers, or forces, or hosts of angels, or sovereign archangels, are not uncreated eternal beings. Rather, they are intelligences who were *created out of nothing* as was the rest of the material order. They accommodated themselves to time-space dimensions so as to be able to minister to human-kind.[29]

It must be said, however, that knowledgeable as Basil was with regard to the then current astronomy, he used his knowledge of science for theological purposes. He showed neither a great deal of interest nor curiosity about the world as such. Hence he had no hesitation in pointing out that since Moses "gave no discussion concerning the shape [of the earth] and did not say that its circumference contains one hundred and eighty thousand stades", such knowledge is quite unnecessary.[30] In a way similar to the attitude of the Psalmists and early Pythagoreans, cosmology for Basil led into worship.

> May He who has filled all things with his creation and has left us in all things clear memorials of his wondrous works fill your hearts with all spiritual joy, in Christ Jesus our Lord, to whom be glory and power forever. Amen.[31]

Thus far, then, we have met three distinct positions in the theology of the early Church which were to have effect on the later development of the Church's attitude toward creation and the relationship of its understanding of nature to Scripture and the faith. First and positively, all creation was considered to be finite and contingent upon God, the transcendent Creator. Second and negatively, when the knowledge of the philosophers about the heavens dis-agreed with biblical cosmology, their cosmology was con-sidered false and discredited. Thirdly, there was the somewhat ambiguous stand that Scripture was considered to be the source of what we may call all "necessary knowledge". Accordingly, while it was considered legit-imate for Christians to accept the knowledge of the philosophers, such knowledge was considered quite secondary to biblical teaching. Hence, believers could be safely ignorant about anything that the Scriptures did not take into consideration.

Cyril of Jerusalem (d. 387) would seem to have followed Basil's lead in his understanding both of cosmology and of the relationship of God to the world. In his Catechetical Lecture IX, "On the Words, Maker of Heaven and Earth, and of All Things Visible and Invisible", he pointed out specifically (and in contradiction to Plato's idea of a creative Demiurge) that the order of the heavens was due to the Creator alone who "hath set them their bounds, and laid out the order of the Universe".[32] God, he said, spread out "the heaven as a veil of his proper Godhead".[33] More important for cosmology, however, Cyril insisted that the heavens were made of earthly substance. God "reared the sky as a dome . . . [and] out of the fluid nature of the waters formed the stable substance of the heaven".[34] Later Cyril expanded on the statement and said, "The heaven is water" and "the sun, moon, and stars are of fire".[35] They were, in fact, constructed for human benefit. The water is held in reserve in the heavens for watering the land when it is tilled. In the summer the sun rises higher in the sky than in winter, making the days longer so men have time for their work. In winter, by contrast, the longer nights contribute to man's rest.[36]

Rejection, Ambivalence, and Ridicule

In contrast to Clement of Alexandria, Basil, and Cyril, we find in Severian, Diodore, Theodore of Mopsuestia, and Chrysostom a complete lack of appreciation for "scientific" cosmology. Severian, Bishop of Gabala (d. after 408), either had little knowledge at all of scientific cosmology or, if he were in possession of such knowledge, chose to set biblical cosmology over against it. He wrote his *Six Orations on the Creation of the World* specifically to proclaim that the construction of the universe followed the biblical story of creation in detail. The heaven which God created on the first day is a two-storeyed structure. There are waters above the heavens. The storeys themselves are divided by a ceiling in between them. The upper storey consists of fire without matter which was analogous to an angel, a spirit without a body. The lower storey is composed of fire and matter. Providence has arranged things in such a way that the heat of the fire moves downwards in order to warm the earth rather than moving upwards as is the case with fires on earth. The heaven we see is the lower heaven which was created on the second day. It is in the form of an envelope or bladder, the outside "skin" of which was composed of crystalline, congealed water to resist the fire of the sun, the moon, and the stars. The inside of the crystalline, congealed water structure is occupied by fire. For the present and until the eschaton, the water protects the heaven from dissolving or burning in the heat. On the last day, it will be used to quench the sun, moon, and stars.[37]

As far as the form of the world is concerned, Severian turned not to Genesis but to Isaiah. Since God "stretched out the heavens as a curtain" and spread them out as a tent or dwelling (Is. 40:22), the heaven is not a sphere or even a hemisphere but its form is that of a tent or a tabernacle. Based on the Genesis report that "the sun was risen upon the earth when Lot came unto Zoar" (Gen. 19:23), Severian concluded that the sun does not ascend (*non ascendisse*) but travels at night through the northern parts of the flat earth where it was hidden by a high wall.[38] In the same vein he understood Ecclesiastes' statement that "the sun goeth down and hasteth to his place where he ariseth" (Ecc. 1:5) to refer to the sun moving south lower on the horizon in the winter than in the summer and taking longer to perform its nightly journey through the north.[39]

Diodore, Bishop of Tarsus (d. 394), also attempted to use biblical data to construct an elementary cosmology. In his writing "Against Fatalism", which we know only from Photius' resumé, Diodore first stressed the idea that the entire world, including the heavens and the stars, was created along with the elements — fire, water, earth, and air. He then objected to the earth being the centre of the world and complained that the astrologers (astronomers) not only divided the heavens into the twelve signs of the zodiac but that they divided the earth according to the same pattern. Based on the revolution of the heavens, Diodore maintained that it was quite impossible for the same regions of the earth to be dominated by the same signs since all the signs pass over the areas of the earth as they revolve above it.[40] Like Severian, Diodore relied on Scripture for his supposition that there must be two heavens. The lower heaven subsists with the earth and forms the roof of the earth. The roof of the lower heaven forms the floor of the upper one. Heaven, therefore, could not be a sphere surrounding the earth but is rather a tent or vault above it.[41]

Diodore apparently passed on his ideas to his student, Theodore, Bishop of Mopsuestia in Cilicia (b. c.428). From Johannes Philoponos, whose cosmology we will discuss later, we learn that Theodore, like Diodore, claimed that the heavens resembled a tabernacle and that, much to Philoponos' dislike, he advocated the Aristotelian idea that the stars are kept in motion by the angels.[42]

In Jerome (c.345–c.419) too we find a definite antipathy to "scientific" cosmology in favour of the kind of biblical imagery which he thought described terrestrial geography in literal terms. Jerome, whose most important contribution to the Church was that of translating the Scripture from the Greek into the vulgar Latin (hence the "Vulgate"), castigated those who followed "the wisdom of the philosophers". He had no patience with those who spoke of the cherubim as representing the two hemispheres, the one standing for the known world and the other for the antipodes. He insisted that our ideas of the world must conform to the biblical geography which demanded that Jerusalem be the centre of the earth.[43]

This same estrangement from a scientific understanding of cosmology and the tendency to conflate biblical imagery with the physical structure of the world may be seen in John Chrysostom (c.347–407) in his *Commentary on the Letter to the Hebrews*, 8:1. In that *Hebrews* portrays Christ as seated at the right hand of the throne of the majesty of heaven, Chrysostom asked, "Where are those who pretend that the heavens move themselves? Where are those who declare that it is spherical? The two opinions find themselves contradicted here."[44]

Like the Eastern Fathers, those of the West for the most part began their discussions of cosmology in the context of the biblical account of creation. Ambrose of Milan (c.339–397) based his cosmological arguments specifically "on the word of God"[45] and began his discussion by repeating Genesis 1:1, "In the beginning, God created heaven and earth". Ambrose was well acquainted, however, with classical cosmology and physics and one senses that his theology and his thought about the nature of the world tend both to complement and influence one another as he considers, for instance, the position of the earth in the universe or the elements of which matter was supposed to be constructed. Substituting the element "heaven" for the usual "air", he claimed that everything in the world was generated from the four elements: heaven, fire, water, and earth.[46] Isaiah's statement that "God hath fixed the heavens like smoke" (Is. 51:6) indicated to Ambrose that God desired "to declare it not of solid but of subtle nature".[47] Although Ambrose may have had Aristotle's fifth "ethereal" substance in mind when he substituted "heaven" for the usual "air", there is no doubt that for him the heavens themselves were of created substance. Like Basil before him, he compared the fire of heaven to the fire on earth. He pointed out that the stars in the skies gleam with the same brilliance as earthly fire. Likewise, he was certain that the water in heaven was the same as that on earth and he substantiated the argument by pointing out that the heavenly waters fell to earth as rain.[48]

For Ambrose the firmament is the spherical heaven which divides the waters from the waters. For him, as for Basil, there was a problem as to how the waters were prevented from flowing off the domed surface of the spherical heaven. There was also a question as to why they did not spin off the swiftly revolving heavenly sphere as it circled around the motionless spherical earth. Rather than answer the questions, however, Ambrose considered them too speculative to be answered. Like Basil he did add, almost as an afterthought, that it was quite usual for a building with a dome-shaped ceiling to have a flat roof.[49] He also took comfort in the fact that it was no more difficult to conceive of the waters being suspended in the heaven than it was to conceive how the earth, which is much heavier, stayed suspended and immobile in the void.[50] In addition to being useful as rain, however, Ambrose, again like Basil, was certain that the heavenly waters, which he finally concluded were held in the heavens by rotation, were necessary to keep the earth from being parched by the "fiery stars".[51]

More in line with accepted cosmology, Ambrose knew that the heaven is a sphere.[52] "The philosophers", he said, "introduced the harmonious movement of five constellations along with the sun and moon, to whose spheres or, rather, round bodies they state that all things are connected."[53] He was also aware of the Pythagorean ideas of the universe given by Cicero (c.102–43 B.C.). Cicero had presented the usual Aristotelian nest of seven concentric spheres inside the eighth and outermost celestial sphere. All were centred on the central and stationary earth which, Ambrose reports, Cicero had counted as the ninth sphere. Cicero, in the Platonic and Stoic manner, identified the universe itself with God (*summus ipse deus*). Otherwise, Ambrose's knowledge of cosmology seems largely dependent upon Aristotle. Thus he recognised that the heavens themselves have uniform and regular circular motion, the seven planets also have retrograde motion. Venus and Mercury themselves are so near the sun that they appear not to be able to move away. The earth is a sphere immobile in the midst of the world and is the centre of gravity.

Perhaps more important for indicating his milieu and for the development of later theology is the fact that, along with Aristotelian cosmology, Ambrose was well apprised of the Pythagorean astrological traditions according to which the planets were thought to influence the fate of humankind, the weather, and the shape of the future. He knew that Jupiter, Mars, and the sun, which is the most important, and the moon, which is nearest the earth, were each supposed to have particular influences. He knew, too, that according to Plato and Cicero, the early Pythagoreans had the planets humming forth their heavenly harmonies in seven tones. Each of the spheres had its own tone (Mercury and Venus produce one together) and the intervals were determined according to the interstices of the planetary orbits and were modulated into an harmonious whole.[54]

> By the impact and motion of those spheres there is produced a tone full of sweetness, the fruit of consummate art and of most delightful modulation, inasmuch as the air, torn apart by such artful motion, combines in even and melodious fashion high and low notes to such a degree that it surpasses in sweetness any other musical composition.[55]

The Pythagoreans were embarrassed, Ambrose recorded, because though they knew full well that the heavenly melodies were being played by the planets — the higher tones by the swifter moving celestial spheres and the lower tones by those which moved more slowly — they were also certain that the music could no longer be heard. People's ears were no longer sufficiently acute to be able to hear the heavenly music. And that was for the best according to Ambrose, for were it otherwise, humankind would be so enraptured by the heavenly music they would cease all labour and a state of complete idleness would result.[56] Although Ambrose seems willing enough to speculate about matters of astrology and finds allusions to astral music interesting, in the end his Christian conscience causes him to confess his basic unconcern about it all. Speculation about such matters, about "subjects alien to our purpose and to divine testimony should be left to those 'who are outside' ''', i.e. the non-Christians (1 Cor. 5:12, 13; Col. 4:5; 1 Tim. 3:7). Rather than becoming interested in the celestial spheres, "We [Christians] should adhere closely to the doctrine laid down by the celestial Scriptures".[57]

Augustine (354–430), too, like Ambrose, his teacher, was well acquainted with the then current cosmology, but for him it was also a matter of secondary import. In his *City of God* he considered the earth as a sphere "suspended within the sphere of the heavens". He could not agree, however, that the opposite side of the sphere (i.e., the antipodes) was inhabited.[58] In the first place, since the earth was a sphere, there would be nothing to prevent the land on the lower side from being completely inundated with water.[59] In addition, there was no evidence at all to indicate that any descendants of Noah could have wandered to the other side of the sphere to live.[60]

In his *Commentary on Genesis*, Augustine's discussion of the waters above the firmament shows a certain ingenuity. The waters are there to be sure. Their particular function was not to cool the whole of the heavens, however, but, with a reference perhaps to the astrological speculation that Saturn is cold,[61] Augustine argued that the function of the waters is to cool Saturn. It was quite logical, as Augustine reasoned, to believe that Saturn needed cooling because of its pace. In that fast-moving objects had a tendency to be heated by the friction of the air, the cooling waters would have been necessary for Saturn because, of all the planets, it had the greatest distance to travel each day. In fact, its rate of velocity around the earth is so extreme that, were it not refrigerated, it likely would be much hotter than the sun which had a much shorter distance to travel. Without the waters, then, Saturn surely would have been burned to ashes. Thus, Augustine was certain that the waters occupied heaven and that they functioned for cooling. He was not at all certain of their form, however. Two alternatives offered themselves as possibilities. They are perhaps congealed (*glaciali soliditate*), as Severian had thought, or they could be of the nature of vapour (*vaporali tenuitate*), as Basil had suggested.[62]

We know that Augustine was much more interested

in the life of the soul than in the form of the world. Nevertheless, his general attitude toward science moved in the direction of accommodating science to Scripture whenever possible. He was certain, for instance, that the statements in Scripture with regard to the heavens could not be explained away by those who believed that the world was spherical, yet he was willing to accept the evidence of science when there was no scriptural evidence to the contrary. In case of conflict, therefore, Scripture had primacy. "The authority of Scripture is much greater than that of the greatest genius of men."[63]

In some of his writings, however, specifically in his *City of God*, where he concentrates on the differentiation between Christianity and paganism, and in his *Confessions*, where his chief concern is with his own soul, Augustine tended to depreciate knowledge of the physical world to the point of rejecting it. In the *City of God*, for instance, while he discussed the nature of earth as a sphere, he made a point of disclaiming any interest in Thales with his water, Anaximenes with his air, the Stoics with their fire, or Epicurus (c.341–270 B.C.) with his atoms.[64] This ambiguity between admitting knowledge of the natural world and of disparaging the value of that knowledge is even more evident in the *Confessions*. He admitted admiration for "the philosophers" who had the "inquisitive skill" (*curiosa peritia*) to "number the stars and the sand, map out the constellations and track the courses of the planets (*vias astrorum*)". They accurately calculated the time, duration, and extent of the eclipses of the sun and the moon and wrote down the rules so that those who followed them could predict the times and nature of the eclipses as well.[65]

Augustine referred to the philosopher's accurate knowledge of the stars, the solstices, the equinoxes, and the eclipses of the sun and the moon in order to rebut the frenzied astrology of the Manicheans. In the end, however, he considered the interest of the philosophers in the things of this world counter-productive. It got in the way of the philosopher's desire to know God. "Their foolish heart was darkened" (Ro. 1:21). "Their discourse about many things concerning the creature is true, but they do not piously seek the Truth, the Architect of the creature, and therefore they do not find him."[66] Thus, in spite of his acquaintance with astronomy and his respect for the astronomers (philosophers), Augustine was extremely sceptical, even judgemental of their learning. Such knowledge was the result of the "experience of the senses". It was knowledge gained by sight which in the divine language was called "the lust of the eyes" (1 Jn. 2:16).[67]

In the same context Augustine faulted those who desired "to know for the sake of knowing". He condemned those (astrologers) who called upon "magical arts" to search out the hidden along with those who tempted God by demanding "certain signs and wonders". Although Augustine did not deny that such things provoked his own interest and created "vain curiosities" within himself, he made a point of disavowing any continuing interest in either the theatre or in the "courses of the stars" (*transitus siderum*). As if to make certain that it was understood that, even in former times, when such things as the theatre and the courses of the stars had indeed interested him, there had been limits to his curiosity, he pointed out explicitly that his soul had never consulted the departed spirits and that he had always detested 'sacrilegious mysteries".[68]

Neoplatonist though he was with a primary interest in the self, the mind, and the "spiritual nature" of things, rather than in the physical world, Augustine, like his Christian predecessors, insisted that the statement, "God created heaven and earth", referred to both the visible and the invisible world. All was created "out of nothing" (*ex nihilo*) whether "spiritual or corporeal".[69] For Augustine the spiritual was, of course, of greater nobility than the corporeal. Nevertheless, and in contradiction to the Platonic idea that the material realm was negative and characterised by decadence and decay, Augustine claimed that matter was "better than if it were nothing".[70] Matter was created by God; being upheld by God, it continued to exist (along with "the spiritual") in a contingent relationship to him. It is because of this dependence (*penderent*) upon God that creation is held back from falling into "unbridled liberty" (*immoderationem*).[71]

Augustine's major emphasis, however, betrays his Neoplatonic heritage. Thus, he interpreted the Genesis account of creation symbolically and allegorically as having its major meaning with reference to the soul. He understood God's commanding light to come into existence anthropologically and soteriologically rather than cosmologically. *"We were beforehand darkness, but now light in the Lord."*[72] The firmament is the "firmament of authority" of divine Scripture. "The heavens shall be folded together like a book (Acts 6:14) which are now stretched over us like a skin."[73] The firmament also divides the waters above the firmament which are "immortal and separated from earthly corruption". Those who live there have had no need of Scripture for "they always see your [God's] face and read in it the meaning of your eternal will".[74] The lights in the heavens are compared to the light of truth and the gifts of faith.[75] The members of the "chosen race" (*genus electum*) are likened to the stars who are to "shine over all the earth".[76]

Thus, for all of his insight, in the end the great Augustine, perhaps more than anyone else, is responsible for pushing the material world to the periphery of Christian vision. Rather than looking to the heavens and the earth as God's creation for which, according to the Genesis account, the people of God were to be responsible, Augustine taught the faithful to turn their eyes inward so that, like the Buddha concentrating on his navel, the main object of Christian concentration became the self.

Back in the East, the writings of the Egyptian monk Cosmas (fl. 6th cent.) indicate that Greek cosmology continued both to be known and to be rejected among Christians. Cosmas, whose surname was Indicopleustes, showed his hand when he entitled the first book of his work, *Christian Topography*, "Against those who, while wishing to profess Christianity, think and imagine like the pagans that the heaven is spherical". His avowed purpose was to condemn those who were so naïve as to think they could mix scientific cosmology with the cosmology of the Bible. Rather than accepting that the heavens rotated daily above the earth, Cosmas held that the heavens moved upward and downward. He admitted, however, that such movement had never been observed. He knew that the planets appeared to move forward, stand still and make retrogressions, but he considered the idea that the heavenly bodies had been assigned "invisible epicycles" which, like vehicles, were supposed to bear the planets along, as silly. Such epicycles for carrying the planets would be necessary only if they were incapable of their own motion. How, he wanted to know, was it possible for the philosophers to declare, as had Aristotle, that the planets are animated and assigned divine souls? Such ideas regarding the whole system of cosmological machinery are ridiculous. "Why", he asked ironically, "have not the moon and the sun received their epicycles?" "Was it, then, because of the scarcity of suitable material that the Creator could not construct vehicles for them?"[77]

Rather than placing the earth in the centre of the universe, an idea which Cosmas thought absurd and contrary to nature but with which he was thoroughly familiar,[78] he, like Clement of Alexandria and Severian, understood the universe to have been constructed according to the plan of the tabernacle which Moses had built on Mt. Sinai. According to Hebrews 8:5, Moses was ordered to construct the tabernacle after the pattern of the "heavenly sanctuary". Therefore it must *ipso facto* typify the structure of the universe. For a pattern of the tabernacle, Cosmas combined the descriptions given in Exodus 25–27 with that of the Letter to the Hebrews. Taking his cue from Exodus where the temple is described as having "inner" and "outer" parts, in a way similar to that of Clement of Alexandria, Cosmas used the "outer tabernacle" to represent the form of the visible world. He set out the arrangement of the inner tabernacle according to the description given in the Letter to the Hebrews. The veil, like the firmament, divides the universe into two parts, the upper and the lower, and portrays the pattern of the kingdom of heaven. The earth, like the table of the shewbread, is rectilinear; its wavy border signifies the ocean which surrounds the earth.[79] The walls of the tabernacle simulate the four walls of heaven; and the roof, shaped like a half cylinder, portrays the vault of heaven. The firmament which divided the universe forms the floor of the upper storey and the ceiling of the lower storey. The lower storey is the place where angels and humankind dwell. The upper storey is the kingdom of heaven to which Christ as *the first of all* had ascended and incorporated a new and living route.[80] This is the true tabernacle set up by the Lord and not by a man (Heb. 8:2).[81] The lower firmament is the place of "the earth, the water, the other elements and the stars". It has the earth for its foundation, the first heaven for its walls, and the firmament for its roof.[82] The sun, moon, and stars are located between the earth and the firmament and are carried along below the firmament by angels who are also in charge of the air, the clouds, and diverse phenomena.[83]

As with Severian, so with Cosmas, the sun does not rise or set; it moves to the northern part of the earth during the night. Since the northern part of the earth is higher than the southern part, it both conceals the sun by night, and hides other heavenly bodies from time to time as well.[84] While the eclipse of the moon is due to the sun passing beneath the elevation of the earth, that of the sun is caused by the interposition of the moon between the sun and the earth.[85] Further, since the sun is hidden during its nightly journey by a part of the earth, Cosmas deduced as a matter of course that the sun is smaller than the earth which conceals it.[86]

With Cosmas, then, we have spelled out in unmistakable terms not only the distinction between "profane science" and "Christian science" but we have a definite expression of a Christian's disdain for the "secular knowledge" of the world. Secular science is pursued according to the "vanity" of the philosophers.[87] Christian understanding is based upon a literal reading of the Scriptures of the Old and New Testaments.[88] It is not surprising that the two had little in common for, according to Cosmas, there should be no association between the faithful and infidels.[89]

Critical Reappreciation, Revival, and Mythicisation

Cosmas' attitude toward "profane science" stands in sharp contrast to that of another Greek who lived in Egypt, Johannes Philoponos of Alexandria. Because of his significance for the rise of science, Philoponos will appear again and again in our discussion. As we now know, Philoponos anticipated seventeenth-century science both in reassessing the theory of impetus and, just as importantly, in anticipating the break of science with Aristotelian metaphysics and cosmology. Philoponos knew Aristotelian thought so thoroughly that he was able to challenge it at its roots.[90]

As Samuel Sambursky in his excellent book, *The Physical World of Late Antiquity*, has pointed out, it was primarily on the basis of the Judaeo-Christian doctrine of *creatio ex nihilo* that Philoponos, who was at that time a Christian teacher at the Academy in Alexandria, challenged Aristotle's doctrine of the eternity of the heavens. That which is created had a beginning and an end and was subject to change. In addition, Philoponos carried the argument of Basil and Cyril — that the fire of the stars was of the same kind as fire upon earth — one step further by adding that what is visible is also tangible. If heavenly bodies consist of earthly elements, Aristotle's division of the world into the super-lunar sphere of eternal, unchangeable "substance" and the sub-lunar sphere, within which objects are subject to generation and change, was obviously called into question. However, since there was no way of sampling the heavenly elements the argument placed one supposition over against another. Philoponos was on solid observational ground, however, when he showed that, rather than displaying perfectly regular and uniform motion and describing eternally identical paths over periods of time, the circles of the stars in the celestial sphere are not concentric. This, along with the observation that the planets move in different directions from the stars, cast grave doubt on the perfection of the heavens in Aristotelian terms.[91]

In addition, although Philoponos had criticised Theodore of Mopsuestia for attempting to argue against the sphericity of the heavens on scriptural grounds, he himself used biblical insights to argue for the contingency of the world.[92] The world is not eternal in itself, he insisted. Rather, it will continue to be preserved as long as God wants it to exist.[93] Hence, rather than being self-subsistent, it is contingent upon God and dependent upon him for its preservation. Thus Philoponos was remarkably perceptive. Unfortunately, however, significant as were Philoponos' empirical observations and trenchant as was his criticism of Aristotle on physics, he was to have no more direct impact upon the cosmology which was to develop in the next 700 years than Aristarchus had had on the previous 800.

After Philoponos' time the Academy at Alexandria was moved first to Athens and from there to Syria. Eventually it was located in Baghdad where it was Islamicised. In Syria Greek manuscripts from the Academy were initially translated into Syriac. Later, when gathered with other Greek manuscripts in Baghdad, they were translated into Arabic.[94] Although some of Philoponos' arguments continued to be known in the West through the writings of his opponent Simplicius (fl. A.D. 530), they were not to be re-appreciated until the breakdown of Aristotle in the sixteenth and seventeenth centuries. It was perhaps because the Arab appropriation of Hellenic learning was concerned for the most part with Aristotle that Philoponos' challenges to Aristotelian thought seem largely to have been forgotten.

At any rate, after having both acquired Aristotelian learning and modified it for their own purposes, it was the Arabs who became the main mediators of Hellenic and specifically Aristotelian thought to the West. In the late seventh and early eighth centuries they migrated through North Africa and crossed the Mediterranean to the Iberian peninsula. By bringing the Arabic translations of Aristotle with them, they set the stage for Spain to become the main outpost from which classical learning was to spread throughout Europe.[95]

Even in the so-called Dark Ages, however, which are dark to us largely because of our lack of knowledge of them, there are evidences that the inspiration given by Hellenic learning had not died out entirely in western Europe. In the generation before the Arab invasion of Spain, Isidore, Bishop of Seville (c.570–c.636), wrote his *De Natura Rerum* and showed that classical learning continued in the West without interruption though certainly with less intensity and perspicacity than it was able to achieve on the basis of Arab translations several centuries later. Both Isidore's enumeration of the seven arts: grammar, rhetoric, dialectics, arithmetic, music, geometry, and astronomy[96] — the first three making up the *trivium* and the last four the *quadrivium* of mediaeval learning — and his delineation of cosmological ideas, which in general were comparable to those entertained by Plato and Aristotle, indicate his grasp of Hellenic knowledge. He knew that the heavens were a sphere made of *aether* and that they were divided into seven distinct zones [spheres] each of which circled on its own while the whole rotated around on an axis once in a day and night.[97]

Although Isidore, like Aristotle and perhaps more like Basil, filled the heavens with divine intelligences, he also gave evidence of knowing the shape and movements of Plato's universe. He discussed the signs of the zodiac and explained that the years and the seasons were designated by the movements of the sun and moon.[98] More particularly, Isidore discussed the movements of the seven planets, the nature and course of the sun, the size, illumination, and path of the moon, lunar and solar eclipses, the circles of the stars, and the positions of the seven erratic planets (*de positione septem stellarum errantium*).[99] His diagram of the universe follows Aristotle's onion model of nested homocentric spheres. His discussion of the geography and climate of the earth, although far from accurate in comparison to present understanding, indicates that his Christian faith in no way detracted from his interest in both the earthly realm and in the heavenly sphere.[100] Like the majority of Christian cosmologists before him, he took account of the waters above the heavens. Indeed, the name "firmament" meant for Isidore that it supported the waters and these were necessary to cool the earth lest the upper fires burned the lower elements. The waters are in the form of an icy solid. They, like the heavens themselves and like the earth, were specifically created *ex nihilo*. Both heaven and earth are of the stuff of creation.[101]

Continuing his discussion of the heavenly bodies, Isidore knew that the moon was much smaller than the sun and that of all the heavenly bodies the moon was nearest to the earth. He designated the order of the planets by a homocentric diagram with the earth in the centre. From the earth outward they were drawn: moon, Mercury, Venus, sun, Mars, Jupiter, and Saturn. He accompanied the diagram with figures to specify the numbers of years necessary for each of the bodies to make a total revolution, not around the world, but under the stars. The numbers which follow the order of the bodies designated by the diagram are: 19, 20, 9, 19, 15, 12, and 30.[102] Isidore's statement, "The stars move with the world, it is not they which move while the world stands still",[103] is interpreted by Dreyer as "a strange mixture of truth and error".[104] However, considering the level of Isidore's cosmological knowledge, he may well have meant the statement to read, "The stars move with the world. They do not move as the planets do; the earth stands still."

With Isidore, then, the attitude that the Bible and the Bible alone gives all necessary answers for cosmology was set aside to the extent that classical astronomy could be remembered and could be accepted to a large extent. At the same time, Isidore was able to take the doctrine of *creatio ex nihilo* along with the biblical insistence on the unity of creation seriously enough to show that elements of Christian theology continued to challenge the Hellenic theological conceptualities of the eternality of the heavens and the division of the world into separate divine and natural realms.

This openness to science displayed by Isidore continued with the English monk, Venerable Bede (c.673–c.735). Bede, as Dreyer tells us, took his cosmology largely from Pliny.[105] He followed the usual practice of Christian writers and began his discussion of cosmology in *De Natura Rerum* with the doctrine of *creatio ex nihilo*. He held not only that the heavens and the earth were created out of nothing but, in addition to the elements of creation mentioned in Genesis 1:1, the angels as well. Thus the angels, air, water, light, the firmament in the midst of the waters (*firmamentum in medio aquarum*), and the bodies of human beings were all created out of nothing. The heavenly bodies were made of light. The creatures and the bodies of people were made either of earth or of water.[106]

Bede, who was acquainted with the Aristotelian physics of the elements and knew that the Greeks (specifically Pythagoras himself) had called the absolute perfect and elegant heavens κόσμος (cosmos),[107] used the "firmament" to divide the upper heavens from the lower heavens. He designated the *superior heaven* which is, he said, "bounded by circles", as the place where the angels dwell and where water in glacial form is to be found. The *inferior heaven*, on the other hand, is non-uniform (in differentiation from the circularity and regularity of the motion of the superior heaven) and, corresponding to its multiplicity of motions, is characterised by a multiplicity of waters.[108]

Bede knew that the Greeks had defined the regular circular orbits of the stars and that these were supposed to turn round on the central axis of the heavenly sphere. Along with Hellenic cosmology, he recognised that the earth is a sphere in the centre of the world with seven bodies circling around it in dissimilar motion.[109] He, like Isidore, designated the relative positions of the planets from earth and their relationships to the signs of the zodiac.[110] Bede also mentioned the Milky Way and discussed the particular orbits, nature, and relative sizes of the sun and the moon in some detail.[111] He ended his *De*

Natura Rerum with a discussion of the winds, the weather, and the geography of the earth.[112]

In his *De Temporum Ratione* in which he dealt with chronology, Bede first set out the Greek and Latin number systems side by side.[113] He then discussed the Roman, Greek, and English systems of months,[114] the signs of the zodiac and the course of the moon through them,[115] and the relationship and nature of the sun, the moon, the equinoxes, and the solstices.[116] Since he knew of only two zones of the earth as habitable, he rejected the well-known discussions of the antipodes as fables.[117]

Although Bede was inaccurate in saying that the moon is larger than the sun,[118] a mistake, according to Dreyer, also made by Pliny,[119] and said that lightning and thunder are caused by the collision of the clouds,[120] by and large one may well agree with Sharon Turner (1768–1847) that *De Natura Rerum* has two great merits. It assembles into one focus the wisest opinions of the ancients on the subjects he discusses, and it continually refers to the phenomena of nature to natural causes.[121] Thus, though Bede was a child of his time, as far as scientific learning was concerned, Turner would seem quite correct in saying, "He collected and taught more natural truths with fewer errors than any Roman book on the same subjects had accomplished".[122]

Both Isidore and Bede show us that by the first part of the eighth century there were scholars in the West who did not consider that the Christian faith and secular learning necessarily contradicted one another. Diametric opposition between biblical cosmology and "scientific" cosmology was still possible, however. As late as the ninth century the Abbot of Fulda, Hrabanus Maurus (d. 856), remained convinced that because Scripture spoke of the "four corners of the earth", the earth must be formed in the shape of a square. Apparently because he thought of the horizon as forming a "circular disk", he conceded to think of the earth as "a wheel".[123] In that he knew that a Euclidean circle could be divided into quadrants, he apparently saw some compatibility between the earth as a disk and its having "four corners". By dividing the circle of the earth into parts, he assigned Europe, Asia, and Africa to the various sectors.[124]

However, by the time Gerbert (d. 1003) became Pope Sylvester II in 999, Bede's cosmology received what can be taken as official sanction. Gerbert himself was a mathematician and an astronomer and knew the subject well enough to construct both celestial and terrestrial globes for his lectures on astronomy.[125] Three-quarters of a century later, as Dreyer notes, Adam of Bremen (fl. 1076) showed that western cosmology was approaching the level that had been achieved in Greece in the fourth century B.C.[126] Thus, in the West by the late eleventh century, cosmological knowledge again included an understanding of the rotundity of the earth and the geocentric system of planetary motions and the causes of the unequal length of day and night at different latitudes. Dreyer's judgement is that by this time cosmology may be considered to have regained the features "held among the philosophers of Greece from the days of Plato".[127] Dreyer goes on to say that although Greek was an unknown language in the West from the fifth century onward, the later writings of Pliny, Chalcidius (fl. 4th cent.), Macrobius (fl. c. 400), and Martianus Capella (fl. 5th cent.) supplied information for anyone who could read them.[128] The fact, however, that Bede at time intersperses his text with Greek words must indicate that in Britain, at any rate, Greek continued to be known to a certain extent at least. In addition both Isidore and Bede would seem to have moved well beyond Plato and to have taken the advances of Eudoxus, Callippus, and Aristotle into consideration as far as cosmology in general was concerned. The fact that both Isidore and Bede were able to designate the periodicities of the planets, describe the zodiac, make notations on the sizes of the bodies and the measurements of the orbits of the sun and the moon and, of more importance, assign the motion of the planets to *natural causes* would indicate that they had an acquaintance with or were able to duplicate at least the work of the later Pythagoreans if not of Ptolemy.

Similar information is to be found in *De mundi coelestis*

terrestrisque constitutione, a work which seems to be from the first part of the ninth century at the earliest and is so parallel to that of Bede that the writing was long attributed to him. In the section *Forma terrae* ("The Form of the Earth") the unknown author shows that the sphericity of the earth could be deduced both from the observation that different lengths of day occur at different latitudes and from the observation that the heavenly phenomena occur at different times for different localities.[129] In the section *De ordine planetarum* ("The Order of the Planets") the orbits of Venus and Mercury are traced as being sometimes above and sometimes below the sun. Reference to the comet, which had been recorded as appearing at the time of Caesar's funeral but which the author took to have been the planet Venus, indicates his familiarity with the history of astronomy.[130] He gives three possible explanations for the supercelestial waters (*De super-coelestibus aquis*), a discussion which had become *de rigueur* for Christian cosmologists. First, they may be held in the hollows of the heavens like water gathered in low places on earth. Second, they may perhaps be in the form of vapour like the clouds. Third, they may be frozen. Their being frozen into ice would correlate with their being a great distance from the sun and near to Saturn which the author, like Augustine, considered to be a "frigid star". However, whereas for Augustine, it will be remembered, the waters were necessary to cool Saturn, for the author of *De Mundi . . . Constitutione*, Saturn is frigid because of its proximity to the waters.[131]

If we take the *De Mundi . . . Constitutione* as an indication of the state of the art in the West prior to the importing of Aristotelian thought by the Arabs, we find that by the early ninth century the Christian writers had absorbed the general cosmology of the Greeks, though without the kind of geometric and mathematical detail of Apollonius, Hipparchus, or Ptolemy. Like the early Pythagoreans, the interest of the Christian cosmologists prior to Bede was, for the most part not in the world as such but in the world as an *illustration* of theological truth. Theology used cosmological data for its own purposes. As the Greeks had used the circularity of the heavenly motions to prove the eternal, uncreated and divine nature of the heavens, which they divided off from the earthly sphere, so the Christian writers used variously the heavenly waters, the fire of the heavenly bodies, and the complex nature of the stars to show the opposite. They used the *created nature* of the heavens and the *unity* of heaven and earth to show that the whole of creation was of a piece. Heaven and earth were parts of a single creation contingent on God who was transcendent but who at times at least was thought to intervene rather directly in world affairs.

Pseudo-Bede attempted to refer the phenomena of nature for the most part to natural causes. In *De Mundi . . . Constitutione*, however, we find that while he first speculated that the heavens may have been constructed so that the waters would gather in hollows, he ended his argument by assigning the task of holding in place the waters needed to cool the heavens to God.[132] This practice of importing God into the system when cosmological explanations proved inadequate was to continue even to the seventeeth and the eighteenth centuries when it was followed by no less a scientist than Newton himself. The idea was finally rejected by Pierre Laplace (1749–1827). Pseudo-Bede's mention of Saturn as the cold planet (*frigor Saturni*) along with his statement that Plato followed the Egyptians in placing the solar orbit immediately outside the moon, may indicate that the kind of Hermetic astrological thinking, which was to become highly important in the late mediaeval and Renaissance European thought, was making itself felt already in the early ninth century.[133]

The twelfth-century document Περὶ διδάξεων *sive elementorum philosophiae* (*Of Philosophical Elements*), which was written by an unknown author, but which was also attributed to Bede, shows a different attitude towards Scripture than that in writings prior to that time. In that the work covers almost the same subjects as *De Mundi Coelestis Terrestrisque Constitutione* and as Bede's *De Natura Rerum*, it is not difficult to understand why it was attributed to him. Its technical detail, however, which includes but moves well beyond what was generally known from Aristotle and even beyond what was known in the West from the later Pythagoreans such as Apollonius, indicates that the work must have been dependent on the Ptolemaic cosmology which was transferred to Europe through Arab sources. Alfargani's summation of the *Almagest* was available about the first half of the eleventh century. The *Almagest* itself was translated from Arabic to Latin in 1175.[134]

The *Elementorum Philosophiae*, as the document is usually referred to, moves into physics and a discussion of the heavens with an excursis on the "rotund" form of the world, its creation and its countries. It explains many of the same phenomena described by Ptolemy though without the detail or mathematics. The author wrote about "the air", "lightning", "the scattered", "the rainbow", "the ether", "the darkening of the moon", "the moon", the means by which it was obscured, its setting and its eclipse. He discussed the sun along the same lines. He showed familiarity with the planets, their epicycles, interstices and movements, including their retrograde motion, the peculiarities of the orbit of Mercury, and the cold temperature of Saturn. He also indicated characteristics of the zodiac, the meridian, the Milky Way, the horizon, and the constellations.[135]

Rather like Calvin later in his *Commentary on Genesis*, the unknown author of the *Elementorum Philosophiae* regarded the waters above the firmament as *contra rationem* (against reason).[136] Were the waters congealed, he said, showing the influence of Aristotle's physics, they would be too heavy for the heavens and the earth would have been the proper place for them. On the other hand, were they next to the celestial fire, they would either have extinguished it or have been dissolved by it. With regard to the order of the heavens, the author realised that the sun is next to the moon and that Venus and Mercury move in nearly the same period round the zodiac as does the sun. He calculated that the sun is eight times as large as the earth,[137] and set out impressive diagrams of the phases of the moon as well as drawings representing the eclipses of both the moon and the sun.

Here, too, we find, for the first time since the pre-Socratics, speculation that the heavenly bodies may have been composed of stone-like material. Thus, while the writer of *Elementorum Philosophiae* speculated that the sun and the stars are made largely of fire, he suggested that they may well contain other elements as well. The sub-lunar sphere he held to be occupied by air, and the space above the moon to be, ether or fire. The cosmos as a whole may be compared to an egg. The earth is analogous to the yolk. Surrounding the earth, like the white around the yolk, is water. Around the water, like the skin around the white, is air, and finally, like the eggshell, there is the celestial fire which encircles it all.[138]

Quite another tune begins to be played in the cosmological symphony by Honorius of Autun (c.1080–c.1156), who wrote *De Imagine Mundi*. Instead of following scientific cosmology, Honorius, it would seem, was inspired largely by Pseudo-Dionysius. With him, then, we begin to see the intrusion of mystical Neoplatonism and Neopythagoreanism into late mediaeval cosmology. Honorius populated his world with angelic and spiritual beings. These, as in Pseudo-Dionysius, are assigned cosmological positions. The upper heaven, which he called the firmament, is spherical in form, adorned with stars, and is round and fiery. It is surrounded by waters which form the clouds. Above the upper heaven is the spiritual heaven which itself was divided into "paradise", the home of the souls of the saints, nine hierarchically arranged orders of angel habitations (as in Pseudo-Dionysius), and finally above it is the "heaven of heavens" (*caelum caelorum*), the place where the king of the angels dwells.[139] The arrangement was to be reflected by Thomas Aquinas' *Summa Theologica* as well as by Dante's *The Banquet*.[140]

Image du monde (1245), the work of a certain Omons (fl. 13th cent.), as Dreyer indicates, is important because it shows that although Aristotle had begun to enter western thought in a massive way from the middle of the twelfth century, other non-scientific trends, which used cosmology to mythicise the world, were also present. Omons' reference to Ptolemy, "King of Egypt", who was responsible for having invented clocks and various scientific instruments and to whom several books including the *Almagest* were attributed, indicates that, with Omons, Hermetic or Hermetic-like writings had begun to be conflated with legitimate astronomy. Thus, while he was aware of the *Almagest*, his cosmology is quite other than that of Ptolemy's geocentric system. He has two heavens. The first is crystalline. The second, above it, is the "empyrean". It is of utmost importance, for there the angels dwell and from it the demons were expelled. The angels' bodies are formed of ether, the air of heaven. Recalling the ancient Pythagoreans, who alone could hear the music of the spheres, and contrary to Ambrose, who was grateful that our sense of hearing had been blunted to the point that we could no longer discern the heavenly melodies, else we would be quite bewitched by them, Omons was certain that children, because of their innocence, continued to be able to hear the heavenly harmonies.[141]

From the middle of the twelfth century onward, the writings of Aristotle began to flow into France from Spain. These were accompanied by the commentaries of Alexander of Aphrodisias (fl. 193–217) and Simplicius, as well as mystical pseudo-Platonic and Arab works on alchemy.[142] So shocked was the West at the importation of this new knowledge, that in 1209 a provincial council in Paris decreed that neither Aristotle's writings on natural philosophy nor his commentaries should be read either in public or in private. The University of Paris passed the prohibition in 1215. The thought of Aristotle, however, soon overcame the opposition. Within forty years of the prohibition, it had so moved into the culture that, as Dreyer tells us, Aristotle was not only accepted but in 1254 orders were issued prescribing the number of hours which should be devoted to explaining his treatises.[143]

Although in 1277 the Bishop of Paris again issued an interdict against a host of Averroist-Aristotelian propositions, his effort was something like trying to hold back the tide with a sand castle.[144] Beginning with the second half of the thirteenth century, Aristotle provided the basis for philosophy in Paris. From then on, and for nearly four hundred years, his thought was to dominate the philosophy of the schools. It was basic to the thought of Albert the Great (1193–1280) and, more importantly, that of his disciple, Thomas Aquinas (1225–74).

Sacrobosco's Sphere

In the meantime, about the year 1220, an Englishman, Johannes de Sacrobosco (d. 1256)[145] or John of Holywood, who was then teaching at the University of Paris, wrote his *De Sphaera (On the Sphere)*. The book sums up the gist of the Aristotelian-Ptolemaic system within the compass of four short chapters, just twenty-four pages in all.[146] For his sources Sacrobosco may have used Alfargani's summation of Ptolemy, *Rudimenta, Differentie scientie astrorum*.[147] It is equally possible, however, that he had access to the *Algamest* itself which, as said, had been translated into Latin from Greek in 1160 and from Arabic in 1175. At any rate, *De Sphaera* was written with such felicity and clarity that it became and remained the basic textbook on astronomy throughout Europe from the thirteenth to the seventeenth centuries.

The text, which is a prime example of just how thoroughly Aristotelian and Ptolemaic thought had captured the European mind half a century after the Arab documents reached Western Europe, begins with a preface in which the four chapters of the book are introduced. Chapter I defines the sphere, its centre and axis, explains the poles of the world, designates the number of spheres in the world, and describes its shape. Chapter II explains the sub-lunar material sphere and the super-lunar celestial sphere and sets out their compositions. Chapter III talks about the rising and setting of the signs of the zodiac, the diversity of days and nights in different parts of the earth, and the division of the earth into climes. Chapter IV, which is the most elaborate, is concerned with the circles and motions of the planets as well as the courses of eclipses.[148]

By an ingenious combination of Aristotelian and Ptolemaic ideas, Sacrobosco taught that the sphere of the world is divided into the northern "right" and the southern "left" hemisphere. The form is Aristotle's nest of nine spheres or what we have referred to as "the onion model". Outermost is the *primum mobile*, then the sphere of the fixed stars (called "the firmament"). Below the firmament are the seven planetary spheres running from Saturn to the moon.[149]

"The machine of the universe" (*mundi machina*)[150] is divided into the super-lunar ethereal region and the sub-lunar elementary region. The former is eternal and unchanging; the latter, as in Aristotle, is subject to continual alteration and is divided into the four elements. *Earth* is in the middle of all; about the earth is *water*; surrounding both earth and water is *air*; and, encompassing the elements — earth, water, and air — is *fire* which, as in Aristotle, reaches to the sphere of the moon. The elements are by themselves altered, corrupted, and regenerated. All are mobile except earth, which is stationary in the centre of the world.

The earthly sphere contrasts, of course, with the heavens, which are of a fifth, immutable essence and immune to all variation. The heavens have two movements. The first is that of the celestial sphere "from east through west, and east again". The second is that of the planets (the inferior stars) which runs obliquely to the other by an angle of 23°. The movement of the celestial sphere carries all the others with it. The planetary spheres, however, whose movements are divided "through the middle of the zodiac", all have their own motion contrary to that of the sky.[151]

The sphericity of the universe is attested to by the equi-distance of the stars from the earth. The spherical form of the earth is shown by the difference in the time of the stars' rising and setting as correlated by different locations of longitude. The fact that a signal on land can be seen by a sailor on the top of a mast of a ship sailing away from land long after it has disappeared from one on deck is proof that the surface of the sea, like that of the land, is curved.

The earth, as Ptolemy had said, is so small that it is "but a point in the universe". Its centrality, like its sphericity, is indicated by the equidistance of the stars from any place at all. The immobility of the earth is "proven" from Aristotle's physics according to which heavy objects fall to the centre. Since earth is the heaviest of the four elements, any movement from its dead centre position, any "ascension", as Sacrobosco called it, would be quite impossible. Testimony for the earth's sphericity and dimensions were taken from Eratosthenes rather than from Ptolemy. Eratosthenes had calculated 700 stades for each of the 360 degrees of the earth's sphere, giving the earth a girth of 252,000 stades, whereas Ptolemy had figured only 500 stades for each degree.[152]

Sacrobosco's second chapter is somewhat more detailed than the first. By making use of the kind of information handed on by Ptolemy, he described first the *equinoctial* sphere, the "equator of day and night", and then the movement of the *primum mobile*, "the ninth and last heaven". As in Plato, the motion of the *primum mobile* is "rational motion". It is eternal and regular. This "rational motion" both defines the proper motion of the universe and, in being passed on downward to the sub-lunar sphere, defines also the proper pattern of thought for human beings. Proper thought forms a loop from the prime mover, through humankind and back to its origin. It goes from the Creator, through the creatures, to the Creator and there rests. In contrast to the motion of the *primum mobile* which is from east to west, planetary movement from west to east is "irrational" or "sensual". It resembles movement "from things corruptible to the Creator and back again to things corruptible".[153] Sacrobosco then discussed the northern and southern spheres of the heavens and the signs of and characteristics of the zodiac. Each of the twelve signs

was designated as having 30° of the 360° circle and hence is
one-twelfth of the 360° circle. Each degree of the zodiac is
divided into 60 minutes, each minute into 60 seconds, and
each second into 60 thirds. The zodiac itself is defined as
being a band 12° in width.

Sacrobosco designated the *ecliptic* as the line which
bisects the zodiac, leaving 6° on either side. This line
defines in general the course of the sun and the moon and
the other planets. He then discussed the *colures*, the two
great circles of the heavenly spheres which distinguish the
solstices and the equinoxes. The *meridian* is the circle
which passes through the two poles of the universe and
through "our zenith". He specified the *horizon* as the line
of division between the upper and the lower hemisphere
and shows the elevation of the poles above the horizon.
After explaining the Tropics of Cancer and Capricorn, he
referred to the Arctic and Antarctic Circles. These are
described in the heavens by the north and south poles of
the zodiac respectively.[154]

Sacrobosco began Chapter III with illustrations from
well-known classical literature which had attempted to
account for the risings and settings of the signs of the
zodiac in poetic verse. He then corrected the misapprehen-
sions involved on the basis of accurate astronomy. He
showed that the oblique ascensions, the inequalities of
days, and the movement of the sun are different in different parts of the earth. He explained that such diverse
phenomena as the length of day and night, the movement
of the stars, as well as the differences in heavenly patterns
as seen from different locations on earth, are all to be
understood in terms of applied astronomy.[155]

In Chapter IV, in which Ptolemy seems to shine through
in every line, Sacrobosco explained the eccentric movement of the sun and the length of the year which,
disregarding a small, imperceptible fraction, is $365\frac{1}{4}$ days.
He then described the equants, deferents, and epicycles
of the planetary spheres all of which were necessary to
account for the planet's stationary, direct, and retrograde
movements. He assigned three circles, namely those

described by the equants, the deferents, and the epicycles, to each of the planets except the sun. Though the number of circles does not tally exactly with Ptolemy (for Ptolemy the equant describes a circle only in the case of Mercury), Sacrobosco got the general idea of Ptolemy's cosmic machinery right. He understood the movement of the moon and its deviations from regularity as well as the cause of the lunar and solar eclipses. In the case of the moon these are due to the shadows of the earth upon it. The eclipse of the sun is due to the imposition of the moon between the earth and the sun and therefore, Sacrobosco explained, it may be observed from one clime but not from others.

Thus, when Sacrobosco compressed the essentials of the whole of Ptolemaic astronomy into the brief compass of his treatise on the sphere, he showed that early in the thirteenth century, in the centres of learning which had been in communication with Arab scholars, astronomy could again be compared with that of the second century A.D. Hellenic world. Sacrobosco, in contrast to his Christian predecessors, gave no hint of any interference of biblical cosmology with "scientific" cosmology. Nor did he seem aware of the fact that classical understanding of the universe was built upon theological presuppositions which were quite antithetical to the teachings of the Christian faith. The Greek theological idea of the ethereal heavens which were considered incorruptible was reiterated. The perfect circularity of the heavens as reflecting both rationality and the truth of God himself over against the corruptible world which represents irrationality was again brought to the fore.

As if to indicate that he was a Christian in spite of his acceptance of pre-Christian Greek astronomical ideas, Sacrobosco ended his treatise by emphasising that the darkness which the Gospels record as covering the land (or earth) from the sixth to the ninth hour during Jesus' crucifixion (Mk. 15:33, Mat. 27:45, Lk. 23:44) was due to a miraculous eclipse which was contrary to nature, "since a solar eclipse ought to occur at new moon or thereabouts". He cited Dionysius the Areopagite (Pseudo-Dionysius) in support. "Either the God of nature suffers, or the mechanism of the earth is dissolved."[156] Nevertheless, here already the fundamental antinomies of the mediaeval synthesis which Thomas was to bring about only by ignoring the basic contradictions between Aristotelian metaphysics, physics and cosmology, and the biblical concept of creation, began to show themselves. Eventually not even the mystery of a miracle was able to provide a saving explanation.

Grosseteste's Challenge to Aristotle

At about the same time that Sacrobosco wrote his *De Sphaera* in Paris, another Briton, Robert Grosseteste, when in Oxford, wrote a book entitled *De Sphaera* as well. The controversy as to whether Grosseteste wrote his *De Sphaera* before or after Sacrobosco wrote his, like the question as to whether Oxford or Paris was the pre-eminent centre of learning at the time, seems to have no definite answer.[157]

More important for our purposes than the date of composition is the content of Grosseteste's cosmology and especially his argument about the composition of the world. Ludwig Baur (1871–1943) is quite correct in stating that, as far as the description of Ptolemaic cosmology is concerned, Sacrobosco's *De Sphaera* elaborates Ptolemy to a greater extent than does Grosseteste. However, in his writings on "The Generation of the Stars", "The Movement of the Heavens", "The Finite Nature of Movement and Time", and "The Comets", Grosseteste's arguments are perhaps of even greater significance than the more descriptive approach of Sacrobosco, simply because at crucial points Grosseteste not only questioned Aristotle but moved directly against him.

Grosseteste, like Sacrobosco, called the world a "machine". The *mundi machina* (the machine of the world) consists of the usual series of concentric circles around the stationary earth. His diagram of the world, like Sacrobosco's description of the world, places the spheres of water, air, and fire directly above the solid sphere of the earth. Then come the usual spheres of the moon, Mercury, Venus, sun, Mars, Jupiter, Saturn, and the stars which, for Grosseteste, were also the firmament (*firmamentum*, i.e., *coelum stellarum*). Outside of and encompassing the whole is the ninth sphere, the Aristotelian *primum mobile*.[158]

In his text Grosseteste took into account the concept of the world as a sphere both internally and externally, the description of the zodiac, and the different heavenly phenomena such as the rising and setting of the constellations. He described uniform motion and designated the position of the seven climes.[159] He explained the movement of the "fixed stars" (*stellarum fixarum*) from east to west including their precession and argued for the figures given by the Arab astronomer Thabit ibn Qurra (c.836–901) over against those of Ptolemy. He elaborated and diagrammed the orbits of the moon and the sun including their eccentrics and eclipses. He described the ecliptic and epicycle of the moon and its phases and pointed out that it receives its light from the sun.[160] His drawings of the eclipses of the sun and the moon plainly illustrate the intersection of the heavenly bodies. The moon blacks out the light of the sun in a solar eclipse while the earth blacks out the light from the moon in the case of a lunar eclipse.

As for Aristotle and Ptolemy, so for Grosseteste, the heavens as such are composed of a fifth essence (*quinta essentia*), also known as a heavenly substance (*corpus coeli*) or ether (*aethera*). The movement of the whole "beyond which are the elementary properties of circular motion" is due to the efficient cause (*causa efficiens*) of the "world soul" which circles around the arctic and antarctic poles. While Grosseteste's idea of the "world soul" would seem to have its source in Plato, his argument that it was the circularity of motion which determined that the world was spherical in shape is directly from Aristotle.[161] All of this, though spelled out with explicit clarity, is not unusual but both the text and the drawings, like those of Sacrobosco's *De Sphaera*, indicate that by the first half of the twelfth century, Ptolemy's universe was part of the standard understanding of cosmology in Europe's main centres of learning.

More important, from a theological point of view, is Grosseteste's astrophysics found in his *De generatione stellarum* (*On the Generation of the Stars*) in which he challenged Aristotle's concept of the eternity, immutability, and essential divinity of the heavens. In the argument Grosseteste used Aristotle's physics to contradict his ideas of eternity. The controversy turned on whether the heavens are simple and hence *eternal* or complex and therefore, according to Aristotle, *mutable*. Grosseteste agreed with Aristotle that there must be a relationship between the nature of a thing and its operation.[162] He turned the argument in on itself, however, and contended that since the stars obviously have different operations (their orbits, i.e., the spheres to which the stars are attached, move in different directions from that of the stars themselves), it follows that the stars are of different natures from the spheres which are responsible for their movement. Taken as a whole, therefore, the heavens are complex rather than simple.[163]

Again Grosseteste used Aristotle's argument that individual bodies are either *simple* (of a single substance) or *complex* (a combination of substances) against the Aristotelian idea that the heavens are simple. He argued that since the stars are bodies, they necessarily have form as well as content, they are complex rather than simple.[164] Further, picking up on a point which Philoponos had already advanced against Aristotle, Grosseteste insisted that the colour of the stars is an indication of their complex nature. While the so-called "fifth essence" or ethereal material is colourless, the stars have colour. "Whatever has colour is a mixture [or compound]. The stars are coloured bodies. *Ergo*, the stars are a mixture."[165] Further, since colour, as Aristotle had defined it, is a secondary quality and secondary qualities have limits, a body with limits could hardly be eternal. And, arguing from astronomy rather than philosophy, Grosseteste stated that while the "fifth element" is transparent, it is obvious from solar eclipses that the moon which blocked out the light of the sun is opaque.

All of this meant for Grosseteste that, rather than being composed of a single, fifth, ethereal, transparent element, the heavens are made *of the elements*. Grosseteste then went on to argue that the composition of the heavenly bodies in turn correlates with their motion. As their composition is complex, so the motion of the spheres is complex and non-uniform. In sum, Grosseteste used Aristotle's own arguments to show that rather than being of a single divine substance, the heavens share with the other elements the diverse nature of creation.[166]

Oddly enough, or in view of what Roger Bacon, also at Oxford, taught, but perhaps not so oddly, Grosseteste ended his argument by calling upon the *doctors of alchemy* (*doctores alchimiae*) to support his case. The alchemists' doctrine is applicable to the argument because their basic principle was that the fifth essence (*quinta essentia*), of which according to Aristotle the heavens were made, was one with the other elements. Rather than being simple and apart, the alchemists were certain that the *quinta essentia* was the fundamental substance of which all other substances were made. Hence it was subject to permutation and change,[167] for it was by way of alteration and modification of the *quinta essentia*, that the other elements came about.

In his discussion on the movements of the heavens (*De motu supercaelestium*), Grosseteste again moved directly against Aristotle. He first called into question Aristotle's concept of the necessity of a prime mover and ended the argument by contradicting Aristotle's idea of the infinity and immutability of the heavens. Grosseteste began by setting out Aristotle's concept that natural motion is perfect, simple, and circular. This implies that the natural form of the body of the world described by natural motion must be a sphere. According to Grosseteste, however, if circular motion prescribed the form of the world as a whole, then it must prescribe the form of its parts as well. If so, consistency would demand that the world be composed

of circular material.[168] In that for Grosseteste the heavens
are complex with regard to their composition as well as
their motion, neither Aristotle's contention that the
heavens are simple nor his concept of the *prime mover*,
which, for Aristotle, was the definition of simplicity itself,
was convincing. Rather, as said above, Grosseteste
reverted to the Platonic idea that a world soul must be
responsible for the motions of the heavens.

From the point of view of logic, Grosseteste's charge
that Aristotle's idea of a prime mover stands in contradiction to his idea of the infinity of the heavens is equally
telling. In accordance with Aristotle's teaching about
change or motion, Grosseteste claimed that all action must
result from that which is the potential (*potentia*) of a
material substance. Further, since all potentiality in
material substance is both finite and the result of that
which is finite, there is no possibility of infinite action
being ascribed to the heavens if they are responsible to a
prime mover.[169]

In his *De finitate motus et temporis* (*On the Finitude of
Motion and Time*) where he argues against the concept of
the eternity of both movement and time, Grosseteste offers
an even stronger argument against Aristotle's concept of
infinity. After putting forward Aristotle's argument for the
perpetuality of motion,[170] he showed first that there is a
basic contradiction between the idea of a first motion and
eternal motion.[171] Second, he claimed that the priority of a
situation of non-motion before motion entails the idea of
time before time.[172] Third, he contended that the position
adopted by Aristotle, who thought of the present *moment* as
the *connection* between the past and the future and then
claimed that there could never have been a *moment* without
a *past* and the *future*, is simply a logical construction built
on the idea of infinite succession which is analogous to
extrapolating local motion into infinity.[173] Grosseteste
then went on to contradict Aristotle's arguments for the
eternity of the world with the same kind of logic. He ended
the writing by asserting that the heavens are finite and, like
human motion and time, they are generated.[174]

Again, in contradiction to Aristotle, Grosseteste's description of comets united the "super-lunar" and the "sub-lunar" spheres. Comets, according to Grosseteste, are composed of sublimated fire which has been separated from its terrestrial nature. They are in the process of being assimilated to the nature of one of the seven planets which are, of course, heavenly bodies.[175] In this way Grosseteste conflated the terrestrial and the celestial. A further mixing of the heavenly and the earthly resulted from Grosseteste's claim that on their journeys through the heavens, the comets were being drawn by celestial "virtue" "as a magnet draws iron".[176] The "virtue" had fallen from the stellar sphere. The explanation is pure fantasy, of course, but the argument does presuppose a universe of a single, created magnitude subject to generation and change. With the same imagination we may even be able to see the "magnetic force" of the planets as a premonition of the force of gravity.

In sum, Grosseteste made a massive contribution to late mediaeval thought both by transferring Aristotelian physics and metaphysics along with Ptolemaic cosmology to his time and by being critical of them at decisive points. Baur might well be right in suggesting that while Grosseteste realised the potential of Aristotle's scientific method, he so feared Aristotle's metaphysics that he did what he could to show its damaging effect upon thought.[177]

Roger Bacon's Cosmological Occultism

Roger Bacon, a student of Robert Grosseteste at Oxford, appreciated "Master Robert", as he called him, both for his mathematics and for his scientific acumen.[178] Besides having learned mathematics under Grosseteste, Bacon was thoroughly grounded in the kind of cosmology inherited from Aristotle, Ptolemy, and Alfargani. These, as we have seen, were the sources for the thought of both Sacrobosco and Grosseteste. In addition, however, and with no less respect, Bacon referred to the cosmological ideas of the Fathers — Cyril, Ambrose, Augustine, Isidore — and also

Dionysius "whose instruction", he says, "the Church now follows".[179] However, Bacon also made reference to "the Chaldeans", "Egyptians", and "Hermes Mercury" or "Trismegistus", the "famous philosopher of Egypt and lands of the south".[180] The "Hermetic cosmology" was based on a neo-Pythagorean, neo-Platonic type of emanative process which encompassed creation, souls, and humankind and which attempted to fathom the future and prescribe divine worship.[181] Thus Bacon was familiar with and seemed to have accepted not only "legitimate cosmology" but also subjects which we would classify as "astrology" as well.

Bacon was fully conversant with the "state of the art" of astronomy in his own time and incorporated a great deal of it in his *Opus Majus*. However, like Clement of Alexandria, Basil, and Augustine before him, and like Thomas Aquinas, his contemporary, he did not regard science primarily as research into the physical mysteries of the universe for the sake of knowledge about the world, but, rather like the early Pythagoreans, he thought of the study of nature as aiding the salvation of humankind. "All wisdom", he claimed, "is constituted with a view to the discovery of salvation for the human race."[182] Thus, in contrast to such Christian writers as Lactantius, Severian, Diodore, Theodore, Jerome, Chrysostom, Cosmas, and Hrabanus Maurus, Bacon was certain that in the search for salvation, it was profitable to make use of "all the sciences, arts, and activities".[183] In his discussion of geography, for instance, he easily combined information from Aristotle, Pliny, Ptolemy, the Arab writers, and the Church Fathers such as Jerome, Ambrose, Augustine, Basil, *et. al.*, with insights from the writings of Scripture. Hence in a statement of admirable candour he stated:

> Since, then, there is a boundless advantage in a knowledge of the places in the world for philosophy, theology, and the Church of God, I wish to compose still another dissertation on places of this kind and to assign more clearly the divisions of the regions: and I

shall follow Pliny rather copiously, whom all the
sacred writers and men of science have followed. But
when I shall have discovered anything definite
through other authors, both the sacred ones, like
Jerome, Orosius, and Isidore, and through others, I
shall not neglect to give those facts that are
necessary.[184]

Bacon, like everyone in Europe doing "serious science"
at the time, was heavily dependent upon Arab writers for
his scientific projects. He knew Avicenna's (980–1037)
Metaphysics, which followed that of Aristotle,[185] as well as
Alfargani's (d. c.820) *Astronomy*, based on Ptolemy.[186] He
apparently had a first-hand acquaintance with Ptolemy's
Almagest as well and referred to the work directly on topics
as diverse as the explanation of mathematics[187] and the
size of the earth in comparison to the universe.[188] The
discussion includes details of the description of the sun and
the moon, their respective sizes, cycles and epicycles,
eclipses and distances from the earth.[189]

Since Bacon was heavily dependent upon Alfargani's
description of the world, it is uncertain as to whether or not
he was aware that Alfargani based his own cosmology upon
Ptolemy. Bacon seems to have treated Alfargani as if he
were a primary source and cited him again and again with
regard to such topics as the size of the earth relative to the
stars, the beginning of day, the diameter of earth, the
dimensions and distances pertaining to the heavenly
bodies and the motions of Mercury.

Alfargani's statement that "all nations that use lunar
months begin the day at sunset" was corroborated by
Bacon with a text from the twenty-third chapter of
Leviticus: "From evening to evening shall ye celebrate
your sabbath" (Lev. 23:32).[190] He excused the inaccuracy
of Alfargani's measurement of the earth as having a
diameter of 6500 miles, a calculation that is less exact than
that of Aristarchus because, as he explained, Alfargani
"omits some fractions, owing to the tediousness of
numbers".[191] He then proceeded to demonstrate his own

mathematical proficiency by correcting Alfargani's figures. This, along with his references to the nature and size of the planets,[192] their characteristics and conjunctions,[193] shows both the depth of Bacon's scientific knowledge as well as his openness to its findings. With all of this, Bacon showed that, by his time, cosmology was assuming a perspective with which we can identify. He knew, for instance, that the earth, which "in itself may possess great quantity", is smaller than the smallest of the stars. Further, in comparison with the heavens, the smallest of the stars "has no quantity of any significance".[194]

As indicated above, however, Bacon was not only a scientist but a scientist with a primary interest in religion. Although he was a Franciscan, his faith was considerably influenced by a renewed interest in Neoplatonic, Neopythagorean mysticism associated with the name of Hermes Trismegistus, "the Thrice-Greatest", also known as "Mercury", the messenger of the gods. In Bacon's time Hermes was considered responsible for the *Asclepius*, a treatise which combined cosmological and astronomical teaching with the relationship of the individual to God. The name "Mercury" evidently provided the impetus for Bacon to begin his account of Hermetic astrology by reference to the orbit of the planet Mercury. Drawing on material from the writings of Albategnus [Albattani] (c.858–929), Thebit [Thabit ibn Qurra] (c.836–901), Archaselis [Alzarkali] (c.1029–1087), as well as Alfraganus [Alfargani] (d. c.830), he argued that the circuit of Mercury "is in an epicycle and in an eccentric circle in a concentric one".[195] He then used the complexity of the orbit of Mercury as the rationale for the introduction of his Hermetic astrology into the discussion with the following paragraph:

> For this reason he [Ptolemy] has reference, as they say, to the law that contains difficult articles and hidden truths, of which kind is the Christian law. But because Mercury signifies writing and writers, and depth of knowledge contained in profound books, and elo-

quence or sweetness of speech and tongue, oratory and its rapid flow, and the explanation of sentences, he indicates that this law will be defended by such authentic scriptures and by so many profound sciences and by such potency of eloquence, that it will always remain firm in its own strength, until the final law of the moon shall disturb it for a time. They say also that this is the law of the prophet who shall be born of a virgin, in accordance with the teaching of all the ancient Indians, Chaldeans, and Babylonians that in the first face of the sign Virgo there ascends a very pure virgin who shall rear a son in the land of the Hebrews, whose name is Jesus Christ, as Albumazar states in his larger Introduction to Astronomy. In morals his authority will be quoted among other authorities on matters pertaining to moral philosophy, because for the matters here mentioned mathematics gives preparation in the service of that philosophy, as will be set forth more expressly in that subject. The virgin birth of the prophet is in full accord with the law of Mercury, because Mercury was created in the sign Virgo, and the dignities or potencies or testimonies or virtues or five fortitudes which are due to the planets in relation to the signs, Mercury has in the sign Virgo, to wit, house, exaltation, triplicity, terminus, face.[196]

Being eclectic in the extreme, Bacon was quite willing to garner evidence for his positions from every possible source. Thus, while he rebelled quite openly against Aristotle's deductive logic and claimed that Aristotle did not "reach the limit of wisdom", he both appreciated Aristotle for having organised all branches of philosophy in his own time and noted that he alone of all the famous philosophers "is stamped with approval by all wise men".[197] More importantly, Bacon cited Aristotle in support of his own Hermetic astrological ideas wherein the influence of the stars was used to explain earthly events. The heavens, according to Aristotle and as interpreted by Bacon, are not only the universal cause of all events but are "the particular cause of all terrestrial things".[198] In the same vein Bacon cited with approval the Arab Averroës (1126–98), who more than any other was responsible for introducing Aristotelian ideas into the intellectual circles of Europe and whose combination of astrology and alchemy was typical of the mix of mythology and science in the late Middle Ages.

> Averroës says in the seventh book of the Metaphysics that the force of the heaven has the same action on putrefied matter, as the force of a father in the semen. Therefore the things generated by putrefaction, although they are animate, are made directly from the heavens, and much more vigorously so than other inanimate things.[199]

Hence, although Bacon was quite specific in dividing what we would regard as "the scientific study of the heavens" into two separate but related areas of thought, *astronomy* and *astrology* (in the non-cultic sense) he also attempted to understand the stars from an astrological point of view. In *astronomy* one used mathematics to construct astral tables and to predict astronomical events. In *astrology*, which was more speculative, one attempted to fathom planetary motion.[200] In studying the heavens "astrologically", however, one attempted to interpret the divine influence of the heavens upon the events of the world and humankind. Hence Bacon was quite straightforward in his astrological investigations. Like the early Pythagoreans, Plato, and Aristotle, he saw the heavens as the place where divine forces are at work. Like them he was certain that the souls of humankind are drawn to respond to the manifestation of divinity in the heavenly movements. They aspire upward in order to imbibe the influences of the harmonious, majestic and eternal display.[201]

So powerful is this display of divinity that in the end, according to Bacon, "the complexions of all things are due to the heavens".[202] Events depend on the stars overhead and the positions of the planets.[203] The quality of the sun and moon along with the positions of the planets intensify vigour and strength or influence its deterioration and loss.[204] Different signs of the zodiac correspond to different parts of the body.[205] The different planets dominate the different hours of the day[206] and determine the appropriate seasons for planting and harvest as well as the proper times for medical treatment from blood-letting to purging. Heat and moisture, cold and dryness, clouds, earthquakes and pestilence, Bacon claimed, are due to comets.[207] When Mars is fiery, men are incited to anger, discord and war.[208] Both Ptolemy and Galen (c.129–c.200), Bacon insisted, connected the position and phases of the moon to health. When it is in conjunction with Jupiter, Jupiter so strengthens nature that the effect of a purgative will be lessened. In conjunction with Saturn, the dryness of Saturn will debilitate the effect of the medicine so that the dry substance is easily retained by the body.[209] In the same way that Galen followed the Egyptian astrologers in calculating that the moon marks the days of sickness and health,[210] so too, according to Bacon, Aristotle taught Alexander the Great (356–323 B.C.) that he should heed the advice of an astronomer.

> Aristotle, the wisest of philosophers, teaches Alexander in the book of Secrets that he should neither eat nor drink, nor do anything without the advice of an astronomer, because there are times selected for all things; for all things have a time, as Solomon, a wiser man than Aristotle, states.[211]

Bacon was not a fatalist, however. Although he held with Aristotle that "God has seen beforehand all things from eternity",[212] he also held that in his eternal foresight God also allows man the ability to change those things he has placed in "the power of man". Therefore, "in contingent things there is a choice".[213] In fact, by knowing the science of astronomy "man can take thought beforehand for all his advantages, and remove the obstacles".[214] Thus, insight into the mystery of the stars injects foresight into human affairs.

Bacon's theosophic astrology included the kind of focus on the sun that, in later Renaissance Hermeticism, made the sun both the centre of the universe and the centre of the cult. Thus he recognised the sun as the supreme power which ruled over the process of creation and generation. He cited Aristotle for support. "Man and the sun generate man out of matter", and since the father only begins generation "by letting the seed fall", it is the force of the sun or the heavens that perfects the generation.[215] Bacon then quoted Averroës for greater elaboration on the subject.

> The sun does more than man in producing a thing. For the force of the sun continues in the seed from the beginning of generation to the end, while that of a father does not, but is confined to one act only, namely, sowing of the seed; and therefore it would accomplish nothing, unless the force of the sun were continuously multiplied and infused, regulating the whole generation.[216]

It is in line with this kind of astrological speculation, whether from Aristotelian, Arab, or Hermetic sources that we can also understand Bacon's penchant for alchemy. The "black art", which will be discussed in somewhat more detail below, incorporated secrets which were supposed to go back to the magic of ancient Egypt. It was based upon the belief that all metals were generated in the womb of nature by different combinations of sulphur and mercury. Experiments were conceived in which attempts were made to transmute metals into one another. This concerned especially sulphur and mercury which, with the help of fire, were supposed to combine into gold at a faster rate than nature could perform the process. In addition, the dream of the alchemists was to isolate the "philosopher's stone". This "elixir", as it is called in *The Mirror of Alchimy* (which, if not written by Bacon, is so close to his ideas that scholars have long attributed it to him), was the "secret of secrets". It was of universal application and was believed to have perfecting and healing powers. Through it, base metals could be perfected and imperfect bodies could be made whole.[217]

The primary supposition behind the "science" goes back to the pre-Socratic Ionians, the atomists, for whom primary matter was of a substantial unity. This primary substance could be generated into different forms while remaining the same.[218] Aristotle had picked up the emphasis and insisted that there is a "universal material element" in all things. Its consistency, whether *compact* or *attenuated*, *heavy* or *light*, determined whether it formed one or more of the four basic Aristotelian elements — earth, water, air, or fire.[219] Hence, Bacon was certain that "experimental science by means of Aristotle's Secrets of Secrets knows how to produce gold not only of twenty-four degrees but of thirty and forty degrees and of as many degrees as we desire".[220] An even greater discovery would be the *medicine* which would both produce a sufficiency of gold for everyone and, more importantly, "would prolong life".

> For that medicine which would remove all the impurities and corruptions of a baser metal, so that it should become silver and purest gold, is thought by scientists to be able to remove the corruptions of the human body to such an extent that it would prolong life for many ages. This is the tempered body of elements, of which I spoke above.[221]

Bacon's alchemistic experiments eventually set a precedent for modern science. Mention of them here indicates that by the last third of the thirteenth century when Bacon wrote his *Opus Majus*,[222] at the very time when Greek astronomy, physics, and metaphysics were beginning to be accepted at the centres of learning like Oxford and Paris, Aristotelian theosophical astrology, Neoplatonic alchemy, and Neopythagorean Hermeticism were beginning to invade the western mind as well. The fact that even such rational thinkers as Sacrobosco could make reference to

Pseudo-Dionysius and that Grosseteste could trust in the arguments of the "doctores of alchemy" is a measure of the influence that this "esoteric science" was beginning to have on late mediaeval thought at a time coincident with the acceptance of the more rational side of Aristotle. This irrationality and rationality were the two sides of the Aristotelian coin which was to become the unstable currency for the mental transactions of the late Middle Ages and the early Renaissance. Eventually the currency was to be the root cause of the bankruptcy of the mediaeval culture which became dependent upon it.

NOTES

1. Dreyer, *History of Astronomy*, Chapter X, "Medieval Cosmology", pp. 207–239. The Arab contribution to the West is discussed below, pp. 118ff, 133ff, 149ff, 168ff.
2. Clement of Rome, *The Epistle of S. Clement to the Corinthians*, Chap. 20, trans. J. B. Lightfoot, *The Apostolic Fathers*, Part I, Vol. II (London: Macmillan, 1890), pp. 70 and 282.
3. *Ibid.*
4. *Ibid.*
5. *Ibid.*
6. Clement of Alexandria, *The Miscellanies*, Book V, Chap. VI, The Ante-Nicene Fathers, Vol. II (Grand Rapids, Michigan: Eerdmans, 1967), p. 452.
7. *Ibid.*, italics added. Cf. Exodus, Chaps. 25–27.
8. *Ibid.*
9. *Ibid.*
10. *Ibid.*
11. *Ibid.*
12. *Ibid.*
13. Origen, *In Genesin Homiliae*, Hom. I.2, *Patrologia Graeca*, ed., F.-P. Migne, Vol. 12, cols. 147–149.
14. Christianity became a recognised religion of the Roman empire in the East under Theodosius I (347–395) and in the West under Gratian (359–383) about 376.
15. Lactantius, Book III, Chap. 24, "On False Philosophy", *The Divine Institutes*, The Fathers of the Church, Vol. 49 (Washington D.C.: Catholic University, 1964), p. 229.
16. *Ibid.*
17. *Ibid.*, p. 228.
18. *Ibid.*, p. 229.

19. George Dragas, "Saint Basil, the Gazeans, and John Philoponos on Creation" (Unpublished paper, p. 1).
20. Saint Basil, *Exegetic Homilies*, Homily 1, The Fathers of the Church, Vol. 46 (Washington D.C.: Catholic University, 1963), pp. 7ff.
21. *Ibid.*, pp. 6f.
22. *Ibid.*, pp. 12–14.
23. *Ibid.*, p. 18.
24. *Ibid.*, Homily 3, p. 42.
25. *Ibid.*, p. 48.
26. *Ibid.*, Homily 1, p. 8.
27. *Ibid.*, Homily 3, p. 49.
28. *Ibid.*, Homily 6, pp. 97f.
29. *Ibid.*, Homily 1, p. 9.
30. *Ibid.*, Homily 9, p. 136. Eratosthenes' third-century B.C. measurement of the earth was c. 250,000 stadia.
31. *Ibid.*, Homily 8, p. 134.
32. Cyril of Jerusalem, *The Catechetical Lectures of S. Cyril*, Lecture IX. 6, A Select Library of Nicene and Post-Nicene Fathers of the Christian Church, Vol. VII (New York: Christian Literature, 1894), p. 52. E. H. Gifford, editor of Cyril's catechetical lectures, refers to Lucretius V.1182 at this point.

    They saw the skies in constant order run,
    The varied seasons and the circling sun,
    Apparent rule, with unapparent cause,
    And thus they sought in gods the source of laws.

33. Cyril, *Catechetical Lectures*, IX. 1, p. 51.
34. *Ibid.*, IX. 5, p. 52.
35. *Ibid.*
36. *Ibid.* IX. 6.
37. Severian, *In Mundi Creationem*, II. 3–4 in John Chrysostom, *Opera Omnia*, MPG, Vol. 56, cols. 441f. Cf. Dreyer, *History of Astronomy*, p. 211.
38. Severian, *In Mundi Creationem*, III. 4–5, *op. cit.*, cols. 451f.
39. *Ibid.*, III. 5.
40. Photius, *223*. *Diodore de Tarse* in *Bibliothèque*, Tome IV, 209a–211a (Paris: Belles Lettres, 1965), pp. 9–14.
41. *Ibid.*, 220b, p. 42.
42. Joannes Philoponos, *De Opificio Mundi* (Lipsiae: Teubneri, 1897), p. 17, pp. 33–59. Cf. below, pp. 109f.
43. Jerome, *Commentarium in Ezechielem Prophetam*, Lib. III. 99, MPL, Vol. 25, cols. 94–95.
44. John Chrysostom, *In Epistolam ad Hebraeos*, Cap. VIII, Homilia XIV. 1, MPG, Vol. 63, cols. 109f.
45. Saint Ambrose, *Hexaemeron, Paradise, and Cain and Abel*, II. 3, The Fathers of the Church (New York: Fathers of the Church, 1961), p. 51.

46. *Ibid.*, I. 6, p. 19.
47. *Ibid.*, p. 20.
48. *Ibid.*, p. 19.
49. *Ibid.*, II. 3, pp. 52f.
50. *Ibid.*, p. 56.
51. *Ibid.*
52. *Ibid.*, I. 3, p. 10; II. 2, p. 50.
53. *Ibid.*, II. 2, p. 50.
54. M. Tullius Cicero, *Somnium Scipionis*, eds. Carl Meissner and Gustav Landgraf (Amsterdam: Hakkert, 1964), IV. 9–V. 11. The seven tones may have presented an analogy to the seven strings of the seventh-century B.C. heptachord, an instrument in vogue when Pythagoras developed the theory. On the other hand, it may also have been the case that the instrument was developed in analogy to the seven chords of the heavenly music.
55. Ambrose, *Hexaemeron*, II. 2, p. 50.
56. *Ibid.*, p. 51.
57. *Ibid.* Italics added.
58. St. Augustine, *Concerning the City of God Against the Pagans*, trans. Henry Bettenson (Harmondsworth: Penguin, 1972), lib. XVI, cap. 9, p. 664.
59. *Ibid.*
60. *Ibid.*, cap. 10, pp. 665–667.
61. Sambursky, *Physical World of Late Antiquity*, p. 161.
62. Saint Augustine, *De Genesi Ad Litteram, Oeuvres Complètes de Saint Augustin*, Tome Septième (Paris: Librairie Vivès, 1873), lib. II, cap. 5, p. 67.
63. *Ibid.*, p. 68.
64. Augustine, *The City of God*, VIII. 5, p. 306.
65. *St. Augustine's Confessions*, trans. William Watts, Loeb Classical Library, 2 vols. (London: Heinemann, 1950, 1951), I, Liber V, Cap. III, p. 212.
66. *Ibid.*, pp. 210, 214.
67. *Ibid.*, II, Liber X, Cap. XXXV, p. 174.
68. *Ibid.*, pp. 176, 178. The phrase, *transitus siderum* (the course of the stars), may well have indicated a former interest in astrological signs.
69. *Ibid.*, II, Liber XII, Cap. XVII, pp. 324–328.
70. *Ibid.*, II, Liber XIII, Cap. II, p. 376.
71. *Ibid.*
72. *Ibid.*, Cap. XII, p. 396.
73. *Ibid.*, Cap. XV, p. 402.
74. *Ibid.*, pp. 404–406.
75. *Ibid.*, Cap. XVIII, pp. 412–416.
76. *Ibid.*, Cap. XIX, p. 418.
77. Cosmas Indicopleustes, *Topographie Chrétienne*, 2 vols. (Paris: Le Cerf, 1968, 1973), Book I. 12, p. 292. Cf. I 5–13, pp. 276–284.

78. *Ibid.*, I. 17, p. 288; IV. 22, p. 566.
79. *Ibid.*, II. 35–38, pp. 340–344.
80. *Ibid.*, IV. 1–3, pp. 532–538.
81. *Ibid.*, IV. 6, p. 540; IV. 9, p. 546. Cosmas assigns the passage to the Apostle Paul.
82. *Ibid.*, IV. 9, p. 546.
83. *Ibid.*, II. 84, p. 402.
84. *Ibid.*, II. 34, p. 338; IV. 11–12, pp. 550f.
85. *Ibid.*, IV. 13, p. 552.
86. *Ibid.*, Vol. II, VI. 6, p. 18.
87. *Ibid.*, Vol. I, II. 100, p. 418.
88. *Ibid.*, IV. 14, p. 552.
89. *Ibid.*, IV. 21, p. 566.
90. S. Sambursky, *Physical World of Late Antiquity*, p. 168.
91. *Ibid.*, pp. 160–162.
92. Philoponos, *De Opificio Mundi*, pp. 36ff.
93. Sambursky, *Physical World of Late Antiquity*, p. 163.
94. Cf. O'Leary, *How Greek Science Passed to the Arabs*, esp. Chapters II–IV, pp. 6–46; pp. 50–52; Chaps. XI–XII, pp. 146–175. O'Leary notes that the Syriac developed in Edessa became one of the main media for the translation process.
95. Cf. *ibid.*, esp. Chapter XIII, pp. 176–181.
96. Isidore of Seville, *Etymologiarum sive Originum libri XX*, Books I, II, III, MPL, Vol. 82, cols. 73–484.
97. *Ibid.*, Book XIII, Caput V, cols. 474–475.
98. Isidore of Seville, *De Natura Rerum*, Cap. XII MPL, Vol. 83, cols. 981–985.
99. *Ibid.*, Cap. XXIII, cols. 995–996.
100. *Ibid.*, Cap. XXXII–XLVIII, cols. 1005–1018.
101. *Ibid.*, Cap. XIV, col. 987.
102. *Ibid.*, Cap. XXIII, cols. 995–996. As Dreyer points out, the figures in the diagram do not designate periods of revolution but "periods after which the planets occupy the same places among the stars"; *History of Astronomy*, p. 221, fn. 3. Isidore's accompanying text indicates that the planets complete their circles in 8, 23, 9, 19, 15, 12 and 30 years respectively.
103. Isidore, *De Natura Rerum*, Cap. XXII.
104. Dreyer, *History of Astronomy*, p. 221.
105. Ibid., p. 223. Cf. Venerable Bede, *De Natura Rerum, Miscellaneous Works of Venerable Bede in the Original Latin*, Vol. VI, ed. J. A. Giles (London: Whittaker, 1843), cap. XIV, "... lege Plinium Secundum ex quo et ista nos excerpsimus".
106. Bede, *De Natura Rerum*, cap. II.
107. *Ibid.*, cap. III.
108. *Ibid.*, cap. VII.
109. *Ibid.*, cap. XIV.
110. *Ibid.*, cap. XVI–XVII.

111. *Ibid.*, cap. XVIII–XXI.
112. *Ibid.*, cap. XXVI–LI.
113. Venerable Bede, *De Temporum Ratione, Miscellaneous Works of Venerable Bede in the Original Latin*, Vol. VI, ed. J. A. Giles (London: Whittaker, 1843), cap. I.
114. *Ibid.*, cap. XII–XV.
115. *Ibid.*, cap. XVI–XXII.
116. *Ibid.*, cap. XXIII–XXX, LVI–LIX.
117. *Ibid.*, cap. XXXIV.
118. Bede, *De Natura Rerum*, cap. XIX.
119. Dreyer, *History of Astronomy*, p. 223, fn. 2. Cf. Pliny, *Natural History*, II. viii, 49.
120. Bede, *De Natura Rerum*, cap. XXIX.
121. Sharon Turner, *The History of the Anglo-Saxons*, 7th ed., 3 vols. (London: Longman, 1852), III, 372. Cf. Giles, "Preface", *Works of Bede*, pp. iii f.
122. Turner, *History*, p. 373.
123. Hrabanus Maurus, *De Universo*, XII. 2, MPL, Vol. 111, cols. 332–334.
124. *Ibid.*
125. Dreyer, *History of Astronomy*, p. 226.
126. *Ibid.*
127. *Ibid.*, p. 227.
128. *Ibid.* Contrary to Dreyer, however, it is quite evident that Bede in the last part of the seventh and first part of the eighth century, as well as Grosseteste in the first part of the twelfth century, used Greek as well as Latin.
129. Venerable Bede, *De Mundi Coelestis Terrestrisque Constitutione* (Dubia et Spuria), "Forma terrae", MPL, Vol. 90, cols. 332–883.
130. *Ibid.*, *De ordine planetarum*, col. 339.
131. *Ibid.*, *De super-coelestibus aquis*, col. 893.
132. *Ibid.*
133. For Dreyer's discussion, cf. *History of Astronomy*, p. 228.
134. Crombie, *Augustine to Galileo, Vol. I* indicates that the *Almagest* was translated from the Greek in 1160, p. 63. I know of no information which pinpoints the text used by the author of the *Elementorum Philosophiae*.
135. Cf. Venerable Bede, *Elementorum Philosophiae* (Dubia et Spuria), MPL, Vol. 90, cols. 1127–1180.
136. Cf. Calvin, *Commentary on Genesis*, p. 79, where he says, "Moses describes the special use of this expanse, 'to divide the waters from the waters,' from which words arises a great difficulty. For it appears opposed to common sense, and quite incredible, that there should be waters above the heaven. Hence some resort to allegory, and philosophise concerning angels; but quite beside the purpose. For to my mind, this is a certain principle, that nothing is here treated of but the visible form of the world."

137. Bede, *Elementorum Philosophiae*, Lib. II, MPL, cols. 1139–1160.
138. *Ibid.*, Lib. I, cols. 1132–1137.
139. Honorius of Autun, *De Imagine Mundi*, LXXXVII, XC, CXXXVIII, CXXXIX, CXL, MPL, Vol. 172, cols. 141–146. Dionysius L'Aréopagite, *La Hiérarchie céleste*, in *Oeuvres complètes du Pseudo-Denys L'Aréopagite* (Paris: Aubier, 1943), Cap. IX, pp. 217f.
140. Thomas Aquinas, *The Summa Theologica of St. Thomas Aquinas*, Part I, Third Number (Q.Q. LXXV–CXIX) (London: Baker, 1912), Q. CVIII, pp. 426–447. Dante Alighieri, *The Banquet*, trans. Katharine Hilliard (London: Kegan Paul, 1889), p. 96.
141. Omons, *Image du monde*, in *Notices et extraits des manuscrits*, T. v., pp. 243–266, referred to by Dreyer, *History of Astronomy*, p. 231.
142. Grosseteste apparently had access to a Greek text of Simplicius in the middle of the thirteenth century. Cf. Crombie, *Augustine to Galileo*, I, 55–63.
143. Dreyer, *History of Astronomy*, p. 232. Crombie gives the first date as 1210, *Augustine to Galileo*, I, 76.
144. Cf. below, pp. 149ff.
145. Sacro = holy, bosco = wood. There is some controversy as to whether John was of Holywood or Halifax or indeed if he were English. He is supposedly buried in the Church of St. Mathurin in Paris. Lynn Thorndike, "Introduction", *The Sphere of Sacrobosco and Its Commentators* (Chicago: University of Chicago, 1949), p. 2.
146. The Latin title of the work is *Tractatus de Spera Magistri Iohannis de Sacrobosco*. For a survey of extant texts, cf. Thorndike, "Introduction", *The Sphere*, pp. 59–74.
147. *Ibid.*, p. 15.
148. *Ibid.*, Proemium, English, p. 118; Latin, p. 76.
149. *Ibid.*, Chap. I, English, pp. 118f.; Latin, pp. 76f.
150. *Ibid.*, English, p. 119; Latin, p. 78.
151. *Ibid.*, English, pp. 119f.; Latin, 79.
152. *Ibid.*, English, pp. 122f.; Latin, pp. 84f.
153. *Ibid.*, Cap. II, English, p. 123; Latin, pp. 85f.
154. *Ibid.*, English, pp. 123–129; Latin, pp. 86–94.
155. *Ibid.*, Cap. III, English, pp. 129–140; Latin, pp. 95–112.
156. *Ibid.*, Cap. IV, English, pp. 140–142; Latin, pp. 113–117.
157. Both writings were apparently written between 1215 and 1230. Baur argues that since Sacrobosco's was the more complete and used a greater variety of sources, it was probably later. Perhaps so, but in that Sacrobosco gives no indication at all of having read Grosseteste's other writings on cosmology, it seems more likely that the two men may have written quite independently and simply used common sources. In *De Sphaera* and his other cosmological writings, Grosseteste used Plato's *Timaeus*, the Aristotelian corpus, Euclid, Ptolemy, and the Arab writers on science. Cf. Ludwig Baur, ed., *Die Philosophischen Werke des*

Robert Grosseteste, Bischofs von Lincoln (Münster: Aschendorf, 1912), Prolegomena, p. 64; Thorndike, *The Sphere of Sacrobosco*, pp. 2–51; Crombie, *Augustine to Galileo*, I, pp. 47f. and pp. 55–63.

Another subject of some controversy, perhaps, is whether Sacrobosco could be described as *Angelicus*, as Thorndike records, or as *der Schotte*, as Baur has it. Thorndike, *Sphere of Sacrobosco*, p. 2; Baur, *Philosophischen Werke Grosseteste*, Prolegomena, p. 64.

For what it is worth, my own opinion would be that though Paris seems to have had greater access to Arab writings including the very important commentaries on Aristotle, the fact that Oxford was prominent in emphasising the importance of mathematics gave it the edge as far as experimental science was concerned. In contrast to such scholars as Albertus Magnus and Thomas Aquinas at Paris, Grosseteste and later Roger Bacon at Oxford only accepted Aristotle's physics and cosmology, which were of a piece with his metaphysics and its attendant theological ideas, only with reservation.

158. Robert Grosseteste, *De Sphaera, Philosophischen Werke*, Cap. 1, p. 11.

159. *Ibid.*, Cap. 2–4, pp. 16–25.

160. *Ibid.*, Cap. 5, pp. 25–32.

161. *Ibid.*, Cap. 1, pp. 11–16.

162. Aristotle, *On Coming-To-Be and Passing-Away*, Loeb Classical Library (London: Heinemann, 1955), II, 10.336a.

163. Robert Grosseteste, *De generatione stellarum, Philosophischen Werke*, Lines 10–25, p. 35.

164. *Ibid.*, Lines 1–20, p. 33.

165. *Ibid.*, Lines 22–23, p. 33.

166. *Ibid.*, pp. 33–35.

167. *Ibid.*, Lines 3–10, p. 36. For Bacon's alchemistic ideas, cf. below.

168. Robert Grosseteste, *De motu supercaelestium, Philosophischen Werke*, Lines 20–28, p. 92, Lines 1–6, p. 93.

169. *Ibid.*, Line 34, p. 98 to Line 35, p. 100.

170. Robert Grosseteste, *De finitate motus et temporis, Philosophischen Werke*, Lines 1–12, p. 101.

171. *Ibid.*, Line 23, p. 101 to Line 8, p. 103.

172. *Ibid.*, Lines 8–26, p. 103.

173. *Ibid.*, Line 26, p. 103 to Line 10, p. 105.

174. *Ibid.*, Lines 11–12, p. 106.

175. Robert Grosseteste, *De cometis, Philosophischen Werke*, Line 22, p. 37 to Line 2, p. 38.

176. *Ibid.*, Lines 14–18, p. 38.

177. Baur has stated that "the emphasis of the heretical character of Aristotle's doctrine in *De finitate* ... is against the attempt of certain 'moderni' [modern philosophers whom one did not respect] to make a Catholic Aristotle out of the heretical Aristotle".

Bauer, Prolegomena, *Philosophischen Werke Grosseteste*, p. 95.
178. Roger Bacon, *Opus Majus*, 2 vols., trans. Robert Burke (Philadelphia: University of Pennsylvania, 1928), I, Part 3, Chap. I, p. 76. Cf. also *ibid.*, Part 4, Chap. III, p. 126 where Bacon refers to Grosseteste's writings on the rainbow, comets, generations of heat, geography and Part 3, Chap. II, p. 78 where Bacon mentions Grosseteste as having "turned into Latin" Greek works.
179. *Ibid.*, Part 1, Chap. XIV, p. 31 and Part 3, Chap. II, p. 37.
180. *Ibid.*, Part 2, Chap. IX, p. 55.
181. *Ibid.*, II, Part 7, Moral Philosophy: First Part, pp. 646, 655, 658. Bacon accepts the reports of Hermes as given by the *Asclepius* on the authority of Augustine, *ibid.*, p. 646. Cf. *ibid.*, pp. 635–662 for Bacon's own Neoplatonic mixture which is spiced with references to Plato, Aristotle, Augustine, Cicero, Trismegistus, Avicenna, Averroës, *et al.*
182. *Ibid.*, Part 7, Moral Philosophy: Fourth Part, Chap. I, p. 787.
183. *Ibid.*
184. *Ibid.*, I, Part 4, Chap. XVI, p. 323. Dreyer notes that Bacon's conclusion in his chapter on geography, that the ocean between the east coast of Asia and Europe was relatively narrow, was copied by Cardinal Petrus d'Ailly (1350–1420) in his *Imago Mundi* and then used by Columbus to persuade the Spanish monarchs to sponsor his voyage to "the Indies", another misconceived experiment with a beneficial outcome. Dreyer, *History of Astronomy*, p. 235. Cf. Bacon's discussion of the geography of India and Asia, *Opus Majus*, I, Part 4, Chap. XVI, pp. 369ff.
185. *Ibid.*, p. 201.
186. *Ibid.*, p. 216.
187. *Ibid.*, Part 4, Dist. 1, Ch. II, p. 117.
188. *Ibid.*, II, Part 7, Moral Philosophy: Third Part, Chap. IV, p. 676.
189. *Ibid.*, I, Part 4, Chap. XVI, pp. 254–259.
190. *Ibid.*, p. 216.
191. *Ibid.*, pp. 248ff.
192. *Ibid.*, pp. 249f., 255ff.
193. *Ibid.*, pp. 392ff., 401.
194. *Ibid.*, p. 201.
195. *Ibid.*, p. 279.
196. *Ibid.*, pp. 279f.
197. *Ibid.*, Part 1, Chap. III, p. 10. Bacon cited Aristotle throughout his *Opus Majus* and records that he was appalled both by objections to the philosophy and metaphysics of Aristotle as interpreted by Avicenna and Averroës and by the fact that those who used them had been excommunicated for long periods. *Ibid.*, p. 22.
198. *Ibid.*, Part 4, Chap. XVI, p. 394.
199. *Ibid.*
200. In the Middle Ages, the terms "mathematician" and "astrologer" were often interchangeable.

201. Cf. above, pp. 19ff, 29f.
202. Bacon, *Opus Majus*, Part IV, Chap. XVI, p. 395.
203. *Ibid.*
204. *Ibid.*, p. 396.
205. *Ibid.*
206. *Ibid.*, p. 397.
207. *Ibid.*, p. 400.
208. *Ibid.*
209. *Ibid.*, p. 401.
210. *Ibid.*, pp. 401f.
211. *Ibid.*, p. 405.
212. *Ibid.*
213. *Ibid.*, pp. 405f.
214. *Ibid.*, p. 406.
215. *Ibid.*, p. 308.
216. *Ibid.*, pp. 394f.
217. Roger Bacon, *The Mirror of Alchimy* (London: Richard Oliue, 1597), p. 1. Cf. H. Stanley Redgrove, *Roger Bacon, The Father of Experimental Science and Medieval Occultism* (London: Rider, 1920), pp. 37f. and Lynn Thorndike, *A History of Magic and Experimental Science*, Vol. V (New York: Columbia University, 1941), p. 537 for discussions of authorship.
218. Cf. above, pp. 5ff.
219. Aristotle, *Physics*, I. vi, 189a–189b.
220. Bacon, *Opus Majus*, p. 627.
221. *Ibid.*
222. Bacon apparently began writing his treatises shortly after 1266. Cf. *ibid.*, Introduction, pp. xi ff.

CHAPTER 4

LATE MEDIAEVAL COSMOLOGY

AT the time Roger Bacon went to Paris from Oxford, the intellectual scene was dominated by Albert the Great and his student, Thomas Aquinas, both of whom had adopted Aristotelianism, especially as delivered to the western mind by Averroës, as the foundation of their thought. Bacon, himself, had no more respect for Thomas than he had for Aristotle. His critique, however, did little to deter the effect of the Thomistic synthesis which forced theological thought into Aristotelian categories with such felicity and thoroughness that it was soon to replace the then dominant Neoplatonically-influenced Augustinianism as the basis of theology and of philosophy and science as well. So strong did the Aristotelian influence become that in spite of formal bans against certain of the Aristotelian claims, the last as late as 1277 (three years after Thomas' death), Aristotelianism was to be the dominant force in the shaping of the late mediaeval and early Renaissance mind until the sixteenth century.

Thomistic Aristotelianism

Thomas' acceptance of Aristotle was not uncritical, however. Much as he relied upon and adopted Aristotle's metaphysics and cosmology, he was profoundly critical of his cosmogony. In agreement with Christian writers from the post-Apostolic period onward, Thomas insisted on the doctrine of *creatio ex nihilo* as over against Aristotle's *aeternitas mundi* (eternity of the world).

Sacrobosco had written his *De Sphaera* at about the same time (or perhaps shortly before) Thomas was born.

Whether or not Sacrobosco was still in Paris when Thomas arrived on the scene in about the year 1245, we can take it for granted that his book *De Sphaera* certainly was. Hence it is highly likely that, prior to engaging himself with Aristotle's cosmology, Thomas would have been introduced to the subject by Sacrobosco's excellent though simplified summary of the Aristotelian-Ptolemaic system. It is evident, at any rate, from Thomas' writings in general and especially from his *In Libros Aristotelis de Caelo et Mundo* (*Commentary on Aristotle's On the Heavens and Earth*)[1] and his *De Aeternitate Mundi* (*On the Eternity of the World*) in particular, that he was thoroughly familiar with Aristotelian cosmology as well as the thought of Ptolemy. The writings make clear that while Thomas accepted Aristotle's concepts of astronomy and physics as a proper explanation of the nature of the world, he was deeply critical of Aristotle's idea that the world existed from all eternity.

As Cyril Vollert has pointed out in his introduction to the translation of Thomas' *De Aeternitate Mundi*, and as said above, it is extremely important to realise that both Thomas and Albert the Great were deeply dependent on Arab scholars, particularly Averroës. Averroës, who more than anyone else was responsible for introducing both Aristotelian philosophy and cosmology to Europe at the end of the Middle Ages,[2] put forward Aristotle's idea of the eternity of the world in the "First Discussion" of his *Tahafat al-Tahafat* (*The Incoherence of Incoherence*). In the argument Averroës defended Aristotle against Alghazali (1058–1111), the most prominent of the theologians of Islam.[3] As Christian theologians had argued for the created nature of the world on the basis of the biblical doctrine of *creatio ex nihilo*, so Alghazali argued on the basis of the Koranic teaching that *the world had its beginning in time*.[4] Consequently, Alghazali had turned down the philosophies of Avicenna and of Aristotle because he considered them dangerous and destructive. Avicenna, like Aristotle, had insisted that the heavens (whose circular motion was incapable of change) had neither beginning nor end. Likewise he argued for the eternity of form and matter.

Interestingly enough, although both Albert the Great and Thomas Aquinas were profoundly influenced by the Aristotelianism of Averroës so far as the question of the eternity of the world was concerned, both agreed with Alghazali as over against Averroës. Albert the Great in particular conceded that from the standpoint of philosophy, it was more probable to believe in the eternity of the world than otherwise.[5] From the *standpoint of faith*, however, Albert had to admit that no creature could have existed from eternity. The third position, which was offered at the time, namely that God created the world and yet that the world exists co-eternally with him, was for Albert, as it had been for Augustine, unintelligible.[6]

The arguments of Thomas in this regard in both his *Commentary on Aristotle's On the Heavens* and in his writing *On the Eternity of the World* are given in the context of his explanation of cosmology as a whole. His *On the Heavens* shows that he both knew and accepted the Aristotelian-Ptolemaic cosmology which was consistent with Aristotle's theological and metaphysical concepts. The writings also indicate that his concern for Aristotle's cosmic system was inspired much more by metaphysical and theological interests than it was by cosmological ones. However, even if his reason for studying cosmology was for the sake of theology, it is evident that Thomas had mastered the main points of the Ptolemaic system. He was aware of the Ptolemaic order of the planets.[7] He knew that Ptolemy had ascribed to the earth an immovable position in the centre of the world.[8] And he understood the difference Aristotle had made between picturing the universe sensibly and knowing it mathematically.[9] In addition, he summarised the explanations of the apparent irregularity of planetary motion given by Eudoxus, Callippus, Aristotle, and Hipparchus[10] and made note of the difficulties that the apparent erratic movements of those wandering stars caused in the Ptolemaic system.[11]

In the end Thomas adopted the fateful Aristotelian

dogma that the earth by nature is at rest in the centre of a world of circling, homocentric spheres.[12] He was, nevertheless, candid enough to cite both Heraclides of Pontus and Aristarchus as having proclaimed, contrary to Aristotle, the idea that "the earth on which we live moves from the west to the east around the equinoctial poles" and that such a movement presupposed that the heaven and the stars were at rest.[13]

In contrast to Sacrobosco who was satisfied to sum up Ptolemaic cosmology without theological inhibition, Thomas objected to Aristotle's conception of the eternity of the world, as had Albert the Great, for theological reasons. It was not possible, he insisted, finally to demonstrate the *aeternitas mundi*.[14] He did not take the matter lightly, however. Neither did he simply dismiss the matter with a dogmatic statement. Rather, he went into a lengthy discussion of the eternity of the world on the basis of the writings of Plato,[15] "the poets", and the opinions of Democritus, Empedocles, and Heraclitus of Ephesus.[16] He capped the argument by showing that Aristotle himself defined part of the world at least [the sub-lunar sphere] as being generated and corruptible.[17] Then, contrary to Aristotle's view that the heavens were incorruptible and eternal, Thomas enlivened his argument by insisting that there must be a differentiation between the eternity of the world and the eternity of God, between God's duration and the duration of that which is generated and corruptible.[18] To back up his claim, he called upon "Ioannes Grammaticus" (John Philoponos) who had shown that the substance of the heavens is generated and corruptible.[19] Philoponos, it will be recalled, based his conviction about the nature of the heavens upon both their complex material substance and the non-symmetry and non-regularity of the movements of the heavenly bodies.[20]

Thomas was well enough acquainted with Aristotle's *Physics* to realise that Aristotle had based his belief in the eternity of the heavens upon the idea of the eternity of motion.[21] Primary motion was eternal, uniform, uninterrupted and, therefore, circular.[22] The impetus for motion

was given by the eternal and motionless prime mover.[23]
However, being Christian, Thomas rejected the argument
because he insisted that God was prior to all things, prior to
motion, to time and, therefore, to the world. If God were
eternal, the world could not be.

In the *De Aeternitate Mundi*, Thomas made the same
point but with greater theological subtlety. Although he
realised, as had Albert the Great, that from the point of
view of philosophy, one could argue for the eternity of the
world, one could not do so from the standpoint of
revelation which tells us that, "In the beginning God
created the heavens and the earth".[24] Faith demands that
"the world had a beginning".[25] In order to express the
contingency of creation on God alone, Thomas translated
the term, *ex nihilo*, not as "out of nothing" but as "after
nothing".[26] It could be argued, of course, that Thomas'
words were meant to imply that there was "a nothing"
before creation. However, his intention was to make it clear
that the world neither *emerges* out of chaos nor *emanates*
from the will of God. Rather, the universe and its dimensions depend on "the mere will of God".[27] The heavens are
what and as they are because "the Creator so willed it".[28]
They were constructed according to "the design of God's
wisdom". Hence, Thomas referred to Isaiah, "Lift up
your eyes on high and see who hath created these things"
(Is. 40:26).[29] Again, in contradiction to Aristotle's argument for the eternity of the world as based upon the
eternity of motion which was traced back to the unmoved
mover who acts in time,[30] Thomas insisted that "time itself
is included within the universality of things that have been
made by God".[31]

Further, in refuting Aristotle's argument that whatever
is incorruptible has the power of existing forever and that
the heavens, which were characterised by circular motion,
are by nature immortal,[32] Thomas turned to a defence
based upon reason and brought in his theology only at the
end of his argument. He made four points:

(1) Incorruptibility applies to the future and not to the
    past.

(2) The statement that the heavens would lapse into
    non-existence if they were not sustained by God
    pertains not to the past but to the future only.

(3) Every effect must have a cause and the cause of this
    effect [of sustainability] is God.

(4) Since the effect is brought about by divine will, it is
    not coexistent with divine nature and hence is not
    eternal.[33]

Thomas' argument was thus a reinforcement of his stand
that God is prior to creation and creation is contingent
upon him. At the same time it is notable that, in light of the
more mystical side of his thought, Thomas here moved
directly against Pseudo-Dionysius, who had advocated
that since God was good he shared his eternal goodness
with the world he had created. Dionysius, whose ideas in
this regard were to be picked up by Nicholas of Cusa, had
argued that the world shares in God's eternity.[34]

Hence, while Thomas was convinced that the Church's
teaching regarding the world as having had a beginning
could not be effectively undermined by any demonstration
based on physics,[35] he also believed that since God was the
cause of all things, both revelation and physics must be
accepted as sources of truth. Where the Church was silent,
however, Aristotle's cosmology could be endorsed as the
basic description of the universe, a universe which was
characterised by simplicity, the heavenly motions of which
were necessarily circular.[36]

Thus, in spite of the fact that Thomas argued against the
eternity of motion, he argued no less stringently than had
Aristotle that the motion of the world could not be
irregular.[37] Thomas did not make it easy for himself,
however. He recognised Aristotle's insistence on the
simple, circular, homocentric motion of the celestial
sphere and the opinion of later observers who noted that
the celestial sphere not only rotated about an axis but that
the axis precessed as well. He even compared Aristotle's
homocentric theory with Ptolemy's epicycles. He explained the motions involved including the precession of

the celestial spheres.[38] He accounted for regular motion, however, by the simple expediency of adding a ninth sphere above the celestial sphere so that the first motion could be attributed to it.[39] Then in typical Aristotelian fashion (fatefully so it was to turn out) he went on to argue that the earth was at rest in the centre of the world surrounded by the spheres of the moon, sun, planets, and the fixed stars.[40]

Hence, although Thomas was familiar with Ptolemy's complicated system of deferents, eccentrics, and epicycles, he used a simplified model of Aristotle's onion universe of nested spheres to represent the construction of the world. His acceptance of Aristotelian cosmology and his reconciliation of it with the Christian faith gave Aristotle's ideas the aura of acceptability, thereby promoting the development of science in an Aristotelian direction. At the same time his combination of theological doctrines with Aristotle's deductive logic had the effect of giving his system such prescriptive force that, when his teachings became accepted as the Church's dogma, any attempt to question them was tantamount to questioning revelation itself.

Thomistic Mysticism

From the above exposition, which is all too brief to do justice either to Thomas himself or to Aristotle's influence upon him, it might appear that it was alone the *rational* and *systematic* aspects of Aristotelianism, and of the Thomism based upon it, that induced the mediaeval and early Renaissance era to accept it as the foundation of its thought. There was, however, another side to Aristotle which Thomas did not neglect. This was Aristotle the mystic, the Aristotle emphasised in Neoplatonism, the Aristotle who held that fifty-five heavenly spirits guided the movements of the heavenly orbs and, as Roger Bacon also believed, guided the ways of the world, human beings and nations.

For Aristotle the universe was both a rational whole and a living inter-connected system.[41] The upper imperishable heaven was the region of the gods.[42] As such the heaven was held to be animated and to contain the principle of motion.[43] The planets were the divine bodies which influenced the development of plants, animals, and people.[44] Thus the world which owed its stability to the rational regularities of motion due to the prime mover was also subject to the unpredictable influence of astral deities.[45]

By the time Thomas inherited Aristotelianism, such divine forces and energies of this kind had long since been given a "Christian" interpretation by Pseudo-Dionysius. They had been "baptised" into the faith and were given biblical names while being arranged in three hierarchies. The first, the Seraphim, Cherubim, and Thrones; the second, Dominions, Virtues, and Powers; and the third, Principalities, Archangels, and Angels. The designations of the first three, as Dionysius explained, were given in reference to God. The names of the second three had to do with a certain kind of government or disposition while the last three had their names in relationship to vocation or work.[46]

Thomas, whose citations from Pseudo-Dionysius are in number second only to those from Aristotle, accepted this combination of mystical Neoplatonism and Neopythagoreanism with such energy that he both apologised for the angelic hierarchies and used the mystical cosmology involved as a basis for piety. He explained the hierarchies by showing the relationship between the orders and pointed out their gracious and natural gifts as well as their perfections and virtues. He referred the statement in Judges 5:20, "*stars remaining in their order and courses*", to the angelic hierarchies which will continue to the day of judgement when, according to the Apostle Paul, "*he shall have delivered up the Kingdom of God and the Father* [RSV, "to God the Father"] (1 Cor. 15:24).[47] However, since Augustine had said that "*there will not be two societies of men and of angels, but only one; because the beatitude of all is to cleave to God alone*",[48] Thomas assured his readers that even human beings by grace may become angels.

Thus prompted by both Pseudo-Dionysius and Augustine, Thomas translated Aristotle's animated heavens, which influence life and events on earth, into "Christian" understanding.[49] "The movements of bodies here below, which are various and multiform, must be referred to the movement of the heavenly bodies, as to their cause."[50] Hence, although the heavenly bodies are corporeal, they can nevertheless act directly on the powers of the soul.[51] It is important to note, however, that in line with the explanation given by Roger Bacon, Thomas was quite insistent that actions of this kind should not be considered deterministic. They were to be regarded as acting immediately on the human intellect by enlightening it.[52] Nonetheless, since the majority of human beings follow their passions rather than their intellects, astrologers are able to foretell the truth in a majority of cases, if only in a general way. This does not apply to particular cases, however, for nothing prevents a man from resisting his passions by free will.[53] Thomas backed up his argument by reference to Aristotle's differentiation between necessity and accident. In a majority of cases, cause is followed by effect, but in a minority of cases it is not.[54]

Thus, for Thomas, as for Roger Bacon, "The heavenly bodies are causes of effects that take place here below, through the means of particular inferior causes, which can fail in their effects in the minority of cases."[55] Here, then, Aristotle the metaphysician, physicist, and astronomer has been replaced by *Aristotle the astrologer*. And it was through adopting *both sides* of Aristotle, as it were, that Thomas opened his "mediaeval synthesis" both to the rational scientific mind and at the same time to the mystical element in mediaeval piety. As with the ancient Pythagoreans, God's activity was discerned in the movements of the heaven. The heavenly bodies were understood to be the seats of angelic beings. Spirits connected heaven and earth and directed fortune or misfortune, destiny or fate. To look to the heavens was to see the movements of these divinities and, in the majority of cases, their wills were done.

Eventually it was this dualism, this dichotomy between order and caprice, that was to make Aristotelianism and the

Thomistic system built upon it, for all its insights, inappropriate for the development of modern science and the modern world. In the end, after much agony and even terror, this basic inconsistency was to disrupt the "mediaeval synthesis", a system which, as it turned out, was not really a synthesis at all but, taken as a whole, a compilation of contradictory concepts. In spite of challenges, however, it proved to be powerful enough to carry on through the era of Copernicus. Before then, the Neoplatonic, mystical elements of the system were to be emphasised and worked out in the poetic power of Dante Alighieri.

Dante's Cosmological Reveries

If Thomas Aquinas framed the "mediaeval synthesis", Dante Alighieri (1265–1321) was its masterful apologist. He so insinuated the system into the minds of the believers that, along with the rationalism of ecclesiastical authority, the whole romantic irreality of Pseudo-Dionysius' cosmic angelic whirls became at one and the same time the constitution of the world and the content of faith. So powerful was the prose of Dante's *Il Convito* (*The Banquet*) and the poetry of *Inferno, Purgatorio, Paradiso* (*The Divine Comedy*) that to question its cosmology, as Cecco d'Ascoli was soon to learn, was to pay for one's temerity with one's life.[56] Dante, who set out his cosmology in the *Il Convito*, knew and cited Aristotle, Ptolemy, and Plato (second-hand from Aristotle) as well as Avicenna, Alghazali, Pseudo-Dionysius,[57] Albert the Great,[58] and, of course, Thomas Aquinas.[59] In his *Il Convito*, Dante appropriately awarded both Albert and Thomas with places in paradise.[60]

Although Dante referred repeatedly to Aristotle's *On the Heavens* and to his *Metaphysics* as well as to the thought of Ptolemy, he used the information he gathered from these writings to allegorise the heavens and the "science" about them into a mystic complex which exploited cosmology for its own purposes.[61] Thus, Dante was quick to improve upon his authorities where necessary. He faulted Aristotle

for having followed "the ancient ignorance of the astrologers" (astronomers) and for thinking that there were only
eight heavens. Dante knew there were ten. He modelled his
universe on Aristotle's nest of homocentric spheres which
surrounded the central and immovable earth. The first
seven spheres from the earth outward were moon, Mercury, Venus, sun, Mars, Jupiter, and Saturn.

Dante was evidently influenced by Averroës who, in his
commentary on Aristotle to which Dante more than likely
had access, had diagrammed the world as consisting of
eight concentric circles and had designated the planetary
spheres from that of the moon to that of the stars to stand
for "individual perception", "communal perception",
"imagination", "judgement", "memory", "passion", and
"anger".[62] And in line with Averroës, Dante allegorised
the seven spheres to refer to the Trivium and Quadrivium,
the academic disciplines of the mediaeval world.[63] The
moon stood for Grammar, Mercury for Dialectics, and
Venus for Rhetoric. The sun designated Arithmetic and
was thus the basis of Pythagorean science. Mars symbolised Music; Jupiter, Geometry; and Saturn, Astrology
(Astronomy). For Dante the eighth celestial sphere symbolised physics and metaphysics. The ninth, the *primum
mobile*, signified moral philosophy or ethics. The tenth,
which surrounded all the others and which was Dante's
special innovation, was "the Empyrean", the dwelling
place of God. Appropriately it typified the Divine Science
of Theology.[64]

More to the point, the kind of Neoplatonic popular piety
which Dante supported, explicated, reinforced, and promoted, was his angelic interpretation of the heavenly
powers. Building on Aristotle but more particularly upon
Pseudo-Dionysius and Thomas, Dante distributed the
heavenly powers into the ecclesiastically designated "nine
orders of spiritual creatures". These coincided with the
nine mobile homocentric spheres of heaven. By altering
the arrangement offered by Pseudo-Dionysius which was
reflected, as we have seen, in Thomas Aquinas, Dante
constructed his first échelon, which is nearest God, of the

Seraphim, Cherubim, and Powers. These corresponded to the persons of the Trinity and were responsible for the *primum mobile*, the sphere of the fixed stars, and the sphere of Saturn respectively. The second hierarchy consisted of the Principalities, Virtues, and Dominions and was assigned to the spheres of Jupiter, Mars, and the sun. The third hierarchy comprised the Thrones, Archangels, and Angels and these were appointed to the spheres of Venus, Mercury, and the moon.[65]

Such were the "nine orders" of contemplating spirits that:

The angels:

> "Matter and form unmingled and conjoined
> Came into being that had no defect." (*Par*. 29.22)[66]

All gazed upward upon the "Light"[67]

> "Beyond all the spheres, beyond Jupiter which
> Like silver seemed with gold inlaid" (*Par*. 18.96).

Beyond the eighth celestial sphere which

> "doth like a glorious wheel move round" (*Par*. 10.145)

and begins like

> "a holy millstone to revolve" (*Par*. 12.3)

is the ninth, the *primum mobile*,

> "the power of the motion of holy spheres
> As from the smith the hammer's craft does come
> Forth from the blessed motors must proceed",
>   (*Par*. 2.127)

itself moving with incomprehensible slowness so as to emulate the restful tenth sphere, the *Empyrean Heaven*, the abode of the Supreme Deity, "that Light which can only be perfectly beheld by Itself".[68]

> "That high Light which of itself is true" (*Par*. 33.54)

is

"he who all the world enlightens" (*Par.* 20.1)

and "announces the unity and stability of God", for, as "the Psalmist says, 'The heavens recount the glory of God, and the firmament announces the work of his hands'" (Ps. 19:1).[69]

In addition, and with Aristotle, Roger Bacon, and Thomas, Dante insisted that humanity on earth was under the influence of the heavenly bodies.[70]

"The heavens your impulses do initiate" (*Purg.* 16.73)
and

"Thence it descends to the last potencies
   Downward from act to act becoming such
   That it makes only brief contingencies
   And these contingencies I hold to be
   Things generated which heaven produces
   By its own motion, with seed and without."
                                        (*Par.* 13.61–66)

For Dante it was not the biblical "from dust you have come, to dust you must return" (Gen. 3:19). but rather, following Plato's *Timaeus*:

"The soul unto its star returns
   Believing it had been severed thence
   When nature gave it as a form." (*Par.* 4.53)

Thus, the Empyrean, the dwelling place of God, is reserved not only for God. It is the home of "the beatified spirits" as well.[71]

Besides this admittedly "allegorical", "moral", "ana-gogical", or mystical meaning of cosmology which for Dante was primary, he also spoke of a "literal" under-standing of the world.[72] Though this was for him decidedly of minor importance, the separate listing presented the bare outlines of a schematised Aristotelian onion model of the world to whose eight spheres Dante added a ninth which, like Ptolemy's outermost sphere, was used to explain the precession of the celestial spheres. And, as we have seen, he also added a tenth, the Empyrean, on his own.[73]

In the centre of the ten spheres is the earth which, like the outermost Empyrean, is immovable. The outermost sphere imparted motion to each of the nine spheres inferior to it

"where the one motion on the other strikes" (*Par.* 10.9)

so that each emulated the movement of the one above while the celestial sphere turned on its axis in a little less than twenty-four hours. The spheres of Saturn, Jupiter, Mars, the sun, Venus, Mercury, and the moon, all of which were moved by batteries of angelic spirits, had movements peculiar to themselves forming

"the oblique circle which the planets convey"
                                      (*Par.* 10.13)

Venus

"the fairest star that moves us to love" (*Purg.* 1.19)

presented a special problem. In order to explain the planet's irregularities and its rising and setting, Dante, like Ptolemy, fitted Venus with both a main sphere and a little sphere or epicycle to which the planet itself was fixed. As the greater sphere revolved around two poles, so, Dante explained, "does this 'little' one". Thus Dante indicated that he knew the particulars of Ptolemy's deferents and epicycles. But rather than go into detail, he added, "How it may be with the other heavens and the other stars, we have not at present to discuss".[74] Nevertheless the world, thus designed in simplicity, harmony, and beauty, was of the order of God himself.

"All things whatsoever they are,
     Have order among themselves, and this is a form
     That makes the universe resemble God." (*Par.* 1.103)

Hermetic Harmonies

The growth of science seems to defy nature in never taking the shortest distance from point to point. Or perhaps, as in an Einsteinian universe where space is "warped" by the presence of ponderable bodies, the intricacies of history are such that we simply are unable to trace anything like a "straight line" or "shortest distance". At any rate, the route of the development of science seems to be circuitous, full of stops and starts, urged on by foreign elements as well as those which we judge to be inherently compatible.

By the time of Dante's death in the year 1321, a thousand years after Constantine had recognised Christianity as a legitimate religion, Aristotle and Plato, who were reflected by Ptolemy, reasserted themselves as the dominant force in the development of western science only to be allegorised, spiritualised, and mythicised. The mythicisation, which had its roots in the kind of Christian Neoplatonism that inspired Pseudo-Dionysius, was to be both supported and advanced by *Hermeticism*. Hermeticism, which is now beginning to become known and accounted for by historians of science, had an influence which, though difficult to measure, seems to have had a profound impact on Renaissance thought and on the kind of science which was brought forth in its milieu. Though at first glance Hermeticism may be regarded as quite foreign and antithetical to science, it had the obvious advantage of urging the human mind to concentrate on the mysterious rather than allowing it to be closed off by Aristotelian rationalism. As we shall see, it may have had other more positive contributions as well.

We have met Hermeticism already as an ingredient of the thought of Roger Bacon. The Neoplatonism of Pseudo-Dionysius which affected both Thomas and Dante clearly resembled it in many respects. There is also evidence that this strange mixture of Neopythagoreanism, Neoplatonism, and Egyptian and Cabalistic mysticism affected Nicholas of Cusa in the early sixteenth century. Copernicus was no doubt familiar with its literature. In the late sixteenth century Giordano Bruno was so inebriated with it that, rather than recant, he went to the stake.[75] In the seventeenth century Francis Bacon came under its sway and it is quite certain that Kepler was persuaded to search for the harmonies of the spheres by the persuasive influence of Hermetic symmetries. Even Isaac Newton was not entirely free of its alchemistic aspects.

As Pythagoreanism in origin was a cult which eventually promoted mathematics, so too from what we know and are beginning to learn about Hermeticism, it seems that this *prisca theologia* or "ancient theology", to use Marsilio Ficino's (1433–99) term, had more than a little influence on the late mediaeval and Renaissance world in which the foundations of modern science developed. As a "cultic science", Hermeticism in the first instance served less as a foundation on which science could develop than as a resource which provided the Renaissance mind with tools for speculation alternative to the propositions of the dominant Aristotelian rationalism of the late Middle Ages.[76] Studies by A.-J. Festugière, D. P. Walker, and Frances Yates indicate that Hermeticism and its sources and variations were as many as its influence was broad.[77] Its central figure was the cultic prophet Hermes Trismegistus.

Hermes Trismegistus, i.e., Hermes the thrice-great or more colloquially "Hermes the Greatest", is the Greek name for the Egyptian god Thoth who was variously known to have been the scribe of the gods, the inventor of writing, and the god of the literary arts. Hermes was introduced to the Renaissance West as a full-blown historical figure by Marsilio Ficino. In the *Argumentum* with which he prefaced the *Pimander* (the name Ficino gave to his 1463 translation of the Hermetic Corpus), Ficino wrote:

> In the time in which Moses was born there flourished Atlas the astrologer, brother of the physicist Prometheus and maternal uncle of Mercury the elder whose nephew was Mercurius [Hermes] Trismegistus.[78]

"Mercurius Trismegistus" or "Hermes Trismegistus", whose total effect upon early Neoplatonism would seem as yet to be unassessed, was not new to the West, however. He was known by the Church Fathers — Athenagoras, Tertullian, Cyprian, Clement of Alexandria, Lactantius, Cyril of Alexandria, and Augustine.[79] They, like Ficino, were assured of the antiquity of Hermes and of the writings attributed to him.

In the early seventeenth century, in 1615 to be exact, Isaac Casaubon (1559–1614) redated the *Hermetic Corpus* and showed that the writings did not arise in ancient Egypt nor did they predate Judaism and Christianity. Rather, they were forgeries by Christian or semi-Christian authors of the second and third centuries which were alleged to be of ancient origin.[80] To the "Renaissance mind", however, both before and after Casaubon's disclosure, the Hermetic literature often revealed the stuff of which the mysteries of the universe were made.

A.-J. Festugière, one of the principal authorities on Hermeticism, has shown that the theology, cosmogony, anthropology, soteriology, and eschatology of the Hermetic doctrines were a combination of Neopythagorean astrology, Neoplatonic theology and anthropology, Stoic moral teachings, elements of Jewish history, Egyptian cabalistic magic, and the cosmology of *The Chaldean Oracles*.[81] Ficino, the translator of the *Hermetic Corpus*, in all seriousness called Hermes "the first author of theology". He was "succeeded by Orpheus and then by Aglaophemus and Pythagoras". Pythagoras' disciple, Philolaus, Ficino explained, was "the teacher of our divine Plato". "Thus", Ficino went on, "there is one *prisca theologia* (ancient theology) from Mercurius [Hermes] to Plato" and this theology was recorded in the Hermetic writings.[82]

Themes from *The Chaldean Oracles*, a theophilosophical text of the late second century, appear and reappear in Pseudo-Dionysius and the Hermetic literature. *The Chaldean Oracles*, which in its own time became a basic religious text for Neoplatonic thought, combined Persian and Babylonian elements with the Platonic understanding of the relationship between creation and the soul. In creation the soul was imprisoned in a "dull body".[83]

Divinity, however, which interpenetrated the world was not necessarily hidden. As with the ancient Pythagoreans as well as Plato and Aristotle, divinity was held to interpenetrate the world and show itself in symmetricity and circularity. According to Plato, the world was characterised by divinity, symmetry, and circularity from the beginning.

> Such was the whole scheme of the eternal God about the god that was to be, to whom he for all these reasons gave a body, smooth, even, and in every direction equidistant from a centre, entire and perfect, and formed out of perfect bodies. And in the centre he put the soul, which he diffused through the whole, and also spread over all the body round about; and he made one solitary and only heaven a circle moving in a circle, having such excellence as to be able to hold converse with itself, and needing no other friendship or acquaintance. Having these purposes in view he created the world to be a blessed god.[84]

In *The Chaldean Oracles* Plato's divine and spiritual realities take on physical form. The Father "fixed a vast multitude of unwandering stars", congregated "the seven firmaments of the cosmos", and circumscribed the heavens "with convex form". He suspended their disorder in six "well-disposed zones"; for the seventh "he cast into the midst thereof the fiery sun". The sun is "the centre from which all [distances] which waysoever . . . are equal". "The sun is a fire, the channel of fire and the dispenser of fire."[85]

Heaven is also the origin of the individual souls which descend from above, are captive to creation for a time and, upon being released, ascend again to their original abode. The soul is a "brilliant fire"[86] which descends from the Father,[87] and is compelled to pass back again through all things,[88] singing a psalm as it ascends[89] to regain its pure paternal symbol.[90]

These same themes were to appear again and again in the Hermetic writings. These were first transferred to the West, it would seem, by the *Asclepius*. Although the original Greek version of the *Asclepius* has been lost, it was known among the Church Fathers in Latin from the second century onward. A second source of Hermetic thought was the literary lore which the Arabs brought with them to Europe along with the writings of Aristotle. These dealt especially with the so-called popular Hermeticism as well as with the related *al Chem* (alchemy). Finally, the third and most important source was the *Corpus Hermeticum*. In 1460 a monk whom Cosimo de Medici (1389–1464) employed to collect manuscripts brought the *Corpus* to Florence and at Cosimo's behest Ficino translated the documents in 1463 from Greek to Latin. He prefaced them with the *Argumentum*.[91]

The *Asclepius*, the Greek name of which seems to have been Λόγος Τέλειος (*The Perfect Word*),[92] is a dialogue between Hermes Trismegistus, Asclepius, Tat, and Hammon. The three are secluded in an Egyptian temple for "it would be impious to divulge to the masses a lesson so filled with divine majesty".[93] The secret teachings are disclosed when the *one [who] is all (unum esse omnia)*[94] begins to speak the divine love (*divina Cupido*)[95] through the lips of Hermes. We may paraphrase the core of his teaching as follows: All descends from heaven to earth. The heaven is governed by God. Though remote, it is perceptible to sense and governs all things. The sun and moon govern generation and decay. They put forth continual effluvia which interconnect the heavenly bodies with the souls of species and individuals. Matter has been prepared by God to be the receptacle of all sensible forms of every appearance. Heaven generates all. Heaven and earth are connected by soul and substance which, in turn, are interrelated with fire, water, earth, and air. Matter is one; soul is one; God is one, and he himself resembles a terrestrial effluvium.[96]

Man is the *magnum miraculum* (great miracle), a being deserving of reverence. Because he takes on the nature of a god as if he were a god,[97] he is both of the divine and of the earth. The divine part despises the earthly part.[98] The Thirty-Six [signs] or Horoscopes impose their influence on individuals. These along with the seven spheres [the planets] are "gods", which are ruled by fortune or destiny and are subject to perpetual movement. All is formed and transformed according to the law of nature.[99] As "the rational animal", man was able to discover how gods could be brought into being by mingling virtue with material nature. He had, in fact, been able to create gods. By divine rites, "our ancestors" had induced souls into their gods so that they had power of good and evil.[100]

The apocalyptic passage of the *Asclepius*, which was written in the genre of an eschatological prophecy, predicts that the religion of Egypt was destined for destruction. The passage was apparently composed both to strengthen the pretence that Hermeticism had originated in ancient Egypt hundreds of years before Christianity appeared on the scene and to encourage the Hermetic faithful. Egypt will be left desolate. "O Egypt, Egypt, there will remain of your religion only an empty tale."[101] "Only the stones will tell of your piety." All good will disappear. Evil will conquer but not eternally. After cleansing the world from evil by fire or flood, war or pestilence, the Lord and Father God will bring the world back to its former beauty. The cosmos will be born anew and with it there will be a renewal of all nature. When that time comes nature will again be worthy of reverence and admiration and at the last God will be adored by all men.[102]

Arab Hermeticism and Alchemy

Arab Hermeticism, as Jaki points out on the basis of Sayyed Hassein Nasr's study of Islamic cosmology, is illustrated by the fifty-two treatise *Summary of Knowledge* (*Rasā'il*), written by the mystical cult called the "Brethren of Purity" (Ilhwān al-Safā').[103] The "Brethren of Purity" or "Sincere Brethren", as F. E. Peters calls them,[104] were a monastic fraternity whose "science" was connected with the kind of Pythagorean-Hermetic doctrines first known in Islam under the corpus of Jabir ibn Hayyam (Geber) (fl. 8th cent.).[105]

In contrast to Arab science in general which was basically Aristotelian, the science of the Brethren was Neopythagorean.[106] To quote Nasr, the Brethren followed the Pythagorean tradition, "especially in their treatment of numbers as a key to the understanding of Nature and the symbolic and metaphysical interpretation of arithmetic and geometry".[107] They thought of the universe as an organism which was hierarchically arranged and possessed of intellect and soul as well as of elements. The unified and harmonious arrangement was expressed in number, form, and music. Thus, "the whole world is composed in conformity with arithmetical, geometrical, and musical relations".[108] Consequently, according to the Rasā'il, "Number", "Geometry", "Astronomy", "Geography", and "Music" are all sub-subjects of "Mathematics".[109]

Being "more Pythagorean" than the Pythagoreans, the Brethren not only grouped their numbers into "unities", "dozens", "hundreds", and "thousands", but related the fourfold grouping to physical nature. Nature encompassed "hot, cold, dry, and moist"; the four elements, "fire, air, water, and earth"; the four humours, "blood, phlegm, yellow bile, and black bile"; "the four seasons"; "the four cardinal directions"; "the four winds"; "the four directions" (which they related to the constellations); and the four basic products, "metals, plants, animals, and men".[110] The whole of creation (which began with the Creator, descended through diminishing states of being and ended with humankind and the elements) was considered to be a generation of numbers arranged hierarchically. The Creator was signified by "1", the World-Intellect by "2", the World Soul by "3", the Original Matter by "4", Nature by "5", the Absolute Body by "6", the Sphere with its seven planets by "7", the four Basic Elements by "8", and the Beings of this world by "9". In a descending scale, then, the numbers whose nature was "single" (in the

Aristotelian sense) both signified and were responsible for the generation of "the 'great chain of Being' ".[111]

So convinced were the Brethren of the significance of the Pythagorean numerology that the Koran itself came within the purview of the system. Each of the letters of the Arabic alphabet which at one and the same time constituted the language of God and the language of the Koran from "a" = 1 to "jgh" = 3000 was given a numerical value. The numerical values attributed to the letters (*'ilm al-jafr*) were then used as the key to interpreting the symbolic significance (*ta'wil*) of the different texts.[112] Further, since as with the ancient Pythagoreans and Neopythagoreans, the movements of the heavens determined the ways of earth, the Brethren's practice of astrology enabled them to read past, present, and future off the positions of the heavenly bodies. Events were controlled by the cyclic motion of the sun, the moon, and the planets. As the apogees and nodes of the planetary orbits circled from one part of the ecliptic to another, or from one sign of the zodiac to another, so in response, events on earth — human, historical, and geophysical — followed the cyclic patterns. All was brought about by virtue of the power determining the conjunctions which occurred in regulated times and circumstances.[113]

Further and strangely, or perhaps not so strangely, like Roger Bacon, Thomas Aquinas, and especially Dante, the Brethren symbolised their cosmic hierarchy in a diagram of the world similar to that which Averroës had produced on the basis of Aristotle. Between the "lowest of the low" at the bottom and "the highest of the high" at the top, between the "left" on the left and the "right" on the right, were minerals, elements, plants, animals, men and angels, characteristics, virtues, evils, satan, prophets, and sacred law. All were arranged in concentric circles around a central square which represented the earth.[114] The whole was referred back to the "universal soul" which was responsible for all changes on earth where all exists in *the other* and all changes into *the other*.[115] The soul, in turn, could express its ministrations through "the angels" who were thought to abide in heaven and "some of whom are actually aspects or various facilities of the Universal Soul".[116] These moved the heavenly bodies around. "The particular soul of each celestial body becomes the guide for that body and the agent in whose activity it participates."[117]

Such were the principles of the Arab science of the *Rasā'il* which, Peters says quite rightly, "are redolent of the Hermetic Neoplatonism practised by Iamblichus and the Syrian School".[118] All is conceived teleologically. The purpose for which both "the rotation of the heavens and the creation of things are produced [is] in order that the Soul may manifest its plenitude in matter and that matter . . . may come to perfection".[119] The "rationality" necessary for both cosmology and the cult which infused the self with the soul of the world was provided by mathematics and informed by astrology.

As astrology combined the heavens with the soul, so the magic of *alchemy* connected the elements with the self. The name would seem most likely to have been transferred from the Arab name for Egypt, *Chem* (black land), where alchemy was thought to have originated. From the time the first text on alchemy appeared in mediaeval Europe, beginning with Robert of Chester's (fl. 12th cent.) translation of *The Book of the Composition of Alchemy* from Arabic into Latin in 1144, interest in the ancient attempts to transform metals by the use of fire grew to the extent that by the end of the century some half a dozen texts had been translated.[120] As we mentioned in our discussion of Roger Bacon, ironic as it may seem in the light of the fact that some of the best known practitioners of alchemy, Roger Bacon early on and Francis Bacon later, set their "experimental method" over against the Aristotelian principles of deduction, the major premises of alchemy are to be traced to Aristotle himself. Aristotle had maintained that nature consisted of one basic or primary "universal substance" or "subject matter", which, when moulded by "such antithetical principles as density and rarity" and "more or less" formed "the elements of fire, earth, air, and water".[121]

"Air", for instance, was the "actualisation of water" and water was "potentially air".[122]

In a similar way alchemists such as Raymond Lull (c.1235–c.1316) could argue that God originally created *"argent"* (quicksilver or mercury) as the first matter and that it gave rise to all other things.[123] The finest part formed the bodies of the angels, the less fine formed the heavenly spheres as well as the stars and planets, and the coarsest formed the four elements — earth, water, fire, and air. Aristotle's fifth *ethereal* element, which for him was confined to the heavens, was matched by Lull's *subtle spirit*. Like "the soul" of *The Chaldean Oracles* it was diffused throughout the world and was believed to be essential to all bodies heavenly and earthly as their active principle.[124] In the belief that, on the one hand, different metals corresponded to the soul (affections and will) and, on the other, to the spirit (intelligence) in humankind, the alchemists attempted to distil the *quintessence* (the fifth element) out of different metals for both chemical and mystical purposes. Were they able to isolate the "fifth element" or the "philosopher's stone", they believed they could use it to transmute any metal at all into gold. Similarly, if it were administered to the body, the quintessence would cause regeneration.

The more Platonic type of alchemy dealt not only with natural elements but with "spiritual entities" as well. By combining ideas of Neoplatonic emanation with Hermetic philosophy, it constructed an alchemistic cosmology which accounted for all things from God to material bodies in one continuous "chain of being". God the Father was compared to the sun; God the Son, to light; and God the Holy Ghost, to the divine heat of fiery love. The first matter, which God created, was no particular thing but potentially *everything*. It was empty darkness which condensed into primitive water. The light which emanated from God penetrated the matter and formed it into a pattern which contained all potentiality. The Holy Spirit which functioned as "divine heat" separated the subtle from the gross by a process of cosmic distillation thus cracking the original mass into four "substances". The first was the "celestial substance" or the *anima*. It consisted of three parts of light to one part of matter. Of it the bodies of the angels, the Empyrean (the highest heaven), the sun and the heavenly bodies were composed. The second substance, the *binarius*, consisted of two parts of light to three of matter. Of it the interstellar heavens were made. The *ternarius*, the least subtle of the three, was put together from one part light and three parts matter. It was the *pneuma* (air, breath, or spirit) and linked the celestial and terrestrial world. Out of the residue of the original mass was formed water and earth, each of which contained but a seed of the original light which emanated from God.[125]

The Hermetic Corpus

The Renaissance attempt to unravel the mysteries of the universe by Neopythagoreanism, Neoplatonic formulae, as well as by alchemistic practices and what we would call "magic" (inherited from both the early post-New Testament "Christian" milieu and from the Arabs) was confirmed and reinforced by the teachings of the Hermetic Corpus. Basic to Hermeticism was the idea of the unification of the *one God* with the *All*. The All included humankind, the heavens, the earth, the elements, and the soul. It embraced theology, anthropology, cosmology, astronomy, alchemy, cosmogony, soteriology, and eschatology, "one matter only, one soul only, one God only" as Hermes had put it in the *Asclepius*.[126]

In the *Pimander*, the first book of the *Corpus Hermeticum* translated by Ficino, the kind of God-world-self identity, which had been proclaimed by *The Chaldean Oracles* and the *Asclepius*, is immediately obvious.[127] God, the *Nous*, exists before nature. The Word, as light, issues from God as his Son. The Word addresses the darkness bringing forth the world and the elements. He brings "the souls" out of himself.[128] The light is constant in number, innumerable in power and came to be an ordered world, a world without limit.[129] Though generally the *Nous* is "God the Father",[130] the *Nous*, ὁ Θεός, which as light is also said to be male and female, brings forth by the Word a second Nous-Demiurge. The Nous-Demiurge is the god of fire and spirit, the one who fashioned the seven governors [the planets] which circle the sensible world and administered it according to *destiny*.[131] The circles, which are under the will of the *Nous*, turn eternally. The elements move downward from this rotation and produce the creatures of earth from air, water and earth.[132] The Nous, Father of all being who is life and light, also bore Man, a being like himself. Man is beautiful and is made in the image of the Father. To him God delivered all his works.[133] Being of a double nature, man is immortal in his eternal essence and mortal in his body.[134]

Since man has within himself the character of the seven governors [the planets], an immortality of which nature is incapable, he is not totally captive to nature[135] and because of this, even in their fallen state, men are of two sorts. There are those who know themselves to be elevated into the good. Conversely, there are also those who follow the carnal desires of the body, wander in obscurity, and suffer the throes of death.[136]

The material body, in contrast to the heavenly bodies, is subject to change. However, when the time eventually arrives when the form humans have will cease to be perceived, then all bodily desires and passions will become quiescent. The desires and passions will be delivered to the demons and the human *corporeal elements* will return to their sources.[137] The human *spiritual essence*, however, will ascend through the circles of the spheres. At each sphere the individual will divest himself of certain of the deformities of the fallen state — passions, vices, ambitions, presumptions, illicit appetites — until, in a state of nakedness, he attains the eighth sphere and, receiving his proper powers, he enters the choir of his companions. He eventually moves from the eighth sphere to the powers and, becoming a divine power himself, he enters into God and becomes God. For the blessed, those, that is, who possess the proper *gnosis* [knowledge], the end is to become God. At the proper but unknown time and by the intervention of God, humanity will be saved. As for the present, the Hermetic message is that the enlightened individual should be a guide to salvation so that others may learn and follow.[138]

Treatise V, *Hermes to His Son Tat, That God is at the Same Time Invisible and Most Visible*, is of importance to our study because it is quite explicit in what it says about cosmology. The mystery of how the invisible God becomes most apparent is revealed by the knowledge that God penetrates all things and so presents himself to ourselves.[139] God makes himself apparent to those whom he wishes to be sure. However, if one is to see God, he must consider the sun, the course of the moon, and the order of the stars.[140] *The sun is the supreme God of the gods in the heavens.* All other gods of heaven yield to him. He is larger than the earth and the sea and he submits to having smaller stars revolving about him. Each star has its prescribed limit and course.[141] In that someone must be the maker of this order,[142] it is the sun which both creates order and preserves it.

The mystery of God can be seen in the intricacies of the human body as well as in the cosmos. Who traced the circles of the eyes? Who formed the nostrils and the ears, the opening of the mouth, the muscles and attachments, the channels of the veins, the bones, skin, fingers, feet, heart, nerves? Who except the Creator God who is Father?[143]

It is of extreme interest, especially in light of the heliocentric theory, to note that there are allusions and statements testifying to both the divinity and the centrality of the sun throughout the Hermetic documents. Other bodies are important but subordinate. The fire of heaven is changed into light which by the working of the sun is shed to all below. The sun is the begetter of all good. It is the ruler of all ordered movement as well as the governor of the seven worlds [planets]. The moon brings forth birth and

growth and works change in matter on earth. The earth in
its turn is the foundation of all, perhaps of the whole good
cosmos. It feeds and nurses all earthly creatures.[144] In
Treatise XI, *Nous* [*The Mind*] *to Hermes*, the interdependent relationship which exists between eternity,
God, the moon, the sun, and humankind continues to be
emphasised. "Eternity is an image of God; the world, an
image of eternity; the sun, an image of the world; and
humankind, an image of the sun.[145]

The most important of the Hermetic documents in
making explicit the kind of cosmology that could very well
have had a direct or at least an indirect influence on
Copernicus is the Treatise XVI, *Asclepius to King Ammon:
Definitions*, which is part of the Turnebus Latin edition of
the *Corpus Hermeticum* of 1554. In it Asclepius divulges
the secrets that his master, Hermes, had taught the King in
the original language and with proper intonation for "the
Egyptian words when spoken are themselves the energy of
the thing said".[146] Asclepius begins his discourse with an
invocation to "God the master, creator, father and encom-
passer of the entire universe, the One who in that he the
One is all and is both One and all things". The One is a self-
duplication [in the One and all] and the two together are the
one and the same unity.[147] The unity is also of the nature of
earth where the three substances — fire, water, and earth
— are all dependent on the same source and evolve into one
another and devolve from one another according to the
influence of the Demiurge which connects the heaven and
the earth. The sun sends down true being (i.e., light and
life) from above and brings up matter from below. Its
beneficent energies penetrate the heaven and the air and
reach to the deepest depths of the earth.[148]

Recognising the sun is not a matter of mental conjecture.
It is rather a recognition of real light rays which shine on
the entire world. Part of the world is above the sun and part
below. The sun itself is stationed "*in the middle of the
world*" [sic] and carries the world as a corona.[149] As a skilled
pilot it guides the chariot of the cosmos, binding it to
himself lest perchance it enter upon a disorderly course.

Order is maintained by reins of light which in themselves are life, soul, breath, immortality, and generation.[150]

Asclepius combines angelology, demonology, and astrology as he explains that the sun which is a continuous and eternal source of light is surrounded by a large corps of demons. These watch over human affairs by means of tempests, cyclones, storms, the vicissitudes of the element of fire, as well as earthquakes, famines, and war.[151] The sun remains supreme. It preserves and provides all space, is responsible for the intelligible as well as the sensible world. It fills the cosmos with the infinite diversity of its figures even while it sustains them with its light[152] and commands their ways by means of troops of demons. Some of the troops are related directly to the sun; others are under orders from the planets. Some demons are good and some evil. Some are a mixture of both. Their character and their essence are reflected in their activities.

Commanded by the stars and given power over the affairs of the world, the demons produce disorder and trouble for cities and nations and especially for each individual. In attempting to mould the souls under their command according to their interests, they enter people's bodies and brains, penetrate to their entrails and torment the soul. Only that part of the soul that is rational escapes their sovereignty. By virtue of having received the light of the divine rays through the mediation of the sun, a soul, or at least a part of it, is enabled to remain stable and escape into the realm of God. Unfortunately, because the demons control the world through the medium of people's bodies, the number of souls saved is small. Thus their rule, according to Hermes, is called "destiny".[153]

To sum up, the intelligible world depends on God. The sun, which penetrates both the intelligible and sensible worlds, receives from God an influx of good to promote creativity. The arrangement of the heavens follows the Aristarchan heliocentric pattern which Copernicus was to adopt in his diagram of the world. The words of Hermes could have been said by Aristarchus and Copernicus alike. "*Around the sun gravitate the eight spheres which are dependent on the sun, the sphere of the fixed stars, the six spheres of the planets and the unique sphere which is around the earth* [i.e., that of the moon]."[154] God is the father of all things, the sun is the demiurge, the creator of all; the cosmos is the instrument by which he accomplishes his work. As God governs the sun by the intelligible substance, the sun in turn governs the other gods [planets]. The demons who are generally considered to be under the command of the planets govern the affairs of humankind and the world. By making use of the "gods" and the demons, God creates all things for himself, and as a part of himself. In the end, since God is all things, in making all things, God makes himself.[155]

This, then, so the late Renaissance scholars of the time were led to believe, represented the very foundation of ancient wisdom on which the Renaissance was founded. It was thought to be older than Aristotle, older than Plato. The *Hermetica* was nothing less than the *prisca theologia*, the original source of illumination from the divine *Mens*. So central was this *gnosis* (knowledge) from the ancient Egyptian wisdom that it was thought to constitute the core of Platonism.[156] Strange as Hermeticism sounds to us, the tone of the "ancient theology" was. not unfamiliar to Renaissance scholars. Strains of its melody had already been played and indeed, at the time, continued to be played by the mystical Neoplatonic and Pseudo-Dionysian astrological elements which both accompanied and undergirded the thought and theology of the late Middle Ages.

Already in the early centuries of the Christian era this mystical mix of history, philosophy, theology, cultic aspirations, and practical magic, which went under the label of "Hermeticism", was known and even approved of by some of the most important of the Church Fathers. Clement of Alexandria (c.150–c.215), Tertullian (c.160–c.230), Athenagorus (fl. 2nd cent.), Cyprian (c.200–258), Lactantius (c.240–c.320), Augustine (354–430), and Cyril of Alexandria (376–444), all spoke of Hermes. They accepted him as a renowned historical figure and testified to him in their writings.[157]

Clement spoke of forty-two books of Hermes Trismegistus, thirty-six of which contained the whole of Egyptian
philosophy and six which discussed the subject of medicine.[158] Tertullian called *Mercurius ille Trismegiste*, "the
teacher [master] of all physicists".[159] He is the one whom
Plato followed most closely.[160] "The Egyptian Mercury"
was supposed to have taught the transmigration of souls.[161]
When separated from the body, the soul was not reabsor-
bed into the soul of the universe as others had apparently
thought but each soul retained its individuality so as to give
"an account to the Father of what it did in the body".[162]
The Christian apologist, Athenagoras, spoke of Hermes
Trismegistus as the most learned of Egyptians. Like
Alexander the Great, he shared the attributes of eternity
and was esteemed as a god.[163] For Cyprian both Plato and
Hermes spoke of God with authenticity. They spoke of the
"one God". However, whereas Plato differentiated between the one God, the angels and the demons, *Hermes
quaque Trismegistus* spoke of "one God who is incomprehensible and inestimable".[164]

The Church Father Lactantius knew of Hermes as the
writer of many books and as one who was much older than
Pythagoras and Plato.[165] He was supposed to have spoken
of divine things and called the only God, "Lord" and
"Father", and the demiurge, "the Son of God".[166] Hermes
came in for particular praise because he used pagan
wisdom to support the truth of Christianity. Lactantius
was especially impressed by the realisation that Hermes
both saw the coming of Christ and testified to his coming
accordingly.[167]

Since he knew little Greek, Augustine, who must have
known Hermes only by way of the *Asclepius*, was ambiva-
lent in his assessment. On the one hand, he condemned
"Hermes the Egyptian (called Trismegistus)" for purvey-
ing the kind of Egyptian magic described in the *Asclepius*
by which statues were supposed to be animated by "a kind
of technique of attaching invisible spirits to material
bodies".[168] Hence, he denounced Hermes as one of those of
whom the Apostle Paul spoke when he said:

> Though they have some acquaintance with God they
> have not glorified him as God, nor have they given him
> thanks: but they have dwindled into futility in their
> thinking and their stupid heart is shrouded in dark-
> ness. (Rom. 1:21)[169]

On the other hand, however, Augustine had apparently
absorbed too much mystical Neoplatonism himself to
dismiss Hermes altogether. He admitted that Hermes had
said much that was true about God. Like Lactantius, he
recognised Hermes as a prophet of Christianity and he
recounts Hermes' lineage accordingly:

> . . . long before the sages or philosophers of Greece,
> and yet after Abraham, Isaac, Jacob, Joseph, and, in
> fact, after Moses himself. For inquiry reveals that it
> was at the time of the birth of Moses that Atlas lived,
> the great astronomer, the brother of Prometheus, and
> the maternal grandfather of the elder Mercury, whose
> grandson was this Mercury Trismegistus.[170]

Cyril of Alexandria seems to have accepted the historical
Hermes without question. He spoke of "the Egyptian
Hermes, also named Trismegistes" as having both learned
from Moses and as having founded the institutions and the
sciences of Egypt. He made laws, designated the districts
of Egypt,[171] and was succeeded by others.[172] Cyril knew of a
literary work entitled *Hermetica* which was compiled in
Athens and consisted of fifteen books.[173] He referred to
Hermes' teaching in the *Asclepius*,[174] and to the work Νοῦς
πρὸς Ἑρμῆν (*The Mind According to Hermes*).[175] According
to Hermes, he reports with approval, God had impressed
order upon disorder.[176]

Thus, when Hermeticism, which displayed an inner and
properly harmonious relationship between the human soul
and the universe as a whole, came to the Renaissance, it
came with ample recommendation. In addition to being
commended by a number of Church Fathers, it recalled the
systems of the ancient Pythagoreans. These in turn were

foundational for Plato's cosmology. Life and its fate, including the interrelationships of the basic elements (wind, water, fire, and earth), the control of the seasons, crops, animals, and the destiny of humankind, were determined by the stars or by the angelic beings connected with them.[177] It identified God with the universe and understood him as existing in conjunction with it. God could be known either by the study of nature or by divine revelation. In Hermeticism, God was the God of light, the centre of all things, and he was identified with the sun from whom all things come and to whom all things go. Those who knew these mysteries and were aware of the basic unity of the *All* were saved by being in unity with the *All* and with God.

The aim, then, of Hermeticism was nothing less than the deification and rebirth of the whole of reality, nature as well as humankind, through the proper *gnosis* (knowledge) of the world-God. "Learned" Hermeticism, which encompassed theology and philosophy, or "theo-philosophy" was complemented by "popular" Hermeticism (astrology, alchemy, and eventually, medicine). By discovering the secret formula, the "fifth element", the *quinta essentia*, its practitioners hoped to be provided with the philosopher's stone — the means for transforming the elements into gold, the elixir for the healing of the body, and the formula for the regeneration of the soul.

Thus, to reiterate and sum up: the ancient theology or *prisca theologia*[178] combined Neopythagorean number mysticism and Neoplatonic world harmony with the divine *gnosis* of Egyptian magic. It illuminated the soul which sought personal salvation. Believers insinuated themselves into the divine without any necessity of a personal God or saviour. They became religiously one with the universe, itself divine. The divine universe was defined by a cosmology which placed it under the intermediate governorship of the stars and the seven planets. These, in turn, were ruled over by the "Nous-God" who existed as life and light. The "Nous-God" had brought forth the "Nous-Demiurge", the god of fire. The Nous-Demiurge was a unity and was represented by the sun in the centre of the world. Being the manifestation of God, the sun illuminated all the other stars, controlled the heavenly bodies and through these, by way of both its light and angelic creatures (demons), controlled the destiny of earth and humankind. In contrast to the perfect unity and order of the heavens, the earth, its elements, and humanity were "diverse".[179]

What more did the late Middle Ages and early Renaissance need but the authority of the Church Fathers, especially that of the great and respected Augustine, to be convinced that Trismegistus, somewhat younger than Moses but older than the sages of Greece, was well worth a hearing? And hear they did. The quest of the late Middle Ages and Renaissance for ancient truth and their discovery of Greek learning whetted their appetites for truth that was more ancient still.

Ficino's translation of the Hermetic Corpus made in 1463 and first printed in 1471, went through sixteen editions before the end of the sixteenth century. Commentaries and secondary material were published to match. Hence, after Plato was translated and Platonism again asserted itself in the Renaissance mind, Hermetic philosophy, which was considered Plato's source, often took precedence over Plato himself.

Though Hermeticism may seem esoteric to us, from the point of view of the early Renaissance, the ideas it fostered were the basis for what A.-J. Festugière has called "the new science".[180] "The new science", in contrast to the "cold", deductive rationality of Aristotle's physics and metaphysics, was "warm", romantic, and personal. Aristotelian science tended to be abstract; it was interested in the knowledge of the *general* and in the *particular* only insofar as it exemplified the *general*. It had little place for observation or experience. "The new science" engaged the individual in the process of investigation and examined the things of this world as if they were intimately connected with life. Astrology might study the stars but, more importantly, it had to do with one's destiny. Alchemy investigated the elements for the sake of personal wealth and/or for the healing of body and soul. The mysteries hidden in nature were at the same time the mysteries of God, the soul and the body, God and creation, heaven and earth, plants and animals, the stars and the elements, the planets and persons. All were conjoined in a great inter-connected chain of being. Cultic practice which included meditation and prayer combined with observation and experience to reveal the mysteries of reality.[181]

As with the Pythagoreans, astrology led to astronomy, so in the Renaissance alchemy slowly issued into primitive chemistry and medicine. Eventually, too, Renaissance astrology moved toward scientific astronomy. As it did, one of the most profound and imaginative minds to help it on its way was that of Nicholas of Cusa.

Cusa's Sacred Circles

Some twenty years prior to Ficino's translation of the *Corpus Hermeticum*, the anti-rationalistic, Neoplatonic mysticism which characterised the fifteenth century was both illustrated and further developed with particular relevance for astronomy by Nicholas of Cusa's *De Docta Ignorantia* (*Of Learned Ignorance*). The work was an elegant attempt to represent all reality — divine, heavenly, and earthly — in terms of geometry. It was also an attempt to maintain a biblical differentiation between God and creation while espousing a Neoplatonically inspired con-cept of harmony between the divine and the creaturely. Although Cusa was unsuccessful in finally distinguishing between the Creator and creation,[182] his stress on the harmony as over against the *infinity* of both God and the world aided and abetted Renaissance longing for the mystical unity of all things. It also served to call into question any absolute knowledge of God or the world.

Cusa was born in Kues on the Mosel River. After being imbued with the mystic theology of the "Brethren of the Common Life" at Deventer, he studied at the Universities of Heidelberg, Bologna, and Padua. He was created a cardinal by his friend, Pope Pius II (1405–64), and appointed to the bishopric of Brixen [modern Bressanone] in the Tyrol.[183]

Cusa had studied mathematics and astronomy under the well-known geographer and mathematician, Paolo Toscanelli (1397–1482), Professor at Padua.[184] In his *De Docta Ignorantia*, completed in 1440, he attempted to hold to the biblical doctrine of creation out-of-nothing along with Neoplatonic pantheistic ideas of unity and harmony. He then attempted to combine those ideas with his own interpretation of Boethius, translation of Euclid's *Elements of Geometry* (*Interpretatio Euclidis Geometriae*) and Thomas Bradwardine's (c.1290–1349) *Speculative Geometry* (*Geometria speculativa*) in order to show that all human knowledge of the world, including that of Aristotle, was inadequate to reality. After citing Socrates who came to realise that "he knew only that he did not know" and "the profound Aristotle" who, with regard to "evident things", held that "we stand before a similar difficulty as a night owl who is obliged to look at the sun", Cusa set out his learned ignorance, *docta ignorantia*, in terms of rationalistic arguments of his own.[185]

Cusa's reasoning was comparatively simple. The "absolute greatest" and the "absolute unity" which constitute the "all possible being" surpasses all human thought.[186] Human beings have to do not with unity as such but only with the multiplicity of the finite. Since examples of this multiplicity are, for Cusa, of less substance than that of absolute unity, there is a disproportionality between the finite and the infinite. This means that that which is known is always *different from* and *lesser than* the basic unity of which the known is but a part. As reality, like God, is perfect unity and simplicity, and as he who is "infinite light" and "life and truth" is unapproachable and "known only to himself", so too reality is basically unknowable.[187]

However, rather than base his epistemology on common sense, convention, or *a priori* categories of mind, as later Locke, Hume, and Kant were to do, or even upon analogy as Thomas had done, Cusa, like the Pythagoreans, attempted to represent reality by means of mathematical symbolisation. He allegorised the identification of God with "ultimate truth" and "infinite rectitude"[188] made by Anselm of Canterbury (1033–1109) into an infinite straight line.[189] He compared the Trinity with a triangle of infinite and equal sides, related the unity of God to an infinte circle, and associated the absolute reality of God with an infinite sphere.[190] Next he showed the basic unity of the fundamental elements of geometry by explaining that, if carried to infinity, an infinite line could be construed to be a straight line, a triangle, a circle, or a sphere. By the same token, an infinite sphere could become a circle, a triangle, and a line; an infinite triangle could become a sphere and a circle; and an infinite circle could become a sphere and a triangle. Then, by borrowing from both Bradwardine's *Geometria speculativa* and Boethius' *De Institutione arithmetica*, Cusa straightened the circumference of a circle into a straight line, divided the area of the circle into triangles, matched one infinite side of an equal-sided triangle with the two others and multiplied the infinite triangles to form an infinite circle which, if duplicated infinitely in relationship to its two poles, formed a perfect sphere.[191] As each figure represented infinity as a whole, so too any part of any of the figures represented infinity as well.[192]

Thus, by using the geometry of infinite figures, Cusa showed, to his own satisfaction at least, that all things, the infinite and the finite, the large and the small, the high and the low, the world and human nature, were both under God's providence (*dei providentia*)[193] and enclosed within a unity. The result of this intricately calculated rationalistic complex, though mathematically suspect, called into question any differentiated system of spheres, whether those of Aristotle or those of Ptolemy, which purported to represent the reality of the world in a finite system of geometry. At the same time Cusa's ideas defined reality in such idealistic terms that not even the heavens passed as proper manifestations of it. "Neither the sun nor the moon nor the earth nor any other sphere describes a sphere."[194]

Equally important for cosmology, if not more so, was Cusa's transfer of the infinite sphere to the actual existence of God (*transumptio sphaerae infinitae ad actualem exsistentiam dei*), a move which shows Cusa to be the "father" of *panentheism*. The doctrine, which in our time has been revived by Charles Hartshorne and Paul Tillich, was worked out in the nineteenth century by K. C. F. Krause on the basis of German idealism.[195] Cusa justified his argument with a citation from "the subtle thinker Parmenides". "God is 'that one for which the fact that it is a particular means that it is all of that which it is' " (*deum esse, 'cui esse quodlibet quod est est esse omne id quod est'*).[196] He then interpreted the statement in terms of geometry. Thus, as an infinite sphere is the perfect figure, it unifies all other figures — line, triangle, and circle — within it so that the whole of it is not larger than any part. It alone is the only one, simple and adequate measure for the whole. Likewise, God is the one, simple, rational ground of the entire universe. (*Deus igitur est unica simplicissima ratio totius mundi universi.*)[197]

Had Cusa stopped there he might have stayed within the bounds of the Christian doctrine that God created the world out of nothing, eternally separate from himself, and made the world eternally contingent upon himself. However, when Cusa went on to explain that all living movement and knowledge come out of God and through him, it is evident that he operated out of Neoplatonic concepts rather than biblical ones.

> With him is a single rotation of the eight spheres no smaller than a single rotation of the infinite spheres because he is the purpose of all movement in that all movement has as its purpose that it comes to rest. He is the greatest rest in whom all movement is rest.[198]

Reality, however, is at best an imperfect participation in God.

> All being aspires to him. In that it is limited and the parts compared, it therefore cannot participate in the final purpose in the same way [as he does in himself]. Nevertheless, some entities can participate in this

purpose by way of other parts, as a line by way of a triangle and a circle becomes a sphere, the triangle by way of the circle and the circle in itself.[199]

With that the doctrine of *creatio ex nihilo* as well as the kind of objections which Philoponos had made to the concept of a divine and eternal universe were pushed aside. The world was once again thought of as *in God*, so that the mind could contemplate the patterns of the universe in the belief that to understand "nature" was to penetrate into the being of God himself.[200]

Cusa's cosmology, like that of Kepler later, was thus shot through with Neopythagorean and Neoplatonic conceptualities. Hence he was certain that God used the arts of arithmetic, geometry, music, and astronomy in the process of creation. As with Kepler, who worked out his planetary laws by means of mathematics, so with Cusa, there was a "scientific advantage" in supposing that since God used arithmetic, geometry, music, and astronomy in creating the world, so we in turn must utilise these "arts" in the examination of creation. In doing so we compare one phenomenon with another in order to investigate the harmony and unity of all things.[201]

Though Cusa's deductions were less than precise, he showed keen perspicacity by setting out what we can only call a "theory of relativity" with regard to motion. Like Aristarchus earlier and Copernicus later, he recognised that "in reality the earth moves even though it doesn't appear to do so simply because we recognise a movement only by way of comparison with something that is stationary".[202] Even more important for cosmology were Cusa's profound speculations regarding motion which took him in the direction of Copernicus and even beyond, toward Einstein. Not only are all things a part of motion, "nothing exists which is not a unity of potentiality and act in connection with motion", but *the centre of the universe cannot be determined*.[203] Because it is impossible to make a proper differentiation between maximum and minimum when considering the varied movements of the spheres, it is quite impossible to say that the "world machine" (*machinam mundanam*) has a fixed and immovable centre and whether the centre is supposed to be the visible earth or air or fire.[204] Further, in the direction of Copernicus, just as "the earth cannot be the centre, so it cannot be without movement".[205] It follows, therefore, that just as comets and the elements of air and fire move, so the earth moves also. As the moon moves a shorter distance from east to west than do Mercury and Venus or the sun, so the earth moves less than the others; but it moves.[206]

Equally radical and certainly of major importance in the history of epistemology was Cusa's insight that to fathom reality we must impose conceptual models upon it. This had two important implications. First, the only centres and poles which exist and according to which movement is determined are those which we presuppose. Second, any understanding of the world which has fixed its centre is bound to be "erroneous". "We all err and because we take it for granted that the old philosophers had the correct conception about the centre and pole and measurement, we remain surprised [which we should not be] that, according to the laws of the old philosophers, the stars do not correlate with their [supposed] positions."[207]

Cusa justified his "relative universe" by pointing out that none of the stars of the eight spheres move as if its sphere turned on designated poles or around a fixed centre. Further, "just as the stars of the eighth sphere move around *the supposed pole, so the earth, moon and planets and stars* move around poles at different distances and in different velocities. Thus one *must conjecture that the pole is where one supposes the pole to be.*"[208]

It followed for Cusa, as indeed it did for Einstein, that the universe is isotropic. We see it as stretching equidistantly from us no matter where we are located in the universe, on the earth, or the sun or on one of the stars. Wherever a person might be, that person would suppose, in a way similar to a person on earth, that "he was in the centre which was immobile and that everything else moved". He would thus "always build new poles whether he found himself on the sun, earth, moon or Mars, etc". Therefore, "the construction of the world (*machina mundi*) is as if it has its centre everywhere and its periphery nowhere". For good measure Cusa added, "and its centre is God who is everywhere and nowhere".[209] The point is more than of passing interest for Copernicus too was to say that since "there are many centres", it is not foolhardy to doubt the centre of the earth's gravity is the centre of the world.[210]

Cusa's universe, all of which is in motion, is given a certain mathematical justification in a note which Dreyer mentions as having been written by Cusa on the last leaf of an astronomical treatise issued in Nuremberg in 1444, four years after the *De Docta ignorantia* was published. After reiterating that it is impossible for there to be any motion which is exactly circular, Cusa discussed the rotation of the earth on its axis as well as the yearly precession of its axis. This precession caused the sun to appear to move from $23\frac{1}{2}°$ to the north and south of the equator relative to the sphere of the fixed stars.

Since the whole universe is in motion, Cusa thought of the sphere of the fixed stars as rotating once in twelve hours, the earth once in twenty-four, and the sun as revolving around the earth 365 times per year.[211] The ratio between the sun and the stars allowed the stars to complete their circles over the earth in twenty-four hours, which gives the same effect as the earth rotating on its axis once each day with the celestial sphere being stationary.

Although Cusa's universe was non-centred rather than earth-centred or sun-centred and his calculations were not entirely accurate, his relativistic universe along with the double movement he attributed to the earth served to call the reigning Aristotelian-Ptolemaic world into question and opened the door for the kind of Neopythagorean cosmology which would reflect the harmony and unity of divinity itself. Thus, whether or not Koyré is correct in saying that Cusa probably inspired Copernicus to "geometrise nature",[212] it is certainly true that Cusa's insistence that sphericity and circularity referred with equal cogency to nature and God both grew out of and reinforced the Renaissance concept of harmony and unity. It was this that stimulated Copernicus to construe the movements of the universe in a system of circles which he intended to be more harmonious than the system of Ptolemy.

NOTES

1. The commentary encompasses Books I–III. iii of Aristotle's *De Caelo*, but omits Book III. iv and Book IV. i–vi that are included in the Loeb Classical Library edition. Cf. Aristotle, *On the Heavens*.
2. Cyril Vollert, Translator's Introduction, St. Thomas Aquinas, *On the Eternity of the World* (*De Aeternitate Mundi*) (Milwaukee, Wis.: Marquette University, 1964), pp. 11ff.
3. *Ibid.*, p. 11 referring to Averroës, *Tahafut al-Tahafut*, trans. from the Arabic with intro. and notes by S. van den Bergh (London: Luzac, 1954), I, xiii, 1–69.
4. Vollert, *Eternity of the World*, p. 11. Cf. Suras 7, 52; 10, 3; 11, 9; 32, 3 in A. J. Arberry, *The Koran Interpreted* (London: Macmillan, 1955).
5. Albert the Great, *Commentarii in Secundum Librum Sententiarum*, *Opera Omnia*, Vol. XXVII, ed. S. C. A. Borgnet (Paris: Vivès, 1894), Dist. I, Art. X, p. 28. Cf. Vollert, *Eternity of the World*, p. 13.
6. Albert the Great, *Summae Theologie Secunda Pars* (Quest. I–LXVII), *Opera Omnia*, Vol. XXXII, ed. S. C. A. Borgnet (Paris: Vivès, 1895), Tract. I, Qu. IV, Mem. II, Art. V. pp. 91–108. Cf. Vollert, *Eternity of the World*, p. 13. Cf. Augustine, *City of God*, XI, 4, pp. 432–433. Augustine's Neoplatonic philosophy lacks the decisiveness of Albert's Aristotelianism. Nevertheless, Albert adds that those who use the phrase "do say something".
7. St. Thomas Aquinas, *In Aristotelis Libros de Caelo et Mundo* (Romae: Marietti, 1952), II, 1. xvii 451[2].
8. *Ibid.*, II, 1. xxvi 530[10].
9. *Ibid.*, II, 1. xiv 143[7].
10. *Ibid.*, II, 1. viii 368[2].
11. *Ibid.*, II, 1. xvii 452[3], 453[4], 454[5]; II, 1. xviii 470[13].
12. *Ibid.*, II, 1. xxvi 527[7], 530[10]; I, 1. iii. 27[7]; II, 1. xvii 452[3]; II, 1. xxviii 538[7].
13. *Ibid.*, II, 1. xi 396[2]. Either Thomas had evidence of which we are no longer aware or, more likely, he may simply have mistaken Heraclides' partial heliocentric system for Aristarchus' total heliocentric one. Cf. above, pp. 32ff.

14. *Ibid.*, I, 1. xxii 221[1].
15. *Ibid.*, I, 1. xxii 227[7].
16. *Ibid.*
17. *Ibid.*, I, 1. xix 185[2].
18. *Ibid.*, II, 1. i 289[2).
19. *Ibid.*, I, 1. vi 60[3].
20. Cf. above, pp. 109f.
21. Aristotle, *Physics*, VIII. ii, 252b.
22. *Ibid.*, VIII. vii–viii, 261b–262a.
23. *Ibid.*, VIII. x, 267b.
24. Aquinas, *Eternity of the World*, pp. 64f.
25. *Ibid.*, p. 66.
26. *Ibid.*, p. 22.
27. *Ibid.*, p. 51.
28. *Ibid.*
29. *Ibid.*
30. Aristotle, *Physics*, VIII. i, 250b.
31. Aquinas, *Eternity of the World*, p. 53.
32. Aristotle, *On the Heavens*, II. iii, 286a.
33. Aquinas, *Eternity of the World*, p. 54.
34. Dionysius, *Hiérarchie Céleste*, IV. 1, p. 199.
35. Aquinas, *Eternity of the World*, p. 50.
36. Aquinas, *Commentary on de Caelo*, I, 1. iii ff.
37. *Ibid.*, II, 1. ix 374[1]–381[8].
38. *Ibid.*, I, 1. ix ff.
39. *Ibid.*, II, 1. ix 374[1]–381[8].
40. *Ibid.*, II, 1. xvi–II, 1. xxiv; II, 1. xxvi–II, 1. xxviii.
41. Cf. above, pp. 25ff, 63ff.
42. Aristotle, *On the Heavens*, II. i, 284a.
43. *Ibid.*
44. *Ibid.*, II. xii, 292b.
45. *Ibid.*, II. xii, 292a.
46. Dionysius, *Hiérarchie Céleste*, Cap. VI–XI, 200B–284D, pp. 205–384.
47. Aquinas, *Summa*, Ia Q. CVIII, Art. VII, p. 444.
48. Aquinas, *Summa*, Ia Q. CVIII, Art. VIII, p. 447 citing *Civ. Dei* xii. Cf. Augustine, *City of God*, XII. 1, pp. 471f.
49. Aquinas, *Summa*, Ia Q. CXV, Arts. 1–6, pp. 506–522. Thomas cites Aristotle, *De Gener.* i, *De Caelo et Mundo* iv, p. 509; Augustine, *De Gen. ad lit.* v, vi; Aristotle, *De Anima* ii, *Metaph.* v, p. 511; Aristotle, *De Gener.* ii, pp. 514f., Aristotle, *Phys.* ii, p. 515; Augustine, *Gen. ad lit.* xii, p. 518; and Aristotle, *Metaph.* vi, p. 521 in this regard.
50. Aquinas, *Summa*, Ia Q. CXV, Art. III, p. 514.
51. *Ibid.*, Ia Q. CXV, Art. IV, p. 516.
52. *Ibid.*, p. 517.
53. *Ibid.*, p. 516.

54. Aristotle, *Metaphysics*, Book VI, 1025b–1028a.

55. Aquinas, *Summa*, Ia Q. CXV, Art. VI, p. 522.

56. As said, Cecco d'Ascoli was the popular name of Francesco degli Stabili, Professor of Astrology (Astronomy) at Bologna. In directing his encyclopedic vernacular poem, "L'Acerba", directly against Dante's astrological theories, he exposed his "heretical" views and was burned at the stake in 1327. Cf. above, pp. xxviii, 8.

57. Dante, *Banquet*, II. XIV, 4, pp. 105f. For Dante, as for Roger Bacon and as later for John Calvin, Aristotle was "the Philosopher".

58. *Ibid.*, III. II, 2, p. 138.

59. *Ibid.*, IV. XV, 5, pp. 304f., II. IV, 2, p. 163.

60. Dante Alighieri, *The Divine Comedy*, trans. Geoffrey L. Bickersteth (Oxford: Blackwell, 1972), "Paradiso", 10. 98–99.

61. Dante, *Banquet*, II. XIV, 1, p. 104.

62. Francesco Perez, *La Beatrice Svelata* (Palermo: Franc. Lao, 1865). The diagram is reproduced between pp. 394–395. According to Averroës' diagram, Aristotle's designation of the eighth sphere is *intellectivae animae pars* which also contains the *substantiarum separatarum intellectio, ibid.*

63. Dante, *Banquet*, II. XIV, 6, pp. 106f.

64. *Ibid.*, II. XIV–XV, pp. 104–122.

65. Dionysius and Thomas have in the first hierarchy: Seraphim, Cherubim, and Thrones. The second order included Dominions, Virtues, and Powers; and the third, nearest the earth, consisted of Principalities, Archangels, and Angels. Cf. Dionysius, *Hiérarchie Céleste*, VI. 2, p. 206, Aquinas, *Summa*, Ia CVIII. 4–6. Dreyer mistakenly has Dante assigning "the Thrones" to the sphere of Saturn, *History of Astronomy*, p. 237. Dante, however, is quite clear, "The motive power . . . of Venus are the Thrones, which, informed with the love of the Holy Spirit, perform their work, that is, the movement of this heaven filled with love" and by which the souls on earth are "inspired to love". Dante, *Banquet* II. VI, 5, p. 79.

66. The selection and translation of this and the following verses is much indebted to Katharine Hilliard's edition of *II Convito* and Geoffrey L. Bickersteth's edition of *La Divina Commedia*. The placement, however, of the verses is my own and I have, on occasion, altered the translation in accordance with the Italian text of *La Divina Commedia* given by Bickersteth.

67. Dante, *Banquet*, II. VI, 4, p. 78.

68. *Ibid.*

69. *Ibid.*, II. VI, 4, p. 79.

70. *Ibid.*, II. V, 1–5, pp. 69ff.

71. *Ibid.*, II. IV, 1, p. 66.

72. *Ibid.*, II. 1, 1–5, pp. 51–54.

73. *Ibid.*, II. XIV–XV, pp. 104–122.

74. *Ibid.*, II. IV, 3, pp. 56ff. For a full discussion of Dante's cosmology

in the literal sense wherein he mentions Aristotle, Ptolemy, the perspectives of arithmetic and geometry, solar eclipses, and the relationship of the moon, sun, and Mars, cf. *ibid.*, III. 1–3 and IV. 1–3, pp. 62–68.

75. Bruno's Hermeticism included a doctrinaire Copernicanism. He was incarcerated in 1592 and, after eight years imprisonment in Rome, was burned in 1600.

76. Cf. A.-J. Festugière's discussion "La révélation dans Thermétisme populaire", in which he contrasts Aristotelian rationalism and Hermetic speculation. A.-J. Festugière, *L'Hermétisme* (Lund: Gleerup, 1948), pp. 12–17.

77. Frances Yates, *Giordano Bruno and the Hermetic Tradition* (London: Routledge, 1964); D. P. Walker, *The Ancient Theology* (London: Duckworth, 1972), and *Spiritual and Demonic Magic from Ficino to Campanella* (London: Warburg, 1958); A.-J. Festugière, *La Révélation d'Hermès Trismégiste*, Vol. I (Paris: Lecoffre, 1944).

78. Marsilio Ficino, Argumentum, *Mercurii Trismegisti Liber de Pimander, Opera Omnia*, 2 vols. in 4 (Torino: Bottega d'Erasmo, 1959), II. 2, fol. 1836, p. 836. Cf. Yates, *Bruno*, p. 2 where she explains that Thoth was identified by the Greeks with their god Hermes and the Latins in turn identified the Greek Hermes with their god Mercury.

79. Athenagoras, *A Plea for the Christians*; Tertullian, *Against the Valentinians* and *A Treatise on the Soul*; Cyprian, *The Vanity of Idols*; Clement of Alexandria, *Miscellanies*; Lactantius, *The Divine Institutes* and *On the Anger of God*; Cyril of Alexandria, *Against Julian*; Augustine, *City of God* and *Confessions*. Strictly speaking, Athenagoras was a "Christian apologist".

80. Casaubon was a Genevan Protestant historian and Greek scholar who had taken up residence in England where he did his work. Yates is of the opinion that the Hermetic writers had their origin in the Hellenistic world of the first to the third centuries A.D. and are most likely the work of Greek scholars who cast their work in a pseudo-Egyptian framework. Yates, *Bruno*, pp. 398–402. Festugière has indicated that the "occult-scientific" aspects of the documents — astrology, alchemy, etc. — go back as far as the third century B.C. The philosophical and theological parts of the works, he thinks, may be dated as coming from the second and third centuries. *L'Hermétisme*, pp. 3ff. Cf. also Walter Scott, "Introduction", *Hermetica*, 4 vols. (Oxford: Clarendon, 1924–36), I, 41ff.

81. Cf. Festugière, *L'Hermétisme*, pp. 22ff.

82. Ficino, Argumentum, *Pimander*, folio 1836.

83. *The Chaldean Oracles* (Gillete, N.J.: Heptangle, 1978), Oracle 18, p. 8.

84. Plato, *Timaeus*, 34. Cf. *Timaeus*, 30, 44, 68, 69, 90.

85. *Chaldean Oracles*, 119–133, pp. 38–41.
86. *Ibid.*, 20, p. 9.
87. *Ibid.*, 90, p. 29.
88. *Ibid.*, 92, p. 31.
89. *Ibid.*, 85, p. 28.
90. *Ibid.*, 158, p. 50.
91. Yates, *Bruno*, pp. 12f.
92. Lactantius, renders the title, *Sermo Perfectus*; Pseudo-Augustinus as *Verbum Perfectum*. Cf. A. D. Nock, "Introduction-Asclepius", *Corpus Hermeticum*, 4 vols. (Paris: Belles Lettres, 1945–1954), II, 275–277.
93. *Corpus Hermeticum*, II, *Asclepius*, 1, p. 297, lines 10–11.
94. *Ibid.*, 1, p. 296, line 12.
95. *Ibid.*, 2, p. 297, lines 15–16.
96. *Ibid.*, 2–3, p. 298, lines 5–25.
97. *Ibid.*, 6, p. 301, line 18–p. 302, line 2.
98. *Ibid.*, 6, p. 302, lines 3–10.
99. *Ibid.*, 19, p. 319, lines 1–10.
100. *Ibid.*, 37, p. 347, lines 5–20.
101. *Ibid.*, 24, p. 327, lines 14–15.
102. *Ibid.*, 25–26, p. 328, line 10–p. 331, line 14.
103. Cf. Jaki, *Science and Creation*, pp. 207f. Seyyed Hossein Nasr, *An Introduction to Islamic Cosmological Doctrines* (Cambridge, Mass.: Harvard, 1964), pp. 25–43.
104. F. E. Peters, *Aristotle and the Arabs* (New York: New York University, 1968), pp. 113–115.
105. Nasr, *Cosmological Doctrines*, p. 35.
106. Peters, *Aristotle and the Arabs*, p. 115.
107. Nasr, *Cosmological Doctrines*, p. 37.
108. *Ibid.*, p. 45 quoting the *Rasa'il*, I. 160.
109. Peters, *Aristotle and the Arabs*, p. 113; Nasr, *Cosmological Doctrines*, p. 42.
110. Nasr, *Cosmological Doctrines*, p. 50 quoting the *Rasa'il*, I. 27.
111. *Ibid.*, pp. 51f.
112. *Ibid.*, pp. 50f.
113. *Ibid.*, p. 80 quoting the *Rasā'il*, III. 246–259.
114. *Ibid.*, p. 71.
115. *Ibid.*, pp. 71f.
116. *Ibid.*, p. 81.
117. *Ibid.*
118. Peters, *Aristotle and the Arabs*, p. 113.
119. Nasr, *Cosmological Doctrines*, p. 81 quoting from *Rasā'il*, I. 73ff. Cf. Pierre Duhem, *Le Système du Monde*, 2nd ed., 10 vols. (Paris: Hermann, 1954–59), II, 169.
120. F. Sherwood Taylor, *The Alchemists* (New York: Collier, 1962), p. 83.
121. Aristotle, *Physics* I, 189a–189b.

122. *Ibid.*, 213a.

123. Taylor, *Alchemists*, pp. 94f.

124. *Ibid.*, pp. 98f. The ancient alchemists appeared to be mainly concerned with making precious metals. Taylor cites two third-century A.D. papyri, which are now at Leyden and Stockholm, by unknown authors, which contain hundreds of different recipes for making gold, silver, precious stones, and dyestuffs. *Ibid.*, pp. 24–27. It was thought that the processes could be activated by the proper combination of mercury, sulphur, and salt and by the use of fire. "*Mercury* was that sharp, permeating, ethereal, and very pure fluid to which all nutrition, sense, motion, power, colours and retardation of age were due." "*Sulphur* was that sweet oleaginous and viscid balsam conserving the natural heat of the parts, instrument of all vegetation, increase, and transmutation and the fountain and origin of all colours." "*Salt* was that dry, saline body preserving mixtures from putrefaction, having wonderful powers of dissolving, coagulating, cleansing, evacuating, conferring solidity, consistency, taste, and the like." *Ibid.*, pp. 156f.

125. Cf. Taylor, *Alchemists*, pp. 172f. Though alchemy was nothing if not mystical, it did not grab at miracle to explain the transformations it attempted to achieve. Rather, it followed "natural procedures" but tried to accelerate them. All metals, it was believed, were generated in the womb of nature by different combinations of sulphur and mercury. The alchemists set up their laboratories in order to *elaborate* the elements of different combinations of "pure sulphur" and "pure mercury" into "pure gold", the "perfect metal", at a considerably quicker pace than was possible in nature itself.

　　For a description of hermetic and alchemistic ideas, combining Neopythagorean, Neoplatonic, and Zoroastrian philosophies that had mixed and matured in the East, cf. Festugière, *Révélation d'Hermès Trismégiste*, Vol. 1, esp. Chapter II, "Les Prophêtes de l'Orient", pp. 19ff., and Chapter VII, "L'Hermétisme et l'alchimie", pp. 217ff.; Walter Scott, *Hermetica*, Vol. I, esp. "The *Hermetica* in the *Anthologium* of Stobaeus", pp. 82ff.; and Peters, *Aristotle and the Arabs*, esp. references to Neoplatonism and Pythagoreanism, pp. 7–10, 81f., 112f., 123–128.

126. *Corpus Hermeticum* II, *Asclepius*, 3, p. 298, line 19.

127. Ficino had fourteen of the fifteen treatises of the *Corpus Hermeticum* and he calls the whole corpus *Pimander*.

128. *Corpus Hermeticum* I, *Pimander*, I. 6–11, p. 8, line 14–p. 10, line 19.

129. *Ibid.*, I. 7, p. 9, lines 5–8.

130. *Ibid.*, I. 6, p. 8, line 19.

131. *Ibid.*, I. 9, p. 9, lines 16–20.

132. *Ibid.*, I. 11, p. 10, lines 5–11.

133. *Ibid.*, I. 12, p. 10, lines 15–19.

134. *Ibid.*, I. 15, p. 11, lines 15–17.
135. *Ibid.*, I. 16, p. 12, lines 7–10.
136. *Ibid.*, I. 19, p. 13, lines 12–19.
137. *Ibid.*, I. 24, p. 15, lines 7–12.
138. *Ibid.*, I. 25–26, p. 15, line 15–p. 16, line 15.
139. *Ibid.*, *Hermes to His Son Tat*, V. 1–2, p. 60, lines 3–15.
140. *Ibid.*, V. 3, p. 61, lines 8–9.
141. *Ibid.*, V. 3, p. 61, lines 11–19.
142. *Ibid.*, V. 4, p. 61, lines 19–24.
143. *Ibid.*, V. 6–8, p. 61, line 15–p. 62, line 18.
144. *Ibid.*, *Nous to Hermes*, XI. 7, p. 150, lines 1–14.
145. *Ibid.*, XI. 15, p. 153, lines 15–17.
146. *Ibid.*, II, *From Asclepius to King Ammon*, XVI. 2, p. 232, lines 7–8. Cf. Scott, *Hermetica*, I, pp. 29ff., for a history of the editions of the *Hermetica*.
147. *Ibid.*, XVI. 3, p. 232, line 18–p. 233, line 3.
148. *Ibid.*, XVI. 4–5, p. 233, line 12–p. 234, line 3.
149. *Ibid.*, XVI. 7, p. 234, lines 8–11. Italics added. Modern astronomy recognises that the corona of the sun reaches at least to the orbit of Jupiter.
150. *Ibid.*, XVI. 7, p. 234, lines 11–16.
151. *Ibid.*, XVI. 10, p. 235, lines 10–18.
152. *Ibid.*, XVI. 12, p. 235, line 25–p. 236, line 1.
153. *Ibid.*, XVI. 13–16, p. 235, line 4–p. 237, line 10.
154. *Ibid.*, XVI. 17, p. 237, lines 11–16. Italics added.
155. *Ibid.*, XVI. 18–19, p. 237, line 20–p. 238, line 6.
156. Yates, *Bruno*, p. 17.
157. Cf. *Corpus Hermeticum*, *Fragments Divers*, Vol. 4 and Scott, *Hermetica*, *Fragments*, Vol. 1 and *Testimonia*, Vol. 4; Yates, *Bruno*, pp. 6–12.
158. Clement of Alexandria, *Miscellanies* VI, iv, pp. 323f.
159. Tertullian, *Adversus Valentinianos*, Cap. XV, MPL, Vol. 2, col. 603.
160. Tertullian, *De Anima*, Cap. II MPL, Vol. 2, col. 690.
161. *Ibid.*, Cap. XXVIII, col. 697.
162. *Ibid.*, Cap. XXXIII, col. 705.
163. Athenagoras, *Legatio pro Christianis*, Cap. 28. 67–70 MPG, Vol. 6, col. 956.
164. Cyprian, *De Idolorum Vanitate*, Cap. VI. 574, MPL, Vol. 4, col. 595.
165. Lactantius, *Divine Institutes*, Book I, Chap. 6, p. 32, and Lactantius, *The Wrath of God* in *The Minor Works* (Washington D.C.: Catholic University, 1965), Chap. XI, p. 87.
166. Lactantius, *Divine Institutes*, Book I, Chap. 5, p. 32; Book IV, Chap. 6, pp. 255f., and Chap. 9, p. 262.
167. *Ibid.*, Book IV, Chap. 6, pp. 255f.; Book VII, Chap. 18, pp. 519f.

168. Augustine, *City of God*, Book VIII, Chap. 23, pp. 330f.
169. *Ibid.*, Book VIII, Chap. 23, p. 332.
170. *Ibid.*, Book XVIII, Chap. 39, p. 814. Note that the genealogy differs somewhat from that given by Ficino.
171. Cyril of Alexandria, *Adversus Julianum*, Lib. I, MPG, Vol. 76, col. 548 B–C.
172. *Ibid.*, Lib. V, col. 769.
173. *Ibid.*, Lib. I, col. 548 B.
174. *Ibid.*, Lib. I, col. 556 A.
175. *Ibid.*, Lib. II, col. 580 B. Cyril's reference is Ἑρμῆς πρὸς τὸν ἑαυτοῦ Νοῦν, "Hermes According to His Own Understanding".
176. *Ibid.*, Lib. VIII, col. 920 D–921 B.
177. Cf. above, pp. 18ff, 60ff, and p. 40 n. 60.
178. Ficino, Argumentum, I. 2, fol. 1836, p. 836.
179. Yates, *Bruno*, pp. 22f., 25, 36, 151–154.
180. Festugière, *Hermétisme*, p. 15.
181. Cf. "La révélation dans l'hermétisme populaire", *ibid.*, pp. 12–17.
182. Hence, it was only in a limited sense that Cusa objected to the dictum attributed to Plato: *ex nihilo nihil fit* (out of nothing comes nothing) which, Jaki points out, can be taken seriously. Cusa's more pertinent objection was that Plato insisted on a multiplicity of "forms of forms", whereas for Cusa there was but one infinite form (*una infinita forma formarum*). It is identical with God and through it God is reflected in the world on the basis of his inherent proportionalities. Nikolaus von Kues, *De Docta Ignorantia, Die belehrte Unwissenheit*, ed. Paul Wilpert, 3 vols. (Hamburg: Meiner, 1970–77), II, Cap. IX. 149, p. 76. Cf. *ibid.*, II, Cap. II. 103–104, pp. 18–22. Thus, the being of creation participates in the being of God as the limited is related to the absolute, the timebound to the eternal. Hence, while Cusa could say, "Who is able to understand that God is the form of being and is not mingled with creation?" (*ibid.*, II, Cap. II. 102, p. 18), so, too, he could say that creation possessed its share of perfection "from the divine being" (*ab esse divino*) (*ibid.*, II, Cap. II. 104, p. 22) and that every creature is "a finite infinity or a created God" (*deus creatus*) (*ibid.*, II, Cap. II 104, p. 20). Thus, there is a lack of clarity in Cusa himself as to the character of the "infinite separation" between the creature and the divine work (*ibid.*, II, Cap. IX. 150, p. 76). G. Heron's translation of *solus deus absolutus, omnia alla contracta* as "Only God is absolute, all else is finite", on which Jaki depends, rather than "God alone is absolute, all else is limited" tends to compound the confusion. Jaki, *Science and Creation*, p. 255; Cusa, *op. cit.*, II, Cap. IX. 150, p. 76.
183. Dreyer, *History of Astronomy*, pp. 282–283. Anton Lübke, *Nikolaus von Kues* (München: Callwey, 1968), pp. 20–30. The "Brethren of the Common Life", who are well worthy of a volume of their own, were pre-Reformation reformers who combined

readings in the "non-Aristotelian" theologians and fathers: Bernard of Clairvaux (c.1090–1153), the Venerable Bede (c.673–735), John Chrysostom (c.347–407), Augustine (354–430), Eusebius of Caesarea (c.263–339), *et al.* with Plato (c.427–347 B.C.), Seneca (c. 4 B.C.–A.D. 65) and Virgil (70–19 B.C.) — and the study of Grammar, Rhetoric, and Philosophy on the basis of Plato's philosophy. These *fratres bonae voluntatis* (brethren of good will), who combined caring for the poor with a work ethic and an endeavour to reform the Church and who could lay claim to such diverse notables as Erasmus (c.1466–1536) and Thomas à Kempis (c.1380–1471), spread their schools from the Netherlands in the north and west to Spain in the south and Polish Prussia in the East. *Ibid.*

184.　Dreyer notes that Toscanelli is supposed to have encouraged Christopher Columbus (c.1451–1506) to take advantage of the sphericity of the world and seek a westerly route to the Indies. Dreyer, *History of Astronomy*, p. 283.

185.　Cusa, *Docta Ignorantia*, I, Cap. I 4, p. 8.

186.　Cusa, *Docta Ignorantia*, I, Cap. II. 6, p. 10.

187.　*Ibid.*, I, Cap. XXVI. 86, pp. 108f.

188.　*Ibid.*, I, Cap. XIII. 34, p. 46. Cf. Anselm of Canterbury, *Truth, Freedom, and Evil: Three Philosophical Dialogues* (New York: Harper, 1967), pp. 108f.

189.　Cusa, *Docta Ignorantia*, I, Cap. XVIII. 52, p. 70.

190.　*Ibid.*, I, Cap. XIII. 35, pp. 46f.

191.　*Ibid.*, I, Caps. XIII–XV, pp. 46–56. Cf. Thomas Bradwardine, *Geometria Speculativa* (Paris: Marchant, 1495 [Biblioteca Vaticana]) and Boethius, *De Arithmetica,* MPL, Vol. 63.

192.　Cusa, *Docta Ignorantia*, I, Caps. XVI–XVII, pp. 58–68.

193.　*Ibid.*, I, Cap. XXII. 67–69, pp. 88–92.

194.　*Ibid.*, II, Cap. XII. 160, pp. 90–92.

195.　Cf. Nebelsick, *Theology and Science*, p. 53.

196.　Cusa, *Docta Ignorantia*, I. Cap. XXIII. 71, pp. 92–94. Wilpert says the reference is to a quote from Parmenides in Bede, *Commentarius in librum Boetii de Trinitate*, Num. XXV (MPL, Vol. 95, col. 397 C). Cf. Wilpert, ed., *Docta Ignorantia*, I, p. 124, n. 71.

197.　Cusa, *Docta Ignorantia*, I, Cap. XXIII. 72, p. 94.

198.　*Ibid.*

199.　*Ibid.*, I, Cap. XXIV. 73, pp. 94–96.

200.　Since Cusa finished writing the *De Docta Ignorantia* on February 12, 1440, he most likely knew of the *Asclepius* but would hardly have been aware of the rest of the *Corpus Hermeticum* which was brought to Florence about 1460 and translated by Ficino in 1463. Cf. Paul Wilpert, "Vorwort des Herausgebers", *De Docta Ignorantia*, pp. XIIf., and Yates, *Bruno*, pp. 12f.

201.　Cusa, *Docta Ignorantia*, II, Cap. XIII. 175–180, pp. 108–114.

202. *Ibid.*, II, Cap. XII. 162, p. 92. The idea, which we know as "Galilean relativity", to contrast it with that of Einstein, was, according to Paul Wilpert, known by William of Conches (c.1084-c.1154) who as early as the twelfth century had pointed out by the example of a ship that movement is only recognisable relative to something else. "Dass Bewegung nur als relative Bewegung erkennbar ist, weiss bereits Wilhelm von Conches, der auch das Beispiel von Schiff bringt." Wilpert, ed., *Docta Ignorantia*, II, p. 133, n. 159. Cf. William of Conches in Bede, *Elementorum Philosophiae*, Lib. II, MPL, cols. 1141B–1142A.
203. Cusa, *Docta Ignorantia*, II, Cap. XI. 156, pp. 84–86.
204. *Ibid.*, II, Cap. XI. 156, p. 86.
205. *Ibid.*, II, Cap. XI. 157, p. 86.
206. *Ibid.*, II, Cap. XI. 159, p. 90.
207. *Ibid.* Einstein reminds us that any theory by which nature is interpreted is "man-made". Einstein, *Out of My Later Years*, p. 98.
208. Cusa, *Docta Ignorantia*, II, Cap. XI. 160, p. 90. Italics added.
209. *Ibid.*, II, Cap. XII, 162, p. 94.
210. Nicolaus Copernicus, *On the Revolutions of the Heavenly Spheres*, Book I.9, p. 521.
211. Dreyer, *History of Astronomy*, pp. 286f. An indication of Cusa's mathematical proficiency is, as Dreyer explains, that his calculations of the sun's annual motion is inaccurate only by a fraction of 1/365. *Ibid.*, p. 286.
212. Alexandre Koyré, *The Astronomical Revolution* (Paris: Hermann, 1973), p. 58.

CHAPTER 5

COPERNICAN COSMOLOGY

WHEN Nicholas Copernicus turned the world inside-out by his discovery of the heliocentric theory, the great astronomer introduced a cosmology which was so new and radical that it could only be characterised as "the Copernican Revolution". So most of us have been taught. But, did he? Whether he did or not, and I shall argue that he did not, his is one of the instances in the history of science that are paradigmatic both of the way theology has influenced the development of science and of the way scientific hypotheses are formed and fare.

Most of us, myself included, were educated to think of Copernicus as a lonely canon of the Frauenberg Cathedral who, by patient observation and intricate mathematical calculations, was inspired to conceive of the heliocentric universe.[1] In the face of ecclesiastical, cultural, and scientific opposition, he then reluctantly published his *De Revolutionibus Orbium Caelestium* (*On the Revolutions of the Heavenly Spheres*), which shocked the world by the boldness of its conceptuality and the originality of its claim. Copernicus, we were led to believe, discovered that the sun rather than the earth was placed in the middle of the universe. The earth, instead of being the centre of the world, was reduced to being one planet among others, the centre only of the orbit of the moon.

Copernicus' Popularity

We now know that little of the above is true. Although Copernicus did spend his years at Frauenberg in relative isolation, he worked out the basic explanation for his heliocentric system as early as the first decade of the sixteenth century. He recorded the fundamental ideas of his sun-centred system in his *Commentariolus (Sketch of the Hypotheses for the Heavenly Motions)* and distributed the writing among friends and interested acquaintances.[2] As the title suggests, the writing set out the basis of the heliocentric theory and listed its principal components. It omitted the mathematical demonstrations,[3] "reserving these", as Copernicus wrote, "for my larger work". The statement indicates that, at this stage, he either planned or was already at work on the *De Revolutionibus.*[4]

According to the Copernican scholar, Edward Rosen, the *Commentariolus* may well have been the reason why, in 1516, Copernicus along with other astronomers and mathematicians was consulted by the authorities in Rome with regard to the reform of the calendar. Copernicus apparently wrote his advice to the authorities at the time. A quarter century later, in his preface to the *De Revolutionibus*, he made note of the fact that the problem remained unsolved because "the magnitude of the year and the months and the movements of the sun and moon had not yet been measured with sufficient accuracy".[5] Hence already in the early part of the sixteenth century, Copernicus had an international reputation. Further evidence of his notoriety is that in 1522 he was approached by Bernard Wapowski (c.1450–1535), secretary to Sigismund I, King of Poland (1467–1548), to comment on an astronomical treatise, *De motu octavae sphaerae tractatus primus (The Motion of the Eighth Sphere)*, written by Johann Werner (1468–1528). Copernicus replied in his *The Letter Against Werner*. The treatise, in which he took Werner to task for his miscalculations, was printed and became widely distributed and well known.[6]

Although we have learned to think that the Copernican theory was revolutionary in its own time, it does not seem to have raised much of a storm either among the astronomers or among the public at large. As said, the heliocentric theory was known among the *cognoscenti* about 1515 with the distribution of the *Commentariolus*. Nevertheless, except for isolated incidents of opposition,[7]

rapid debate about and wholesale rejection of the theory
did not appear until decades after the *De Revolutionibus*
was printed. It was first published in 1543. In 1566 the
work underwent a second edition. However, it was not
until 1616, coincidental with the "first hearing" of Galileo,
and nearly sixty years after it first appeared, that the
volume was placed by the Roman Church authorities on
the *Index of Forbidden Books*. Rosen's evidence, which
shows that shortly after publication it had become one of
those "workaday manuals for practical astronomers in all
countries", would seem to indicate that for the first half-
century of its life, the work enjoyed relative and largely
unopposed popularity.[8]

Also, contrary to our usual understanding of the importance of Copernicus as a discoverer of a revolutionary
theory of planetary motion, the heliocentric hypothesis
was neither unique with him nor was his version of the
theory particularly convincing. As Copernicus himself
explained in the "Preface and Dedication" to the *De
Revolutionibus*, it was simply an arrangement based on the
movement of the earth that represented "the revolutions of
the celestial spheres" more firmly than the "circles" that
his predecessors had conceived to "demonstrate the astral
phenomena".[9] For many of his contemporaries the
Copernican theory was, however, simply one hypothesis
among others; and this, as we shall see below, was exactly
what Osiander's preface to the *De Revolutionibus* described
the theory as being.[10]

Thus, rather than the heliocentric hypothesis having
been sprung upon an unsuspecting world with the publication of *De Revolutionibus*, the evidence indicates that both
Copernicus and his theory were known subjects of discussion in learned circles and among the populace at least
ten or even twenty years before the book came off the press.
There is evidence that as early as 1533, a decade before the
publication of the *De Revolutionibus*, the theory, as described in the *Commentariolus*, had been discussed in
Rome. There is also a record that Copernicus, the *Stern-
gucker* (star-gazer), was one among a number of ecclesias-

tics who were satirised in a play before a Shrove Tuesday audience in the town of Elbing, located just five kilometres from Frauenberg, about the year 1531. The farce, it seems, was composed and produced by one Willem de Volder (1493–1568) who had grecised his name to Gnapheus. Gnapheus had fled the Inquisition in The Hague and found refuge in Elbing. He thus had reason enough to heckle the ecclesiastical establishment in general. Although the play apparently did not single out Copernicus for particular derision, the fact that he was featured in the piece at all indicates that the "star-gazer" was well-known to the local populace at the time. The point of the play seems to have been that Copernicus and the rest of the ecclesiastics were worthy of ridicule because they spent time and resources on useless esoteric occupations.[11]

By the year 1539 the Copernican doctrine had entered the popular mind to such an extent that it could become subject to an off-hand comment by no less a person than Martin Luther (1483–1546) in Wittenberg. According to the June 4, 1539 entry in Luther's *Tischreden* (*Table-Talk*), the Reformer is recorded to have said:

A new astrology [astronomy] has been thought up which would prove that the earth is moved and goes around, not the heaven or the firmament, sun and moon: just as when one sets on a wagon or in a ship and is moved, though it may seem that he sits still and rests, the earth and the trees go by and move themselves. But in our time it would seem to be the case that whoever would be clever must think up something strange. The fool will turn the whole art of astronomy inside out! But, as the Holy Scripture reports, Joshua ordered the sun to stand still and not the earth.[12]

In equating the non-movement of the moon with that of the sun, the firmament, and the heaven, Luther did not get it quite right. Nevertheless, the statement leaves little doubt that Luther understood the main substance of the

Copernican theory. It also leaves little doubt that for Luther, as for the early post-New Testament writers who had commented on cosmology, the Bible took precedence over "scientific theory".

Like Martin Luther, John Calvin, the Genevan Reformer, who must have known about the Copernican theory, remained geocentric in his cosmology. Although there is no evidence for Calvin's having faulted astronomy in general or Copernicus in particular, we know of one instance in which he derided those "who say that the sun does not move, and that it is the earth which shifts and turns itself".[13]

Eventually, as Herbert Butterfield has pointed out, Protestantism rather than Roman Catholicism became the ally of science in the seventeenth century. However, ironic as it may seem as far as the Copernican theory was concerned, for the first half century of its life, that is, until almost the end of the sixteenth century, certain of the leaders of the Church in Rome were more sympathetic to the new scientific hypothesis than were those in Wittenberg or Geneva.[14]

Since, as our investigation will show, in its own time the Copernican theory was somewhat less than convincing, such scepticism is quite understandable. Thus, one probably should not fault Luther or Calvin in the sixteenth century any more than one should condemn Cardinal Robert Bellarmine (1542–1621), who warned Galileo in the first years of the seventeenth century that he should teach the Copernican theory only as speculation and not as fact. Why give up biblical concepts — and on this point, interestingly enough, Luther, Calvin, and Bellarmine all agreed — for a revolutionary theory which had little or no evidence to support it?

Just as in Copernicus' own time there was no official opposition to his theory from the Church of Rome, so there was no controversy regarding the hypothesis which divided itself along confessional lines. This lack of confessional partisanship in the matter is amply illustrated by events related to the publication of the *De Revol-*

utionibus. In the late 1530's and early 1540's, Ermland, the province in which Frauenberg was located, had come under the influence of the staunch Catholic prelate Bishop Johannes Dantiscus (1485–1548) and was becoming more and more anti-Lutheran. Nevertheless, in 1539 the Lutheran mathematician Georg Joachim von Lauchen (1514–76), who assumed the surname Rheticus, was welcomed by Copernicus to Frauenberg. Rheticus was a protégé of Luther's disciple, Philip Melanchthon (1497–1560) and was Professor of Mathematics at the University of Wittenberg. He eventually became responsible for the publication of the *De Revolutionibus* itself.

During his first stay in Frauenberg, Rheticus familiarised himself so well with the Copernican theory that he summed up and published its principles in his *Narratio Prima (First Statement)*. After returning to the University of Wittenberg, Rheticus travelled to Frauenberg a second time where, in 1540 and 1541, he spent fifteen months as a guest of Copernicus. During this time he both edited and hand-copied the 424 page *De Revolutionibus* and, even more importantly and in corroboration with Copernicus' friend and superior, Tiedemann Giese, Bishop of Kulm (1480–1550), he persuaded Copernicus to allow the *De Revolutionibus* to be published.

Early in 1542 Rheticus carried the copy first to Protestant Wittenberg where he had the first two chapters, which dealt largely with mathematics, published, perhaps for use in his own instruction at the university.[15] In May 1542 he took the entire manuscript to Nuremberg and arranged for it to be published by Johannes Petreius (1497–1550), the Protestant printer-publisher who had made a reputation by publishing scientific works. During 1542 Rheticus was called to take up his duties at a new post as Professor of Mathematics at the University of Leipzig. At that juncture the Lutheran minister Andreas Osiander (1498–1552), who had a hobby of mathematics and astronomy, both saw the work through the press and provided it with a preface which he hoped would help the work to be accepted.[16]

The *Narratio Prima*, written by Rheticus during his first

stay at Frauenberg, was published in 1540, three years before the *De Revolutionibus* came off the press. It is an admirable display of his own excellent understanding of the content and importance of the Copernican system. In contrast to Osiander's anonymous "Preface" to the *De Revolutionibus*, which commended the Copernican hypothesis as a *possible theory*, Rheticus, like Copernicus himself, considered the Copernican heliocentric theory to be a proper expression of the construction of the universe. The hypotheses, he said, agreed "so well with phenomena that they can be mutually interchanged, like a good definition and the thing defined".[17]

The publication of the *Narratio Prima* is itself an indication that the usual picture of Copernicus as a canon hidden away in remote Frauenberg and sitting in fear and trembling and in dread of ecclesiastical persecution because of his heliocentric theory is patently untrue. Copernicus had, no doubt, agreed to allow Rheticus to compose and publish the writing. Although Rheticus did not call Copernicus by name in the *Narratio Prima*, the comparison of his "teacher" with the great Ptolemy and his claims that this teacher had made astronomical observations, lectured on mathematics in Bologna, was now a resident of Frauenberg and was an intimate acquaintance of Tiedemann Giese, left no doubt as to Copernicus' identity.[18] In spite of this notoriety, there was no hint that Copernicus faced persecution or even censure by ecclesiastical authorities. On the contrary, there was every sign that Copernicus received encouragement for his theory not only from his friend Giese, but even from his sometime adversary, Dantiscus.[19] More important, perhaps, Nicolaus Schoenberg (1472–1537), who at the time was in Rome, encouraged him as well.

The best indication that Rome posed no threat to Copernicus is found in a letter to him from Schoenberg dated November 1, 1536. The letter, which Copernicus was later to mention in the prefatory material to the *De Revolutionibus*, indicated that his theory was well known to the Vatican, probably from the *Commentariolus* well before the time *De Revolutionibus* was published. Schoenberg, who is known to have had a relation of trust with both Pope Clement VII (1478–1534) and his successor, Pope Paul III (1468–1549), not only indicated interest in the theory but urged Copernicus "to communicate your discovery to the learned world".[20]

Especially interesting, if not astounding, is the evidence from the title page of a manuscript which Pope Clement VII had presented to Johannes Albertus Widmanstadius (1506–57), his private secretary. The page records a note of appreciation to Widmanstadius for the explanation of the Copernican theory which Widmanstadius had addressed to the Pope and other dignitaries in the Vatican Gardens in 1533.[21] Hence, at that date, at any rate, there is nothing to suggest that Copernicus had anything to fear from Rome. This, in addition to the fact that the Bishop of Kulm, Tiedemann Giese, was, along with Rheticus, primarily responsible for persuading Copernicus to allow his work to be published, would seem to indicate that the possibility of ecclesiastical recrimination was remote indeed. Rather than expressing massive opposition to the theory, Protestants and Roman Catholics worked together to bring it to light.

Another interesting indication of inter-confessional co-operation in the matter is that when Rheticus journeyed to Nuremberg to deliver the manuscript to the printer, he was equipped with several letters of recommendation addressed to the leading patricians and Protestant clerics of that city written by no other than Melanchthon, Luther's younger colleague.[22] The attitude with which the theory was greeted in the Protestant city is revealed in a letter from one T. Forsther, a citizen of Nuremberg, to a friend, J. Schrad in Reutlingen:

> Prussia has borne us a new and wonderful astronomer, whose teachings are already being published here, a work of approximately one hundred sheets in length wherein he assures and proves that the earth itself moves and the heavens are at rest. A month ago I saw

two printed sheets. The proof-reader of the printing is
a certain *Wittenberger Magister* [Rheticus].[23]

It is true that Copernicus hesitated to publish his *De
Revolutionibus* and had to be persuaded by friends to allow
the book to be printed. His reluctance, however, was
apparently due not to any fear of ecclesiastical recrimination but because of possible ridicule by the "Aristotelians". The "Aristotelians" were Ptolemaic astronomers
who, in the middle of the sixteenth century, were as
convinced as was Ptolemy himself in the first century and
as convinced as those who were to be responsible for trying
Galileo in the seventeenth century, that it was absurd to
think that the earth both rotated on its axis and revolved
about the sun.

As we have seen, *Magister* Rheticus, because of a call to
fill the prestigious Chair of Mathematics at the University
of Leipzig, was unfortunately not able to complete the task
of seeing the entire manuscript through the press. He
turned the responsibility over to the Lutheran Minister,
Andreas Osiander of Nuremberg who, like himself, was an
advocate of the Copernican theory. Osiander, who knew
Copernicus well enough to correspond with him, not only
superintended the printing of the work, but provided it
with an anonymous preface, "To the Reader, Concerning
the Hypotheses of this Work".

The preface which Osiander added (whether with or
without Copernicus' knowledge is uncertain, but quite
certainly without his agreement) recognised the novelty of
the theory, pointed out that, even before publication, it had
already "received a great deal of publicity", and noted that
"certain of the savants" (Luther, perhaps, though more
likely certain Aristotelian astronomers) had taken serious
offence at the hypothesis because they thought it wrong to
question traditional disciplines. Most importantly, how-
éver, at least from Osiander's point of view, the heliocentric theory was to be considered as *one hypothesis among
others*. He rightly saw that it was "calculated from the
principles of geometry". Contrary to Copernicus' own

intention of having hypotheses correspond with reality, for Osiander, "it is not necessary that these hypotheses should be true, or even probable; but it is enough if they provide a calculus which fits the observations".[24]

Although Koestler pronounces Osiander's preface perhaps "the greatest scandal" in the history of science, there is no evidence that Osiander intended to betray Copernicus. Letters, to which Koestler himself refers, indicate that Osiander had written to both Copernicus and Rheticus (the latter was at that time in Frauenberg) about the necessity for just such a preface as he later provided.[25] Although no replies are extant, the evidence would indicate that both Rheticus and Copernicus rejected Osiander's interpretation. Rheticus had made his position clear in the *Narratio Prima* and, as we shall see more fully below, Osiander's idea that the theory was only a "probable hypothesis" was diametrically opposed to Copernicus' own understanding.[26]

In his own "Preface and Dedication to Pope Paul III", Copernicus also put forth his work as a mathematical hypothesis. He understood "hypothesis", however, in the sense of a *theory that reflected the reality of the world*. Hence, he criticised those astronomers who had put forth various systems of circles for not having been able "to establish anything for certain that would fully correspond to the phenomena". Although he was quite aware that his ideas would not be universally appreciated, that some people would likely try to refute him by "shamelessly distorting" the sense of "some passage of Holy Writ", and that others might "laugh" at his theory, he was certain that the mathematicians would appreciate what he had done. After all, "Mathematics is written for mathematicians," he said.[27]

While Copernicus was careful to dedicate his work to the Pope and meticulously credited the proper Roman Catholic officials, Schoenberg and Giese, for having been instrumental in persuading him to publish, it would be quite wrong to interpret this as a bribe to the ecclesiastical authorities. The dedications were more than likely intended as foils against the orthodox Aristotelians whose whole understanding of physics was put in peril by the heliocentric theory and from whom Copernicus correctly anticipated a certain amount of derision.[28] He apparently continued to work on the calculations of the *De Revolutionibus* and modified the trigonometry until the last moment. This would seem to indicate that he too may well have had a certain hesitation about the theory which he attempted to rectify. A letter of Rheticus dated June 2, 1541 which states that Copernicus was "enjoying quite good health and is writing a great deal", may or may not refer to the revision of the *De Revolutionibus*.[29] We know, however, that even when the document was finally released for publication in August, 1541, it was less than satisfactory. Not only did the theory stand in "opposition to the general opinion of the mathematicians", as Copernicus himself had said, but there were internal inadequacies that may have caused him to be less than completely satisfied with it. If so, it may well have been his own dissatisfaction with the theory itself, rather than the fear of any opposition it might provoke, which explains the main reason for his having kept his thoughts hidden not merely for nine years (as was mandatory for the Pythagoreans) but, as he said, for nearly "four times nine years".[30]

Nevertheless, the fact that, in a letter to Achilles Pirmin Gasser (1503–77), who wrote the "Foreword" to the second edition of the *Narratio Prima* printed in Basel in 1541, Rheticus himself suggested that the *Narratio* "could ... be considered heretical (as the monks would say)",[31] would seem to indicate that the "Aristotelians" were as prone to apply censure to heterodox astronomy as was the Church to heterodox doctrine. Rosen reports without mentioning names that two of the most widely read sixteenth-century scientists recommended the destruction of the *De Revolutionibus* and the "whipping of its author". Further, if it is true, as Rosen goes on to assert, that "the foremost Roman Catholic astronomer of the time" rejected Copernicanism, there is evidence that the opposition Copernicus expected was indeed forthcoming. There is no indication, however, that such opposition was enough to cause real difficulty for the theory until late in the century. The fact that such hostility was in the offing does show nonetheless that, rather than being the "Timid Canon" that Koestler portrayed Copernicus as being, he was courageous enough to release the book for publication once he became persuaded that he had done as much as possible to "get it right".[32]

Our usual view of Copernicanism is conditioned by later history. When we consider such events as the opposition of the Dutch Calvinist Gisbert Voetius (1589–1676) and his followers to Cartesianism (which they identified with Copernicanism) at the universities of Leyden and Utrecht from 1639–45, the burning of the Hermeticist-Copernican Giordano Bruno in 1600, the first trial of Galileo in 1616 and his condemnation in 1633 for his Copernican ideas, we transfer the somewhat fear-filled atmosphere of that era to the time of Copernicus half a century before. As a youth I was told that the old canon kept the book hidden under his mattress and brought it out only on the day of his death. There is evidence to indicate that Copernicus was delivered a copy of the *De Revolutionibus* in printed form just prior to his death. There is little evidence, however, that fear of ecclesiastical censure caused him to delay publication. Hence, in contradistinction to Koyré's statement that the secret was well kept[33] and, in line with his other statement, that neither the Pope nor anyone else was shocked by the system,[34] the evidence that Copernicus was so deeply concerned about ecclesiastical censure that he kept his hypothesis to himself would seem to be found wanting.

The Renaissance Influence

As we cannot lock up Copernicus with his astronomical instruments in his tower at Frauenberg after he took up residence there as a canon of the cathedral, so we cannot confine him to his rooms at the Italian universities he attended in an attempt to shield him from Renaissance thought. His instruments consisted only of the parallactic instrument which was used mainly for observing the moon, the quadrant for measuring the position of the sun, and the astrolabe or armillary sphere for checking the locations of the stars.[35] Not only did they leave much to be desired as far as precision was concerned,[36] they were less important to him in the development of his heliocentric cosmology than was the mathematics he learned at the University of Cracow, on the one hand, and the astronomy and Neoplatonic and Neopythagorean influences of Renaissance Italy, which he encountered at the universities of Bologna and Padua, on the other. We may never know the real reason why Copernicus put the sun in the centre of the world in place of the earth. Indeed, considering the fact that discoveries are seldom traceable to their origins with absolute certainty, he himself may not have known. It would seem quite certain, however, that his heliocentric hypothesis did not depend upon astronomical observation and mathematics alone.

Copernicus insisted, of course, that it was the disagreement of mathematicians with one another in their researches that had moved him "to think out a different scheme of drawing up the movements of the spheres of the world".[37] Nevertheless, it was not as straightforward as that. His real objections to the schemes he found unsatisfactory were two-fold. Those systems that had relied on concentric circles, e.g., of Eudoxus, Callippus, or Aristotle, failed fully to correspond *to the phenomena*. Those that had relied on eccentrics, i.e., the systems of Hipparchus and Ptolemy, contradicted "the first principles of regularity of movement".[38] It was, in fact, this *contradiction* between "regularity of movement" and the pattern of planetary movements of the Ptolemaic system, a contradiction which indicated a *disharmony* within the system, that prompted him "to think out a different scheme". Thus *aesthetics*, a sense of what was right, proper, and necessary, rather than mathematical error or observational discrepancy, caused Copernicus to substitute his own system of circles for that of Ptolemy.

Aristotle's system of homocentric spheres, which had been built on the schemes of Eudoxus and Callippus, was inadequate as astronomers had realised from Heraclides onward. The spheres, all of which turned around the central earth, even though they were thought to turn in hundreds of directions, made for a system which was far too rigid to account for the irregularities observed in the behaviour of the planets. The Ptolemaic system attempted to "save the appearances", i.e., to take account of the irregularities of motion observed, by a series of eccentrics, deferents, epicycles, and equants. It was especially the eccentrics and the equants which offended Copernicus' sense of unity and regularity. It was because this *sense of unity*, which was so characteristic of the Renaissance cast of mind as exhibited, as we have seen, both by Cusa and by the Hermeticists, was offended by the Ptolemaic system that Copernicus sought a more unified scheme, a scheme which would comply with the Renaissance insistence that the heavens, being divine, display perfect harmony between the circularity of pattern and the regularity of movement.

So profound was this demand for harmony that, in the end, Copernicus was persuaded to publish even though his own system of the universe was at least equally complicated and was less accurate than the Ptolemaic hypothesis. Hence Copernicus himself was quite straightforward when he claimed that it was because the Ptolemaic system so contradicted "the first principles of the regularity of movement" as to be a monstrosity that he was persuaded to embark on the reformation of the plan.[39] Ptolemy, in short, insulted his Renaissance-inspired sense of symmetry.

Hence we do a disservice to our understanding of the Copernican theory if we isolate Copernicus from his context. More particularly, we miss our opportunity to understand the process by which heliocentricity came about as a pertinent example of how science was both motivated and compromised by the *theologically charged atmosphere* of the Renaissance and do not see the way theories arise in general if we attempt to shield Copernicus from the Renaissance thought world. In consequence, we could very well miss the truth of the matter if we were to make Copernicus into either a modern scientist or into a thinker upon whom the Renaissance culture, with its identification between harmony and divinity, had little or no effect.

The Renaissance, with its insistence upon the unity and harmony of all reality and its romantic acceptance of the past as a sure guide to truth, was *ipso facto* a multi-coloured fabric of idealised history, mystical religion, and quixotic "science". It was a world in which alchemy was the search for the divine essence which was thought to be the basis of and the unification of all material reality. Astrology was the "science" of heavenly divine influences of the stars and planets upon earthly events. Astrology and astronomy were so closely allied that the terms themselves continued to be interchangeable right up to and throughout the seventeenth century. The divine was thought to interpenetrate and press its influences upon reality. "Science" was the search for the divine mysteries by which the universe was moulded and within which it was encompassed.

Nevertheless, it would be difficult indeed to classify Copernicus as one of the Renaissance "scientists" to whom Festugière refers as doing the kind of science whose "sole purpose was to lead to God".[40] Aleksander Birkenmajer is probably quite accurate in saying that "contrary to the majority of the astronomers of his time, Copernicus was never an astrologer".[41] Rosen offers supporting evidence by pointing out that in contrast to Rheticus and also, by the way, in contrast to Tycho Brahe, Johannes Kepler, Galileo Galilei, and even Isaac Newton, Copernicus is not known to have cast a single horoscope.[42] However, one did not have to espouse astrology to be deeply affected by Renaissance culture, Even Birkenmajer admitted that Copernicus had familiarised himself with astrology at Cracow. Birkenmajer quickly minimised the effect of that familiarisation by adding, "The contact never became more than casual and did not go beyond his young years".[43]

Perhaps, but since Copernicus spent ten impressionable years in the effervescent atmosphere of Renaissance Italy, it is hardly coincidental to find him well enough acquainted with the Neopythagorean literature of that time to celebrate his own heliocentric hypothesis, not with a diagram which replicated his own system of deferents, eccentrics, and epicycles, but with the perfectly symmetrical diagram of homocentric circles around the sun described in the Neopythagorean Hermetic literature. As far as astronomy itself is concerned, the diagram represented Aristarchus' heliocentric system of simple concentric circles rather than Copernicus' own much more complicated hypothesis. However, the fact that in the paragraph which accompanies his diagram of the seven concentric orbits centred on the sun (the inner six representing the planets and the outer one the fixed stars with the orbit of the moon centred on the earth), Copernicus wrote an ode worthy of Hermes himself is evidence enough that his familiarity with Hermetic thought was more than superficial. The paragraph is so filled with Hermetic concepts that Ficino himself would gladly have claimed authorship.[44]

> In the centre of all rests the sun. For who would place this lamp of a very beautiful temple in another or better place than this wherefrom it can illuminate everything at the same time? As a matter of fact, not unhappily do some call it the lantern; others, the mind and still others, the pilot of the world. Trismegistus calls it a "visible god"; Sophocles' Electra, "that which gazes upon all things". And so the sun, as if resting on a kingly throne, governs the family of stars which wheel around. Moreover, the Earth is by no means cheated of the services of the moon; but, as Aristotle says in the *De Animalibus*, the earth has the closest kinship with the moon. The Earth moreover is fertilised by the sun and conceives offspring every year.[45]

Although, as we have stated, it is extremely difficult to assign the place of Hermeticism in the development of science, it is certainly true that Copernicus, as Yates has pointed out, was living within the Neoplatonism of the *prisca theologia*.[46] Alexandre Koyré (1892–1964) may have gone too far in emphasising that the real motive which inspired the mind and soul of Copernicus was his view of the sun in a religious, Neopythagorean and Neoplatonic way: "he adores it and almost deifies it".[47] There is, however, ample evidence for such influences in the milieu in which Copernicus was educated. It was a culture in which cultic elements associated with the study of the stars were reinforced by the revival of ancient wisdom. Greek cosmological concepts, which were founded on the belief that the harmony and form of the heavenly spheres was reflected in the divinity of the Maker, were part of the atmosphere that Copernicus, along with his teachers, breathed. The heavens above reflected their thoughts within. The harmony, order, and splendour of the eternal heavens which marked the ways of God brought comfort to their souls. Moreover, the discovery was not new. It was a renewal of ancient wisdom, a rebirth, a renaissance of the wisdom of those older than Ptolemy, even of those older than Aristotle, Plato, and the Pythagoreans, valuable as their knowledge was considered to be. It was a reappreciation of knowledge of the mysteries of the universe going right back to Hermes Trismegistus who was thought to have lived a generation after Moses. The literature had been translated for all to read. The sun, reflecting the light of God, was placed in the middle of the world. The six planets, including the rotating earth, circled round under its control. The orbit of the moon encircled the earth; and the seventh sphere, that of the stars, enclosed the whole. Such a universe had long since been set out by Aristarchus; and, though Copernicus knew it and used a diagram which fits Aristarchus' specifications to illustrate his own universe, he did not admit that he knew it, at least insofar as the published edition of his *De Revolutionibus* was concerned.[48]

Surely the fact that Copernicus spoke of the sun as "the lantern", "the mind", "the pilot of the world", which "governs the family of stars which wheel around", would seem to indicate that he did more than tip his hat in the direction of the romantic Neopythagoreanism of Renaissance Italy.[49] If so, it was hardly a coincidence that, rather than bring the heavens to earth, as Galileo was to do with his laws of dynamics, Copernicus raised the earth to the heavens so that our planet could be regarded as one of the wandering stars.[50] What the earth lost in being the centre of the world was more than compensated for by its joining the heavenly spheres and participating in the movement of "perfect circularity".

It is in this light, even if allowance is given for the Renaissance manner of describing nature in florid language, that we may understand the reason why the introductory paragraphs to Book One of *De Revolutionibus* sound less like the work of a cold, calculating mathematician than of one who is enchanted with the mystery of the harmony and beauty of the heavens. It is but a small step from the Neoplatonist and Neopythagorean conception of the heavens as reflected divinity to Copernicus' own description. "The godlike circular movements of the world and the course of the stars" are seen to explicate the whole form. The fact that the heavens "contain all the beautiful things" is made clear by "their very names". *Caelum* (heaven) is the name of that "which is beautifully carved" *Mundus* (world) stands for "purity and elegance".[51] So taken is Copernicus by the beauty and splendour of it all that he eagerly reports that "many philosophers have called the world a visible god".[52]

Nevertheless, Copernicus was not caught in astrology. Although he defined astronomy as a "more divine than human science", he also insisted that it leans on "nearly all the other branches of mathematics". " Arithmetic, geometry, optics, geodesy, mechanics and whatever others, all offer themselves in its service." Rather than speaking of the stars as ruling over human fate as all astrologers were prone to do, Copernicus was certain, like Newton later, that contemplation of them causes "wonder at the Artificer of all things".[53]

Whether or not Copernicus, like the ancient Pythagoreans, turned his thoughts to the heavens because their beauty and order were reflective of divinity, he certainly saw beauty and order there and attempted to fashion a system which would do these qualities justice. Like the Pythagoreans, then, he was ultimately concerned to have the harmony of the heavens reflected in the geometry of the system which was drawn to represent it. Like them, too, however, he eventually moved from rêverie and admiration to geometry and mathematics.

It was when Copernicus turned to represent the world in terms of form and figure that he showed himself to be a superb geometer and mathematician. He agreed with Plutarch whom he quoted to emphasise the enigma facing the astronomer: "So far the movement of the stars has overcome the ingenuity of the mathematicians."[54] Nevertheless, it was as a mathematician that Copernicus turned the Ptolemaic world inside out.

Brilliant as was his mathematics, however, his primary concepts about astronomy were based neither upon the particulars of measurement nor upon the results of observation. Rather, his most important concept, which was the *regulating principle* for his whole system, the principle which eventually condemned it to inaccuracy, was the *principle of circularity*. It was built upon notions inspired by Plato and Aristotle. And in the Renaissance, it was incorporated in the thought of the Neoplatonists and the Hermeticists as well as by those who continued to insist upon the physics of Aristotle. Hence Copernicus followed the statement, "The movement of the celestial bodies is regular, circular, and everlasting — or else compounded of circular movements",[55] with another which sounds as if it may have come directly from Aristotle himself.

> For the motion of a sphere is to turn in a circle; by this very act expressing its form, in the most simple body, where beginning and end cannot be discovered or distinguished from one another, while it moves through the same parts in itself.[56]

The Development of "Heliocentricity"

When and where Copernicus first began to think seriously about his "heliocentric" system is as difficult to ascertain as are his motives for developing it.[57] By the end of the fifteenth century Cracow had gained a reputation as a good place to study mathematics and astronomy. Hard times had fallen on the universities of Prague and Vienna with the result that a good number of peripatetic students and other interested persons brought their books and astronomical instruments to the city. Copernicus went up to the University of Cracow in 1491 to begin his study of mathematics. It was there, as far as we know, that his acquaintance with astronomy began. Birkenmajer, who is an unabashed apologete for Copernicus' originality, reports that the two theories of cosmology taught at Cracow at the time were Aristotle's theory of homocentric spheres and the Ptolemaic system. Both were geocentric but whereas the Aristotelian system consisted of a nest of fifty-five concentric spheres which turned and influenced one another in order to explain the apparent irregularity of planetary motion, Ptolemy used a whole series of eccentrics, circular orbits, epicycles, and equants to "save the appearances".[58]

However, according to Ernst Zinner's fascinating *Entstehung und Ausbreitung der Coppernicanischen Lehre* (*The Establishment and Propagation of the Copernican Doctrine*), astronomy at Cracow when Copernicus was a student there between 1491–93,[59] as everywhere in Europe at the time, was under the influence of the combined teachings of the Viennese professor Georg Peurbach (1423–61) and his student and colleague Regiomontanus (Johann Müller) (1436–76). Zinner shows that at Cracow, the Professor of Astronomy, Albert Blarer von Brudzewo (1446–95), interpreted Peurbach's planetary theory and noted in particular the sun's influence upon the movement of the planets, especially as it affected the angle of their retrograde motion.[60]

Peurbach had published his *Theoricae novae planetarum*

(*Planetary Theory*) in Nuremberg in 1472 or 1473. The book was destined to go through fifty-six editions and by the time Copernicus took up mathematics and astronomy at Cracow, it had replaced Sacrobosco's *De Sphaera* as the basic textbook in astronomy throughout Europe. The publication dealt with the sun, the moon, the seven planets and their characteristic phenomena. It explained the theory of altitude, gave a description of the solid celestial spheres, illustrated them by way of Ptolemaic planetary models, and interpreted the motion of the eighth sphere. Most importantly, Peurbach adjusted Ptolemy's astronomy according to the mathematical notations of the Alfonsine Tables.

This in itself would have assured Peurbach a place in history as a major contributor to astronomical theory. The work was of especial importance at the time because it showed the limitations of the Ptolemaic system. Peurbach's second work, *Tabulae Eclipsum* (*Ecliptic Tables*), is even more astounding than the first for demonstrating the author's ability to combine theory and mathematics and coordinate these with observation. In the book, which Peurbach probably wrote in 1459 but which was not published until 1514, he rearranged the Alfonsine Tables so as to be able to use their notations to designate the times of the occurrences and the duration of the eclipses of the sun and the moon with comparative accuracy. Also, as in his better known *Planetary Theory*, so in the *Ecliptic Tables* Peurbach adjusted the Ptolemaic notations according to the more exact measurements given by Arab astronomers. Here he followed the Toledan Tables in particular. The result was a series of notations which, because they were much more exact than those of Ptolemy, served to call the *Almagest* into question. In addition when Peurbach, like Ptolemy, coordinated theory with notation and observation, he laid foundations for astronomy as an experimental science. Peurbach climaxed his efforts by producing, along with Regiomontanus, the *Epitome of the Almagest* which both simplified the *Almagest* and supplied it with corrected notations. Very importantly as it turned out, the authors pointed out Ptolemy's erroneous calculation of the distance of the moon from the earth at different points in its orbit.

Thus if Zinner is correct, which seems likely, Peurbach and Regiomontanus had a direct relationship to the study of astronomy at Cracow and at least an indirect influence on Copernicus. That influence was to continue when in 1496, without having completed a degree at Cracow, Copernicus went up to the University of Bologna ostensibly to study law but, as Birkenmajer says, "for the purpose of pushing on with his studies in astronomy".[61] He took with him a copy of the edition of the Alfonsine Tables by Regiomontanus which he had purchased in Cracow about 1493.[62]

In 1492, just four years before Copernicus enrolled, the University of Bologna was the site of the well-publicised dispute between Marsilio Ficino and Alexander Achillini (1463–1512).[63] Ficino, it will be recalled, was the translator of the *Corpus Hermeticum* and of Plato's *Dialogues*. He was the head of the Platonic Academy of Florence which had been founded by Cosimo de Medici as well. As far as astronomy was concerned, Ficino, in good Hermetic fashion, was the champion of heliocentric speculations. In his Hermetically inspired *De Sole* (*The Sun*) printed in Florence in 1493, the year following the debate, and the year Copernicus went up to Bologna, Ficino published his claim that the sun was the heart of the world.[64] He likened it to a king occupying the central position toward which the planets moved and before which they paraded.[65] The sun was the pilot of the heavens and the criterion of divinity for the heavenly bodies. All the bodies turned to it for their direction.[66]

The impact of the meeting between Ficino and Achillini is evident from Achillini's answer to Ficino's challenge. In 1498 Achillini published his *De Orbibus* (*On the Orbits of the Planets*)[67] in order to re-emphasise and re-establish the Aristotelian-Ptolemaic cosmology largely on the basis of Averroës' explanation of Aristotle's *De Caelo*. In particular, and as if to answer Ficino directly, Achillini claimed that it was quite illegitimate to set the sun in the middle or to compare the *heavenly* sphere with the *earthly* one.[68] The idea of heliocentricity, then, rather than being "newly discovered" or even "rediscovered" by Copernicus, was public property and a matter of discussion both before and during Copernicus' years in Italy. The idea was propounded and attacked from philosophical, cultic, and astronomical points of view. The singular importance of the sun had been suggested by the writings of the astronomers Peurbach and Regiomontanus and these in turn set the stage for astronomy from Cracow to Bologna and even Ferrara where Copernicus pursued his academic efforts.

Whether or not Neopythagorean-Hermetic speculation had any influence on Regiomontanus' thoughts with regard to the control of the sun over the movement of the planets cannot be documented. We do know, however, that he had doubts about the limitations of the reigning Aristotelian-Ptolemaic cosmology and, in a letter to Giovanni Bianchini (d. 1466), he expressed his desire for a new system to be worked out on the basis of observation. In that both Domenico Maria Novara (1454–1504), who was Professor of Astrology at Bologna during the time Copernicus was a student there, and Pellegrino Prisciano (b. c.1450), who became Professor of Astrology at Ferrara where Copernicus took his degree in law in 1503, claimed to be students of Regiomontanus, Copernicus was in the stream of the most advanced cosmological speculation of the time.[69]

Whether or not Copernicus knew Prisciano is not documented although there has been a good deal of conjecture as to the reason why he took his degree at Ferrara rather than at Bologna.[70] There is, however, documented evidence that Francesco Patrizzi (1529–97), who in the Preface to his 1597 edition of the *Hermetica,* recommended to Pope Gregory XIV (1535–91) that the Hermetic teachings replace those of Aristotle in the Church, taught the *Hermetica* along with the philosophy of Plato in Ferrara from 1597 onward. At Bologna, Copernicus studied mathematics and astronomy with Novara and he evidently became more of a colleague to him than a student. A. C. Crombie's statement that it was Novara, "a leading Platonist", who taught Copernicus "the desire to conceive of the constitution of the universe in terms of simple mathematical relationships",[71] seems borne out by the record. On March 9, 1497, shortly after he had purchased a copy of Peurbach and Regiomontanus' Epitome of the *Almagest*, Copernicus and Novara together made the first of the relatively few astronomical observations which Copernicus recorded.[72]

The purchase of the book is important because it was in the *Epitome of the Almagest* that Peurbach and Regiomontanus had noted the large discrepancy in respect to the distance of the moon from the earth between the full moon and the first quarter. As a result Ptolemy had provided the moon with a disproportionally large epicycle in relation to the size of its eccentric deferent. In checking out the distances by observation, Novara and Copernicus noted that the earth-moon distance was, at the two phases, all but invariant. They confirmed thereby that Peurbach and Regiomontanus were right and that Ptolemy was wrong.[73] This, along with his knowledge of the heliocentric hypothesis argued for by people like Ficino, whose apology for the heliocentric system was well enough known so that Copernicus would no doubt have been familiar with it, may well have caused him to question the Ptolemaic system as a whole.

Ptolemy's miscalculation of the moon's distance, which Copernicus notes in his *De Revolutionibus*, and even Copernicus' acceptance of the corrections which Peurbach and Regiomontanus made of Ptolemy on the basis of the Alfonsine Tables, did not bring him to admit doubt with regard to Ptolemy's observational notations in general.[74] Although Crombie seems correct in stating that Copernicus took the data for his own system not from Ptolemy's *Almagest* but from Peurbach and Regiomontanus' *Epitome of the Almagest* as well as from Gerard of Cremona's (c.1114–87) Latin translation of the *Almagest*,[75] Copernicus never once mentioned any inaccuracy in Ptolemy's mathematical notations as a reason for wanting to alter the system. On the contrary, as we shall see, he had nothing but compliments for Ptolemy's measurements and he preserved as much of Ptolemy's system as was possible.

More surprising is the fact that even heliocentricity was not Copernicus' concern. In fact, precisely speaking, his system was not heliocentric. Rather, it was centred on the supposed *centre of the earth's orbit*, a mathematical point which Copernicus set adjacent to the sun.[76] With this in mind we can understand, perhaps, the reason that in the dedication to Pope Paul III, with which Copernicus prefaced the *De Revolutionibus*, he placed much more emphasis upon the movement of the earth than upon the necessity of centring the planets on the sun.[77]

One could argue, of course, that Copernicus was more worried about the movement of the earth than about the position of the sun because the idea of a moving earth was antithetical to the major concepts of Aristotelian physics and astronomy.[78] Copernicus had no trouble, however, setting Aristotle aside in this respect. He readily admitted that he knew of the idea of the moving earth from the history of astronomy and he knew that history from the early Pythagoreans to Ptolemy with admirable thoroughness. Philolaus had attempted to show that the earth, along with the sun and moon, orbited a central fire. Heraclides, whom Copernicus referred to as "Pontus", and Ekphantus depicted the earth as rotating on its axis "like a wheel" but without orbital motion ("movement of locomotion").[79]

The history of astronomy also revealed to Copernicus that the heliocentric idea had precedent. Since he knew his history and stressed that he knew it, it does not surprise us to learn that in the first manuscript of the *De Revolutionibus*, he mentions the third-century B.C. heliocentric theory of Aristarchus of Samos. It is somewhat disappointing, however, to note that he deleted any reference to Aristarchus in the copy that went to the publishers. Although Copernicus admitted in the published version of the *De Revolutionibus* that he had found in the writings of

Plutarch "others" who were of the opinion that the earth moved,[80] he expunged from the record the fact that the main "other" (whom Plutarch had in fact mentioned at some length) was Aristarchus whose heliocentric system was exactly that which he represented in the diagram he drew to symbolise his own system. The sun was placed in the centre and was surrounded by the perfectly circular and heliocentric orbits of the seven planets. The moon was set in orbit around the earth and the whole was surrounded by the immobile sphere of the fixed stars. Copernicus' own system in which the planets moved on epicycles attached to deferents, which were themselves eccentrics, was much more complicated, of course.

The passage in the original manuscript of the *De Revolutionibus* which is struck through with black ink so that it was not reproduced in the copy delivered to the printer reads:

> Although we acknowledge that the course of the sun and moon might also be demonstrated on the supposition of the earth being immovable, this agrees less with the other planets. It is likely that for these other reasons Philolaus perceived the mobility of the earth, which also some say was the opinion of Aristarchus of Samos, though not moved by that reasoning which Aristotle mentions and refutes.[81]

It is tempting to think that Plutarch's reference to Aristarchus in his dialogue, *The Face on the Moon*, may have given Copernicus pause. In the dialogue Lucius had been accused of turning the world upside down for saying the moon was a solid body. Asked to elucidate his views, he began by saying:

> Oh, sir, just don't bring suit against us for impiety as Cleanthes thought that the Greeks ought to lay an action for impiety against Aristarchus the Samian on the ground that he was disturbing the hearth of the universe because he sought to save [the] phenomena by assuming that the heaven is at rest while the earth is

revolving along the ecliptic and at the same time is
rotating about its own axis.[82]

However, in that Copernicus seemed much less concerned,
nor need he at the time have been concerned, about being
accused of impiety than of being taken to task by the
Aristotelians, he, or whoever was responsible for deleting
the reference to Aristarchus, may simply have wanted
Copernicus to be known as the author of heliocentrism.[83]

Whatever the reason for the deletion, the passage, along
with Copernicus' "Ode to the Sun" and the circumstantial
evidence from his studies in Italy, would seem to leave
little doubt that he was well aware of a good measure of
speculation about a sun-centred system with its concom-
itant earth movements from both the history of astronomy*
and from Renaissance literature.

Heavenly Harmony

Although the Copernican system is renowned for having
placed the sun in the centre of the universe, the exact
position of the sun was really of secondary importance.
Copernicus' prime concern was another. His main interest
was to fashion a system which would reflect the exact
agreement between circularity and regularity of motion
which was the *sine qua non* of Greek astronomy and was
basic to their theology and rationality as grounded upon
the thought of the Pythagoreans, Plato and Aristotle. In
Copernicus' own time this demand for the unity and
harmony of the heavens had been re-emphasised by Aristotelian Thomism, Neoplatonism, and Hermeticism. It
was celebrated by Dante, accentuated by Cusa, and lauded
by Ficino who, in order to express it, had placed the sun in
the centre of his Hermetically inspired astronomical system. It was because Copernicus found that Ptolemy's
circles did not reflect the unity and harmony of the heavens
in terms of perfect circularity and regularity of motion that
he found the system wanting and set out to replace it.

Thus, Copernicus' primary objection to the Ptolemaic cosmology was neither the inaccuracy of its mathematics nor any error with regard to its notations of the planetary positions. Rather, to repeat, Copernicus took exception to the system because of its *lack of harmony*. Although he had been aware of the inaccuracy of Ptolemy's notations since his student days, in the *Commentariolus* (the full title of which Rosen appropriately translates as "Nicholas Copernicus' Sketch of His Hypothesis for the Heavenly Motions"), he boldly stated that the theories of Ptolemy were consistent with the numerical data. He pointed out, however, that the system lacked symmetry and that this was the reason for his desire to propose his own hypothesis.

Yet the planetary theories of Ptolemy and most other astronomers, although *consistent with the numerical data*, seemed likewise to present no small difficulty. For these theories were not adequate unless certain equants were also conceived; it then appeared that a planet moved with uniform velocity neither on its deferent nor about the centre of its epicycle. Hence a system of this sort seemed *neither sufficiently absolute nor sufficiently pleasing to the mind.*

Having become aware of these defects, I often considered whether there could perhaps be found a more reasonable arrangement of circles, from which every apparent inequality would be derived and in which *everything would move uniformly about its proper centre*, as the rule of absolute motion requires.[84]

In order to re-establish the absoluteness of circularity which was, for Copernicus, essential to his aesthetic judgement of harmony, i.e., that which was "pleasing to the mind", he set out on his quest for "a more reasonable arrangement of circles" which would both explain the "apparent inequalities" of planetary motion and be a system "in which every thing would move uniformly about its proper centre, as the rule of absolute motion requires".

Rheticus captured the intention of his "teacher", Copernicus, in his *Narratio Prima*:

> My teacher saw that only on this theory could all the circles in the universe be satisfactorily made to revolve uniformly and regularly about their own centres, and not about other centres — an essential property of circular motion.[85]

The rule of absolute motion required of Copernicus that he eliminate Ptolemy's equant, the device which, as indicated in our discussion of Ptolemy, was a mathematical point off centre from the geometric centre of a planet's deferent. Ptolemy had used the equant to explain the difference between the centre of regular motion and the geometric centre of the planet's orbit. For Copernicus, however, such a device was against everything he had learned about the harmony of celestial motion and geometry. It was a direct affront to the idea of harmony stressed by the ancient Pythagoreans through Plato and Aristotle to the Renaissance Hermeticists alike. All believed that the heavens reflected the pattern of divine perfection.

Saving the Circles

Having eliminated the equants in order to follow the demand that everything "move uniformly about its proper centre as the rule of absolute motion requires",[86] Copernicus, as he explained in the *Commentariolus*, adopted the pattern of explication Euclid had used in his *Elements of Geometry*. He first set out the seven basic axioms or assumptions on which his system was to be based and then explained them. The assumptions were:

(1) The heavenly bodies do not have a single common centre of motion.
(2) The earth is not at the centre of the universe but only at the centre of the orbit of the moon and of terrestrial gravity.

(3) The sun is the centre of the planetary system and also the centre of the universe.

(4) The earth's distance from the sun is minute compared to the distance to the fixed stars.

(5) The apparent diurnal revolution of the firmament is due to the daily rotation of the earth on its own axis.

(6) The apparent annual rotation of the sun is explained by the fact that the earth, like the other planets, orbits around the sun.

(7) The apparent irregular movements of the planets, their stopping (stations) and moving backward (retrogressions) are due to the planets and the earth orbiting the sun in different periods of time.[87]

Thereafter, as Koyré explains with admirable brevity, Copernicus, in just seven short chapters, set forth the sequence of the celestial spheres, dealt with the earth's triple motion, explained the advantage of referring all motions to the fixed stars, described the mechanism of planetary motion and gave the data for the dimensions of the epicycles and circles.[88] The scheme, of course, was no more than the description of the Aristarchian heliocentric system with the addition of Ptolemy's epicycles so that, as the first axiom prescribed, the heavenly bodies did not have a single centre of motion but each deferent and epicycle had its own centre. Copernicus knew that the multiplicity of centres already represented a compromise when compared to Aristotle's system of homocentric spheres but the compromise was necessary in order to bring the system into closer compliance with observation.

Callippus and Eudoxus, who endeavoured to solve the problem by the use of concentric spheres, were unable to account for all the planetary movements; they had to explain not merely the apparent revolutions of the planets but also the fact that these bodies appear to us sometimes to mount higher in the heavens, sometimes to descend; and this fact is incompatible with the principle of concentricity. Therefore it seemed better to employ eccentrics and epicycles, a system which most scholars finally accepted.[89]

The Copernican innovation, then, was to impose Ptolemy upon Aristarchus.[90] He explained his position by first stating that no one should suppose that he had "gratuitously asserted, with the Pythagoreans, the motion of the earth". He then described the circles and epicycles of the moon and the planets. Thereafter he gave notice that he had reserved mathematics (which he took largely directly from Ptolemy) for the larger work (*De Revolutionibus*) and closed the writing with a paragraph in which he enumerated the circles (deferents and epicycles) which were necessary for his system.[91]

> Then Mercury runs on seven circles in all; Venus on five; the earth on three, and round it the moon on four; finally, Mars, Jupiter, and Saturn on five each. Altogether, therefore, thirty-four circles suffice to explain the entire structure of the universe and the entire ballet of the planets.[92]

One of the best summary descriptions of the system as it was later worked out in the *De Revolutionibus* is given by Rheticus:

> My teacher dispenses with equants for the other planets as well [as also in the case of the moon], by assigning to each of the three superior planets only one epicycle and eccentric; each of these moves uniformly about its own centre, while the planet revolves on the epicycle in equal periods with the eccentric. To Venus and Mercury, however, he assigns an eccentric on an eccentric. . . . These phenomena, besides being ascribed to the planets, can be explained, as my teacher shows, by a regular motion of the spherical earth; that is, by having the sun occupy the centre of the universe, while the earth revolves instead of the sun on the eccentric.[93]

We now know, of course, that Copernicus was extremely generous with himself as far as his count of the circles necessary for his system was concerned. In actuality, if Koestler has counted correctly, Copernicus' system demanded forty-eight different circular movements, eight more than the forty which Peurbach had advanced for the Ptolemaic system. Zinner has counted thirty-eight circles and Koyré at least forty-one.[94] After enumerating the circles Koyré, like Koestler, went on to explain that, from the point of view of the number of circles or spheres involved (Copernicus does not differentiate between them) the system, as seen from a general point of view, was more complicated than that of Ptolemy.[95] It would seem that of all the astronomers who bothered to count, only Kepler, who by the way was extremely *pro-Copernican*, estimated that the number of actual circular movements in the Copernican system was less (ten less) than in the Ptolemaic one.[96]

All things considered, the general consensus is that the Copernican system demanded at least as many circles as the Ptolemaic plan, if not more. From our point of view, Copernicus may have achieved an aesthetic advantage in following Aristarchus and in placing the planets, including the earth, in orbit around the sun. Aesthetics, however, is a matter of choice. If simplicity in terms of numbers has any validity, Copernicus made no gain at all over Ptolemy.

Copernicus' own basic explanation of the circles of the planets around the sun in the *De Revolutionibus* is confusing simply because he referred only to their major orbits at their deferents.

Thus the orbital circle of Mercury will be enclosed within the orbital circle of Venus — which would have to be more than twice as large — and will find adequate room for itself within that amplitude. Therefore if anyone should take this as an occasion to refer Saturn, Jupiter, and Mars also to this same centre, provided he understands the magnitude of those orbital circles to be such as to comprehend and encircle the Earth remaining within them, he would not be in error, as the table of ratios of their movements makes clear. For it is manifest that the planets are always nearer the Earth at the time of their evening rising, i.e., when they are opposite to the Sun and the Earth is in the middle between them and the Sun. But they are farthest away from the Earth at the time of their evening setting, i.e., when they are occulted in the neighbourhood of the Sun, namely, when we have the sun between them and the Earth. All that shows clearly enough that their centre is more directly related to the Sun and is the same as that to which Venus and Mercury refer their revolutions.[97]

Thus, Copernicus followed the lead of Aristarchus who had improved on Heraclides' partial heliocentric system in which only Venus and Mercury circled the sun by developing the first complete "heliocentric" system of which we are aware. Copernicus, in turn, improved on Aristarchus by adding Ptolemy's epicycles and eccentrics. Although the result was at least as complicated as the Ptolemaic system, it did have two definite advantages. The first was that Copernicus displayed the main movements of the planets with greater simplicity and harmony than Ptolemy. The second was that the Copernican system allowed for a more accurate measurement of the distance of planetary orbits from one another than the Ptolemaic one.[98] When, however, Copernicus added the epicycles there were at least as many circles involved. Even more serious, because Copernicus refused to use equants — the feature of the Ptolemaic theory which robbed it of its unity and harmony — his system was actually *less accurate*, i.e., it described the actual movements of the planetary system with less precision than the Ptolemaic plan. To make matters worse, Copernicus attempted to compensate for eliminating the equants by reintroducing Ptolemy's eccentrics. This both caused the planets to wobble in their orbits and made the orbit of Mars, for instance, less circular than that which Ptolemy had described.[99]

Kuhn's explanation is that in the Ptolemaic system, where regular motion was centred on an equant, the movement of the heavenly bodies, if calculated from the exact geometric centre of their orbits, would move against their orbits at different rates and "wobble". However, if in the Copernican system motion were likewise calculated from the orbital centres, the eccentrics which Copernicus used would cause the epicycles and hence the planets which were supposedly attached to them to wobble in their orbits as well. It would seem, therefore, that Kuhn is quite right when he says, "It is hard to imagine how Copernicus might have considered this aspect of Ptolemaic astronomy monstrous."[100]

Although it is difficult to believe, the facts would seem to indicate that, although Copernicus eliminated the equant which explained irregular motion because he found motion of that kind quite unacceptable, he reintroduced that same irregular motion with the adoption of the eccentrics although in his explanation of his system he did not admit having done so. Hence, instead of improving upon Ptolemy, his system displayed the same kind of irregularity that he found objectionable in the Ptolemaic plan, and on the basis of which he decided to reform the system in the first place. To make matters worse, the orbit of Mars actually bulged more at the quadrants of periodic time in the Copernican system than they did in the Ptolemaic[101] — an illustration of the inaccuracy which resulted from Copernicus' attempt to press the heavens into a geometry which would reflect the harmony of circularity and regularity of motion. Thus, in his attempt to achieve harmony, Copernicus not only sacrificed accuracy but, in the end, he lost out on the harmony as well.

Much as Copernicus advocated *saving the appearances*, therefore, there is little doubt that his primary interest was in *saving the circles*. The fact that he reintroduced the eccentrics in what appears to be an attempt to eliminate a number of epicycles in his original scheme (an eccentric deferent plus one epicycle would equal the variation of motion of a circular deferent and two epicycles) meant that he had not lost sight of the criterion of simplicity nor had he given up his attempt to represent reality as closely as his "circles" would allow. He apparently considered the eccentrics a lesser evil than multiple epicycles. However, in adopting them in the system as worked out in the *De Revolutionibus* he lost the aesthetic advantage, which according to both the *Commentariolus* and the preface to the *De Revolutionibus* had been the impetus for the whole effort.

As described in the *Commentariolus* the system was "concentrobiepicyclic", i.e., a system of *concentric* deferents each with two or more epicycles attached in tandem to their perimeters.[102] The planets rode on the perimeter of the outer edge of an outer epicycle, the inner centre of which was carried along on the edge of the first epicycle. The centre of the first epicycle in turn was carried around by the edge of the deferent whose centre was coincident with the centre of the universe.[103] In the *De Revolutionibus*, however, the system became "eccentrepicyclic". The outer epicycle was eliminated and in order to compensate for the movement it would have imparted to the planet, the centre of the deferent was moved off the centre of the universe so that the deferent became an eccentric in relationship to the centre of the planet's movement. Thus, whereas in the first system Copernicus attempted to maintain the concentricity of all motions around their own centres, in his more developed system he was concerned only for the uniformity of the motion of the planet around the centre of its orbit which was coincident with the centre of the universe even if the motion of individual deferents was eccentric to that centre. To repeat, although Copernicus objected to the Ptolemaic system because "it appeared that a planet moved with uniform velocity neither on its deferent nor about the centre of its epicycle" and conceived his own theory so that "everything would move uniformly about its own proper centre", he lost the "aesthetic advantage" which was the *raison d'être* of the whole effort by reinserting the eccentrics.[104]

It was just because Ptolemy realised that eccentrics did

not allow for uniform motion around the proper centres of the circle involved that he invented the equant, that mathematical point off centre from the proper centre of the circle from which uniform motion was to be observed. Copernicus eliminated the equant but reinstated the eccentric which was as responsible for the non-uniformity of motion in his system as it was in the Ptolemaic one. He then developed his system of circles in accordance with the data of the corrected but still inaccurate Alfonsine Tables and made observations which assured him that the heavenly movements fit his geometric patterns. Hence, in contrast to Einstein who, as T. F. Torrance has pointed out, insisted that "science is an attempt to make the chaotic diversity of sense-experience correspond to a logically uniform system of thought"[105], for Copernicus the "logically uniform system of thought" predetermined his "sense experience" or at least his geometric representation of it.

In modern epistemology we have become aware that all our observations of reality are "theory laden", i.e., we see things with our minds. Thus, we look for things we believe to be there and within "acceptable" parameters are able to "see" the things we look for. In this event, it should not surprise us that Copernicus was convinced that his doctrine, which described the movements of the planets on paper, was a proper representation of the heavenly movements. However, in view of the fact that he knew that the Alfonsine Tables, on the basis of which he calculated his measurements, were inaccurate and that he must have been aware that the eccentrics of his system ruined its symmetry, we may now understand better the reason why he was reluctant to release his work for publication. Although he finally offered it as an orderly account of the world which has "a wonderful commensurability" and "a sure bond of harmony for the movement and magnitude of the orbital circles such as cannot be found in any other way",[106] there can be little question that he must have remained dissatisfied with the system until the last.

We judge Copernicus too harshly if we think of him as

a modern astronomer. He was, rather, the last of the Pythagoreans and was less concerned about the "wobble" of the planets, exact measurements, and the relationship between geometry and observation, than he was about the inter-harmony of the geometry of circles by which the heavens must at all costs be represented. Holding on to as much of Aristotle as possible, Copernicus adjusted his divinely given circles to observation only as far as the circularity and uniformity of the system would allow.[107] Thus, in one sense, Copernicus was even more conservative than Ptolemy. In line with the Renaissance re-emphasis on unity and harmony, he wished to reinstitute the harmony of geometry and motion along with the concentricity of the main orbits of the planets which Ptolemy, in the light of observation, had long since discarded.

To repeat, although Copernicus effectively turned the Ptolemaic world inside out and made minor changes in Ptolemy's description of the motion of the moon, by and large he had no quarrel with Ptolemy's observations or measurements. In his *Letter against Werner*[108] he praised Ptolemy, saying that "since Ptolemy based his tables on fresh observations of his own, it is incredible that the tables should contain any sensible error or any departure from the observations that would make the tables inconsistent with the principles on which they rest".[109] He went on to castigate anyone who, in trying to determine the motion of the celestial spheres, would disregard the observation of the ancient astronomers.

We must follow in their footsteps and hold fast to their observations, bequeathed to us like an inheritance. And if anyone on the contrary thinks that the ancients are untrustworthy in this regard, surely the gates of this art are closed to him. Lying before the entrance, he will dream the dreams of the disordered about the motion of the eighth sphere and will receive his deserts for supposing that he must support his own hallucination by defaming the ancients.[110]

In his *Narratio Prima*, Rheticus would seem to agree completely with his "teacher". After asserting that Copernicus fully intended to imitate Ptolemy, he also assured his readers that Ptolemy could well be followed.[111]

> For Ptolemy's tireless diligence in calculating, his almost superhuman accuracy in observing, his truly divine procedure in examining and investigating all the motions and appearances, and finally his completely consistent method of statement and proof cannot be sufficiently admired and praised by anyone to whom Urania is gracious.[112]

In sum, Copernicus set out his system with the same purpose as that of the Pythagoreans, Plato, and Aristotle, "to show how the uniformity of motions can be saved in a systematic way".[113] His system of circles was not a result of observations, of which he made comparatively few. Rather it was the result of a genial geometrical arrangement which followed Ptolemy as far as possible, but which attempted to rearrange the system in order to harmonise the movements of the heavens so that "the first principles of the regularity of motion" could be saved.[114]

The Relationship of Theory to Reality

Devoted as Copernicus was to developing a system which would reinstate the classical concept of harmony and "save the circles", he clearly had no intention of abstracting his geometry from the actual motions of the heavens as such. He was, in fact, deeply critical of schemes which did not "fully correspond to the phenomena".[115] Osiander, on the other hand, who saw the *De Revolutionibus* through the press, was of quite the opposite opinion. For him, as he expressed it in the anonymous preface with which he supplied Copernicus' work, "It is not necessary that these hypotheses be true, or even probable but it is enough if they provide a calculus which fits the observations".[116] The comparison of Copernicus, who was supported by

Rheticus, with Osiander, whose ideas of the relationship between theory and reality can be traced back to Aristotle, presents us with a classic contrast in the way theory and reality are thought to be related.

Although there was a fundamental disagreement between Osiander and Copernicus as far as their understanding of the relationship between theory and reality is concerned, there can be no doubt that Osiander added the "Preface" to the *De Revolutionibus* as a gesture of good will. As he explained in letters to both Copernicus and Rheticus, letters which we know about by way of Kepler, his intent was "to appease the Peripatetics [Aristotelians] and theologians whose contradictions you fear".[117]

From the correspondence we can deduce that, for Osiander, truth was a matter of revelation as articulated in the articles of faith. Scientific theory, on the other hand, was simply a symbolic representation of reality. According to Kepler, Osiander in his letter to Copernicus dated April 20, 1541 treated Ptolemy's theory of eccentrics and epicycles as "hypothesis" in exactly the same way he was to treat Copernicus' theory in the "Preface" to the *De Revolutionibus*.

> With regard to hypotheses, I have always thought that, rather than being articles of faith [*articulos fidei*], they are only the basis of calculation, so that it makes no difference if they are false provided they present the phenomena exactly.[118]

Again, according to Kepler, Osiander wrote Rheticus on the same day and repeated the same message in slightly different words:

> The Peripatetics [Aristotelians] and theologians will easily be appeased if they are told that a variety of hypotheses are able to explain the same apparent motions and that those which have been published are really certain but that they calculate most appropriately the apparent composite motions.[119]

Thus it is obvious that Osiander's policy of appeasement was not only motivated by expediency, but coincided with his own judgement of "scientific" hypotheses in general whether they were those of Ptolemy or those of Copernicus. In Aristotelian terms both Ptolemy and Copernicus were, according to Osiander, "mathematicians" rather than "physical astronomers". Aristotle differentiated between the physical astronomer and the mathematician on the basis of the relationships between the lines and figures they used to reflect reality and reality itself.[120] For Aristotle, whereas the physical astronomer attempts to represent reality with his drawings and schemes, the mathematician is not concerned with these concepts *qua* boundaries of natural bodies. Rather, "he [the mathematician] abstracts them from physical conditions; for they are capable of being considered in the mind in separation from the motions of the bodies to which they pertain".[121] Further, a point of considerable importance for Aristotle as for Osiander, was that "such abstraction does not affect the validity of the reasoning or lead to any false conclusions".[122] According to Osiander, Copernicus was doing mathematics as indeed he was. Copernicus, however, attempted to use mathematics as the language of physics.

Rheticus, who knew Aristotle's distinction between the mathematician and the physicist, also knew of the place and importance of hypotheses.[123] He was aware that "the results to which the observations and the evidence of heaven itself lead us again and again must be accepted".[124] In other words, theory must be corrected by observation. He also recognised, however, that hypotheses were not simple abstractions from the reality observed.

> Propositions assumed without proof, if once they are perceived to be in agreement with the phenomena, cannot be established without some method and reflection; and the procedure for apprehending them is hard to explain, since in general, of first principles, there naturally is either no cause or one difficult to set forth.[125]

Thus, as Torrance points out, the formulation of scientific theory is indeed troublesome.

> It may take very intricate and complicated processes of thought to arrive at it, but the elemental forms reached will be minimal and basic and will have the effect of illuminating a great variety of otherwise incomprehensible facts, and will thus represent a vast simplification of our knowledge over a wide area.[126]

According to Rheticus, Copernicus conceived his hypothesis in *relation to* but not *from* the data which were later used to verify them. Their appropriateness depended on their ability to conform to the truth of past observations, on the one hand, and to serve as the basis for astronomical predictions, on the other.[127] Such hypotheses, then, although they were not simply abstracted from the observational data, were tested by ascertaining their conformity with observations both past and future. So far so good, but like all hypothetical constructs, whether valid or invalid, the Copernican hypotheses tended to force the data into their own prescription. Copernicus intended his system to be "realistic", so realistic, in fact that, as we have pointed out, according to Rheticus' explanation in his *Narratio Prima* "the hypothesis of my teacher agrees so well with the phenomena that they can be mutually interchanged, like a good definition and the thing defined".[128]

Rheticus then went on to contrast Copernicus' "realistic theory" with Averroës' whose judgement of Ptolemy followed Aristotle's definition of a "mathematician". Accordingly, for Averroës, "The Ptolemaic astronomy is nothing so far as existence is concerned; but it is convenient for computing the non-existent."[129] Rheticus, of course, was of a quite contrary opinion. He was, however, far too astute to think that the Copernican system would be readily accepted. He thought it too sophisticated for the "untutored". It was to be expected that the ones whom the Greeks called "'those who do not know theory, music, philosophy and geometry'" would object to Copernicus' system; and he advised that their shouting should "be ignored".[130] The fact that Copernicus himself asked Pope Paul III to disregard objections to his theory which might come from those who were "ignorant of mathematics" indicates that he too was aware that objections would most likely be raised to his system.[131] There is little doubt, however, that he considered the theory to be "true". He was convinced that its geometry reflected the regularity and circularity of the heavens. He was also certain that his mathematics, which was based upon Ptolemy or, to be more precise, which was based upon the Ptolemaic notations as corrected by Peurbach and Regiomontanus, reflected reality closely enough at least for his system of circles to be accepted as accurate.

Copernicus, after all, was primarily a mathematician. Thus, rather than depend on observations of his own, Copernicus, as Taliaferro has indicated, simply used Ptolemy's values [as corrected] and transposed them according to his own scheme. To take the case of the outer planets, the movement of the epicycles which centre on the deferent in Ptolemy's system corresponds to the revolutions of the planets about the sun in his own. The radius of the deferent then corresponds to the planet's mean distance from the sun. Also, with regard to the periodic time and radius, the orbit of the epicycle's centre on the deferent about the earth in Ptolemy's system was exactly that of the planet about the sun in Copernicus' scheme (if the zodiacal anomalies are ignored, which they were). In other words, Copernicus combined the epicycle and the eccentric with reference to the mean sun so that they were exactly equivalent to Ptolemy's eccentric and equant with respect to the earth.[132]

Copernicus, to his own satisfaction or at least according to his intention, summed up the whole history of astronomy and re-established the Pythagorean demand for harmony between geometry and motion which Ptolemy had broken with his equants. It was a truly magnificent feat of mathematical genius. Unfortunately, because the eccentrics had to be maintained for the sake of simplicity, the planetary orbits remained irregular.[133] In the case of Mars at least, that irregularity was compounded by the fact that the orbit bulged more at the quadrants of its periodic time than it did in the Ptolemaic model.[134]

The Copernican Non-Revolution

To repeat, Copernicus sacrificed accuracy for the sake of desired elegance, an elegance that could not be substantiated either by observation or by the mathematics involved. The demand for that elegance, it would seem, was elicited by a deep sense of the "rightness" of the Neoplatonic-Neopythagorean understanding of unity and harmony along with the Hermetically inspired placement of the sun in the middle of the world from where it could express its primacy over the earth and the other planets and indeed over the whole cosmos as then understood. The scheme, in other words, was brought about in the first instance not on the basis of observational or mathematical data but through re-interpreting the symbols and numbers by which the universe was represented.[135] Since, however, in Copernican heliocentricity, genial as we know the system to have been, the symbolisation had to follow the demand of harmony both in terms of the coincidence of the centres of circularity and regular motion and in terms of a coincidence between theory and actuality, success was ruled out simply because the heavenly "circles" were not really circular. Therefore, any scheme which was based on circularity was *ipso facto* bound to fail both in terms of the inner harmony of the system and in terms of the accuracy of its representation. Thus, elegant as it attempted to be or really because it attempted to reflect an elegance to which the heavens did not conform, the system was "scientifically" untenable. As Kuhn puts it, it was simply too inaccurate to work.[136]

Little wonder, then, that the system had scant appeal. Copernicus' arguments had no appeal to laypersons who, even if they understood them, "were unwilling to substitute minor celestial harmonies for major terrestrial discord".[137] In this sense, though, without excusing the mendacity of the whole episode, we can understand Cardinal Bellarmine, who in 1616 upbraided Galileo for having accepted the Copernican position as *truth*. Bellarmine represented the mediaeval Church's Aristotelian understanding in respect to the centrality and immobility of the earth. He noted that the Copernican system disagreed with biblical evidence,[138] and since it was without proof, he could quite properly insist that Galileo teach the heliocentric theory as *an hypothesis* only and not *as fact*.[139]

More importantly, as far as science is concerned, Copernicus' argument "did not necessarily appeal to astronomers".[140] A prime example was Tycho Brahe who, along with Hipparchus and Ptolemy, must be reckoned as one of the most persistent and accurate of astronomical observers of all time. Tycho's notations were to become the basis for Kepler's discovery of the elliptical orbits of the planets, a discovery which eventually saved the heliocentric system. He refused, however, to adopt the Copernican principle of an orbiting earth as a *sine qua non* of the system simply because at the time there was no way of determining any parallactic motion in the observation of the fixed stars as the earth supposedly changed positions in its relations to them.

It was not until 1838, some three centuries after the publication of the *De Revolutionibus*, that telescopes became accurate enough to observe any change of angle between the earth and the fixed stars as the earth moved from one extreme of its orbit to the other.[141] Hence Tycho found himself in the same position as those who had rejected Aristarchus' heliocentric theory some seventeen hundred years previously and who had argued that the non-existence of an observable "parallactic motion" implied that the universe is many, many times larger than it was thought to be. Interestingly enough, the argument which Copernicus put forward to explain the enormous distance necessary between the earth's orbit and the fixed stars, i.e., the size of the universe, so that the parallax need not have been observable, came right out of Aristarchus;

and it was as unconvincing in the sixteenth century A.D. as it was in the third century B.C.[142]

Copernicus explained the immensity of the heavens in relation to the earth by saying, "In the judgement of sense perception the earth is to the heavens as a point to a body and as a finite to an infinite magnitude".[143] Since "points", "finite", and "infinite" are of no measurable quantity, the statement meant nothing except that the distance to the fixed stars was very great indeed and that one should not expect to measure any differentiation in angle in observing them, no matter where the earth was located in its orbit beneath them. Copernicus attempted to elucidate the immensity with another proposition which, although ill-ustrative, was convincing only if one believed his theory in the first place. He explained that the magnitude of the world was such that, great as the distance is between the sun and the earth or between the sun and any other planetary sphere, "this distance as compared with the sphere of the fixed stars, is imperceptible".[144]

The actual distance from the earth of the celestial sphere which was needed for the Copernican system was more than 1,500,000 earth radii. When this figure is compared to the 20,110 earth radii that had been given by Alfargani and was the then currently accepted measurement, it is not difficult to understand the scepticism with which astron-omers greeted the Copernican theory. The Copernican system demanded that the universe be more than seventy-five times as large as even the most generous estimates of the time.[145] Even among astronomers, then, the Copernican system, like the original heliocentric theory of Aristarchus, seemed "too hare-brained" to be taken seri-ously, as Koyré has put it.[146]

As a possible alternative Tycho Brahe, who was the best astronomer of the day and whose notations in the hands of Kepler saved the Copernican system from the fate of joining that of Aristarchus on the junk heap of brilliant but useless theories, adopted an expanded partial heliocentric theory of the type first proposed by Heraclides of Pontus. Whereas Heraclides, it will be remembered, had Mercury and Venus orbiting the sun and the sun with the two planets orbiting the earth, Tycho put all the planets except the moon in circular orbits around the sun. He then put the sun trailing the planets in orbit about the stationary earth and at a great enough distance so that the orbit even of the outermost Saturn would not intercept that of the moon. The system had all the advantages of the Copernican system without the tremendous disadvantages — physical, practical, and theological — of the moving earth.[147]

In the end, then, even the best astronomers found the Copernican theory unconvincing. In addition, of course, as we have indicated, the Copernican harmonies did not really satisfy the two primary criteria of a valid scientific theory, *simplicity* and *accuracy*. Rheticus, like Copernicus himself, saw the system as being simpler than that of Ptolemy. Hence, he quoted the Greek physician Galen's version of "Ockham's razor", " 'Nature does nothing without purpose' ".[148] He went on to ask, "Should we not attribute to God, the Creator of nature, that skill which we observe in the common makers of clocks? For they carefully avoid inserting in the mechanism any superfluous wheel."[149] As we have seen, however, so far as the number of circles was concerned, the Copernican system offered no obvious advantage over the Ptolemaic one.

Kuhn puts the matter well, saying that the Copernican arguments "could and did appeal primarily to that limited and perhaps irrational subgroup of mathematical astronomers whose Neoplatonic ear for mathematical harmonies could not be obstructed by page after page of complex mathematics leading finally to numerical predictions scarcely better than those they had known before".[150] Zinner makes the same point. After indicating that the Alphonsine Tables, which Peurbach and Regiomontus used in thier summary of the Ptolemaic system and on which Copernicus had depended, were not known to be inaccurate by astronomers in general including Copernicus, he asks, "Why should they [the astronomers] change their views in order to describe the heavenly processes less adequately than heretofore?"[151]

Thus, although the Copernican theory was judged to be wrong according to science and common sense, it appealed to those whose scientific imagination and common sense had been *distorted* to believe that which by all counts was irrational. In time, however, some of the "facts" which these distorted minds perceived were proven to be true. Eventually the seven basic axioms which Copernicus set out in his *Commentariolus* all proved to be more or less valid in respect of the planets, except the first: "The heavenly bodies do not have a single common centre of motion", by which Copernicus justified his use of epicycles.[152] Strictly speaking the statement is true even for Kepler's system of eliptical orbits since eliptical orbits do not have a centre as such, but have dual foci. However, Copernicus' point was that the epicycles which centred on the circumference of the deferents had different centres from the deferents themselves. The deferents were roughly centred on the sun. I say "roughly centred on the sun" because as Copernicus finally developed the system in the *De Revolutionibus*, the only way he could achieve the semblance of the *circular harmony* he desired was to locate the common centre of the deferents of the planets on a point which marked the supposed centre of the earth's orbit. This was located somewhat off the side of the sun itself. Hence in a literal sense, Copernicus' third axiom: "The sun is the centre of the planetary system and also the centre of the universe", was negated.

The above investigation of the evidence would seem to suggest that the question of whether or not and to what extent Copernicus was swayed by the Neoplatonic-Neopythagorean-Hermetic literature of his day to revive Aristarchan heliocentricity and put the sun in the centre of the world, must finally be given a somewhat ambiguous answer. There is no doubt that he was aware of the Hermetic literature which celebrated the centrality of the sun and there is no reason to believe that either his mathematics or his observation would necessarily have persuaded him to adopt the heliocentric model of the universe. At the same time he never succumbed to Hermeticism as such. Copernicus' own ode to the sun in which he repeated the well-known Hermetic epithets in reference to it — "the lantern", "the mind", "the pilot of the world", "the visible god", "resting on a kingly throne" from where it "governs the stars which wheel around" — sound as if he, like Ficino, could well have placed the sun in the middle of the world for religious and philosophical reasons rather than for astronomical ones. As we have seen, for Ficino, the sun in the centre of the world was "the universal generator", "nourisher", and "mover", "the very signification of God".[153]

Nevertheless, in contrast to Rheticus, without whose assistance the Copernican "nocturnal study"[154] would probably never have seen the light of the sun, and in contrast to Kepler without whom the theory would probably have been forgotten, Copernicus gave no evidence of being a Hermeticist. Although his imagination and his search for harmony, like that of his teacher Novara at Bologna, may very well have been stimulated by Neoplatonic, Neopythagorean Hermetic conceptualities, his arrangements of the planets and his explanation of their relationships were purely mathematical. Thus, while there is evidence for Koyré's statement, referred to above, that Copernicus adored the sun and for his contention that Copernicus' geometrising of nature was probably inspired by Nicolas of Cusa,[155] it is also true, as Butterfield has pointed out, that Copernicus was extremely conservative. Butterfield, it seems, is quite wrong in applauding the Copernican system for its evident simplicity. He is quite right, however, in showing that Copernicus went back to Aristotle.[156] Copernicus as a true Renaissance person thus combined the interest in unity and harmony with the search for truth in antiquity. Although it is not known why he adopted the heliocentric model, once having adopted it he bent his astronomy to fit it and refused to give it up in spite of the fact that he must have realised its inadequacies. If so his reason for adopting the heliocentric system was beyond reason. It lay within the realm of presupposition, the presupposition of the elegance of heliocentricity and circularity to which his reason was persuaded to comply.

The Collapse of Circularity

So far as Aristotle was concerned, the heavenly bodies were "simple" rather than complex. There were also "spherical". The "natural movement" of "simple" as well as spherical bodies was "circular" in contradistinction to "rectilinear". Thus following Aristotle, Copernicus wrote that the movement of a "simple" (heavenly) body was "none other than circular which remains entirely in itself as though at rest".[157] It was because Copernicus presupposed that the heavenly orbits were necessarily circular that he saw a "wonderful commensurability" and a "sure bond of harmony" between the movement of the planets and the magnitude of the orbital circles".[158] Copernicus was so convinced of the "commensurability" between the form of the heavenly spheres, the regularity of their motion and the pattern of their orbits, that he held to the supposed heavenly harmonies in spite of the fact that even his own system was inharmonious. This "commensurability" had been espoused by astronomers from the early Pythagoreans to Ptolemy. In the late Middle Ages and the Renaissance it was re-emphasised in Hermeticism and Aristotelian-inspired Thomistic theology. Dante, Nicholas of Cusa, and Copernicus followed in train. The fact that Copernicus' presuppositions both prevented him from taking the inharmonious relationships of his system seriously and compelled him to see commensurability where none existed prevented him also from discovering the irregularity of planetary motion. This in turn prevented him from bringing about the "Copernican revolution" for which he is given credit.[159]

We usually think of the Copernican system as being heliocentric because he said it was. As we have seen, however, Copernicus responded to the classical and Renaissance insistence on regularity and harmony with a system of geometrical elegance so uncompromisingly that, in spite of what he had to say about the sun in the centre of the world ("in the centre of all rests the sun"), he did not actually put it at the centre.[160] Rather, he centred his universe on a point which represented the "centre" of the earth's orbit. To complicate the matter still further, the mathematics involved demanded that the point, which represented the centre of the earth's orbit and on which the orbits of the other planets were centred as well, rotate in a circle of its own around a second mathematical point.[161] Finally the second mathematical point orbited in a circle round the sun.[162]

It may be somewhat ironic to realise that Copernicus' rotating mathematical point on which he centred the orbits of the planets resembled nothing so much as Ptolemy's rotating equant of the orbit of Mercury to which Copernicus had made vehement objection. Thus, Copernicus replaced Ptolemy's multiple equants with a single orbiting equant of his own. It was this "equant" which he supposed was the very centre of his system, the centre of both geometry and motion. The fact that this equant rotated around another mathematical point which in turn rotated around the sun so complicated things that one would have thought the complexity would have made him call the whole system into question.[163] However, the rotating point that allowed his system to follow a concentricity of pattern in approximate harmony with the regularity of motion apparently persuaded him to overlook even the strict demands of the harmony he desired his system to display. Since, according to his own measurements, the central rotating point moved in perfect circularity and with regular motion, the all-important circularity, but it alone, was maintained and this was apparently quite enough to allow him to think of his system as a valid representation of the universe.

We now know that Copernicus' "central equant" was not the centre of either geometry or regular motion. However, the fact that Copernicus thought it was inspired him to develop his system and to hold on to it after he had developed it. Even though his conception of the universe was false and in spite of the fact that by and large it was rejected in his own time, it reflected reality well enough to be fruitful. When Kepler squashed the circles of Copernicus' primary deferents (the circles which described the orbits of the planets about the sun and that of the moon about the earth) into ellipses, the heliocentric system proved to be correct. To express it more accurately, the helio-focused system of Kepler replaced the "equanto-centric system" of Copernicus. Nevertheless, by distorting history, we credit Copernicus for having developed heliocentricity.

By placing the planets in elliptical orbits around the sun with the sun as the main focus of the ellipses, Kepler did away with the system of multiple circles presupposed by Copernicus' first axiom, "The heavenly bodies do not have a simple common centre of motion". He retained the sense of the other six: (2) the earth is a planet and the (approximate) centre of the moon's orbit; (3) the sun is the "centre" or at least the central focus of the planetary system; (4) the universe is immense compared to the earth–sun distance; (5) the daily apparent revolution of the stars is due to the rotation of the earth on its axis; (6) the apparent annual rotation of the sun [through the ecliptic] is due to the earth's rotation about the sun; and (7) the apparent irregular movements of the planets are due to the different planets and the earth orbiting the sun with individual periodicities.

In general these were nothing more nor less than the axioms which undergirded the heliocentric system of Aristarchus of Samos. Copernicus' rediscovery of them, even though for the sake of accuracy he compromised their simplicity with his first axiom (that announcing the epicycles), brought them back to consciousness and allowed them to become the basis for further experimentation and eventually to become the foundation of modern astronomy.

In the end, then, we cannot agree with Rosen who said that Galileo and Kepler "preserved the solid underpinnings of the *Revolutions*, discarded its extraneous trimmings and added the new wings which completed the structure of Copernican cosmology".[164] It would be more accurate to say that Kepler discarded the heart of Copernicanism (his harmony between uniform motion and circularity), trimmed the system back to its Aristarchan foundation, squashed Aristarchus' circles into ellipses, and founded the first workable heliocentric or actually "heliofocused" universe.

The Use of Hypothesis

The Copernican theory represents an excellent example of what Einstein was talking about when he referred to physical concepts as being "free creations" of the human mind.[165] Such hypotheses may or may not later prove useful in the development of science but their original inception is the result of what Michael Polanyi referred to as a "heuristic leap".[166] Hypotheses arise in a leap of faith based upon a conviction that may or may not have its impetus in the hitherto observed data of science. They result in a theory that, more often than not, is not verifiable under circumstances contemporary with it. If the theory is worthwhile it will be fruitful in generating the kind of interest and experiments that will prove its worth. In the process of proof, those aspects of the theory which reflect reality, e.g., in Copernicus' case the centrality of the sun and the movements of the planets about it, will be retained but other aspects of the theory itself may be either forgotten or changed quite beyond recognition. However, in that the original theory was the impetus on which the evidence for "the proof" was based, its inadequacies will often be ignored and the whole theory will be mistakenly remembered as having been *true*.

Comparison with Kepler may help elucidate this matter. Kepler, of course, was even less of an observational astronomer than Copernicus. He, however, was adamant in basing his calculations on the observations of Tycho Brahe, who night after night for some twenty years had noted the positions of the stars from his observatory,

Uraniburg. When, in 1599, Tycho was invited by Emperor Rudolph II in Prague to become his court astronomer, he took his notations with him. A year later Tycho invited Kepler to join him, and when Tycho died in 1601 Kepler was appointed Imperial Mathematician. He eventually gained access to Tycho's extremely accurate observational data.

Try as he might to follow his own Neopythagorean-Hermetic presuppositions and force the rotations of the planets into circular orbits, Kepler found that the orbit of Mars which, as we have seen in the Copernican system, bulged appreciably at the quadrants of its periodic time, resisted his subtlest mathematical manipulations. It deviated from the circular by a mere eight minutes of an arc (equal to just one-fourth of the diameter of the moon as seen at its mean distance from the earth) but it deviated. In contrast to Copernicus, however, Kepler, who believed in harmony at least as much as Copernicus, was not wedded to the Aristotelian circles. Therefore, rather than continuing to "save the appearances" by creating another epicycle for Mars or by increasing the eccentricity of the deferent which would simply have extended the Copernican universe of circles on circles, he allowed the heavenly patterns to break free from the confinement imposed upon them by the presupposed circles and followed the data of observation. By showing that the notations which defined the orbit of Mars described a simple ellipse, he revolutionised astronomy.

The process of discovery was extremely painstaking. In 1604, just three years after Tycho's death and after trying hundreds of possible geometric configurations, Kepler made his discovery and accounted for it in the first of his three laws of planetary motion: Mars followed an ellipse rather than a circle and the sun was not located at midpoint in the orbit but was situated slightly nearer one end than the other.[167] The fact that the original term "ellipse" (Greek *elleipsis*) comes from the verb *elleipein* meaning "to fall short", "to be imperfect", or "to be defective", may help us understand why, from the early Pythagoreans to

Copernicus, such a figure for heavenly motion was considered monstrous. To be so persuaded was to shut one's eyes to the possibility of such an abrogation of heavenly perfection, and the only alternative was to ignore observational deviations from the circular and treat those irregularities as *apparent* rather than *real*.

In his second law defining the velocity of the planets, Kepler showed that the *regular* motion of the planets was calculated not in relation to the linear movement of the planet but in relation to the area enclosed by its orbit.[168] Rather than have each planet describing equal arcs in equal times (the kind of motion which could supposedly be calculated from Ptolemy's equants, for instance, and according to which Copernicus had defined "regular motion"), Kepler demonstrated that an imaginary line (a vector) drawn from any particular planet to the sun would sweep over equal areas in equal times. This meant that the nearer the planet was to the sun in its elliptical orbit, the greater was its velocity. The concept of uniform or regular motion in the Greek and Copernican sense was seen to be no more than a geometrical construct that had no basis in reality. The Greeks and, following them, Copernicus had maintained this "regular motion" in spite of contradictory observational evidence because it was part and parcel of the theological and philosophical conceptuality which attempted to project the simplicity and rationality "of God" upon the movement of the heavens.

Kepler's third law, which is ancillary to the interest of our present discussion, compared the periodicities of the planets and their distances from the sun. The ratio of the squares of the orbital periods of any particular planet was defined as equal to the cube of the mean distance of the planet from the sun.

Thus, Kepler saved the "heliocentric" theory by destroying the Copernican demand for circles and the harmony of pattern and motion on which it was based. In doing so, however, he established a kind of harmony of which the ancient astronomers and Copernicus could only dream. This harmony was not of geometry and motion as designated by preconceived patterns but a harmony which, when translated into mathematics, showed nature to have an order of its own. That order could be penetrated only by ignoring preconceived theological and philo- sophical misconceptions and by moving below the then obvious aspects of phenomena on the strength of subtle clues given by the phenomena themselves. Ironically enough, Kepler's search for harmony came from the same Renaissance-Neopythagorean-Hermetic influences with which Copernicus, too, was familiar. Kepler, who allowed his sense of harmony to be reformed by observation, followed his mathematics and revolutionised astronomy. Copernicus, whose ideas of harmony circumscribed his data, was fated to continue to propagate the ancient, erroneous Aristotelian-Ptolemaic system of complicated circles.[169]

Thus, to repeat, Kepler, whose Neopythagorean- Hermetic ideas demanded that the sun be the centre, proved that the sun-centred system of Copernicus was "true" by destroying its basic tenet, the concentricity of the geometry of planetary motion and the regular motion of the planets in terms of which "harmony" was defined. Only when Kepler showed that the god-like circles were ellipses, i.e., that the orbits of the planets were "defective", was the "Copernican system" saved. In Greek terms, the actual orbits of the planets "fell short" of circularity and perfection. They had two foci rather than one. That would have been monstrous indeed to Copernicus' Renaissance mind.

To state the matter somewhat differently for the sake of emphasis, Copernicus' primary concept was that the heavenly bodies followed perfect circles. Actually, how- ever, the planetary orbits were "defective", i.e., ellipses. Secondly, Copernicus objected to the Ptolemaic system because Ptolemy used "equants" to explain the non- coincidence of the centres of the geometry of the heavenly bodies and the regularity of their motion. Since there is no coincidence of the centre of motion and the centre of the geometry of ellipses, Kepler saved the Copernican system by showing that, in this instance, Ptolemy was right and Copernicus was wrong. Thirdly, Copernicus centred both the geometry of the planetary orbits and the regularity of planetary movements on a mathematical point which he calculated to be the centre of the earth's motion, a point which itself orbited a second point. This second point (which we have termed the Copernican "universal equant") in turn orbited the sun. However, Kepler showed that planetary motion had no single centre and that each planetary orbit had two foci. One of the foci of each elliptical orbit of each planet was located near the centre of the sun, while the other was located outside the sun between the sun and the planet. Whereas Copernicus had, for all intents and purposes, avoided the sun in the geometry of his system, Kepler showed that it occupied the position of the main focus of the ellipse. Thus Kepler "proved" what the Hermeticists had proclaimed for over a thousand years, that the sun was *the pilot* of the heavens, the commander of the planets which guided them according to its power!

Kepler showed every sign of being a Neopythagorean Hermeticist. Like the Pythagoreans and Plato, he even listened for the melody of the spheres.[170] Copernicus too gave indications of having been well acquainted with the mystical world-view of Hermeticism. However, once he conceived the model of his system of ellipses, Kepler's work, like that of Copernicus, was a pure and ingenious mathematical achievement. Kepler proved Copernicus right by showing where he was wrong. His own model which enabled him to reflect reality by means of geometry and mathematics enabled him to abandon the "divine circles" as so much theological and philosophical myth-ology which had imprisoned both Copernicus and his science within its prescription. So powerful was Copernicus' trust in the prescription which had united theology, philosophy, and science from the ancient Pythagoreans onward, that the only possible alternative he was enabled to fathom was one that perfected, rather than abandoned, circularity of geometry and regularity of motion. Since, however, the system was based upon false premises, the more perfect the system became with regard to its own inner logic, the less descriptive it was of the reality it sought to represent. Hence, the more true it was in its own terms, the more false it became in terms of reality.

In a strict sense, then, when we compare Kepler with Copernicus, we should speak of Kepler's "heliofocused series of ellipses" which he based on Copernicus' distorted attempt to combine the heliocentric system of Aristarchus with the eccentrics and epicycles of Ptolemy. Aristarchus, Ptolemy, and Copernicus were able to see the world only so far as their theologies allowed God's "perfect circles", whether dictated by ancient Pythagorean mysticism or by Aristotelian physics, to be incorporated into their systems. Aristotelian astronomy itself pivoted upon Pythagorean mystical concepts of the world. These became a part of the theology of Thomas Aquinas. The mystical ideas were resuscitated by the Neoplatonists and Hermeticists of the Renaissance and were a powerful force in shaping the Renaissance mind. In the case of astronomy the Renaissance mind, whatever else it achieved, was so misshapen by a 2000-year-old "theological" perversion — the belief that the circles of God represented the quintessence of divinity — that it prevented the heavenly movements to be seen for what they were. The "circles" so defined beauty, harmony and, indeed, all rationality and reality that, until Kepler allowed the heavens to force his mind to conform to their inherent pattern, even observational data was skewed according to the perception of circularity.

Eventually, then, the heavens that "declare the glory of God" (Ps. 19:1) were seen to declare it in terms of creation and not of divinity. The form of the heavenly movements was *elleipsis*, exactly that form which Greek and the renewal of Greek thought in the Renaissance could not allow because *elleipsis* meant *imperfection*. Hence Kepler's discovery underscored the realisation that Christian astronomers insisted upon from the beginning, namely that the heavens were not of godly stuff but of earthly reality with a contingent, rational order of their own. With that the heavenly movements shed the halo of harmony defined in terms of circularity and regularity, and astronomy became science which understood those movements in appropriate terms.

The Copernican theory, then, magnificent as it was as a demonstration of single-mindedness and mathematical genius, is a prime example of how the same theological dedication that may inspire us to turn our eyes to the heavens to discover the wonderful works of God may also prevent us from seeing those works as they are. It shows, too, as Kuhn has pointed out, that sometimes at least revolution in science comes about by default rather than by design.[171] Theories which may be fictitious in origin and largely fallacious in content may prove later to be fruitful if a number of their basic tenets are true.

Theory and Truth

Scientific theories are not, however, simply fictitious as interestingly enough both Osiander and the well-known French physicist and philosopher Pierre Duhem (1861–1916) would seem to suggest.[172] The job of the astronomer, claimed Osiander in his preface to Copernicus' *De Revolutionibus*, is first to gather up the history of astronomical observation. Then, however, since he cannot discover the true causes of the movements involved, he is "to think up or construct whatever causes or hypotheses he pleases such that, by the assumption of these causes, those same movements can be calculated from the principles of geometry for the past and for the future too".[173]

> And as far as hypotheses go, let no one expect anything in the way of certainty from astronomy, since astronomy can offer us nothing certain, lest, if anyone take as true that which has been constructed for another use, he go away from this discipline a bigger fool than when he came to it.[174]

Rosen has pointed to Pierre Duhem's "Essai sur la notion de théorie physique de Platon à Galilée" ("Essay on

the Notion of Physical Theory from Plato to Galileo") as
an example of Osiander's thought.[175] In that article Duhem
takes the side of Osiander, Bellarmine, and Pope Urban
VIII (c.1568–1644) over against Copernicus, Galileo, and
Kepler. The former agree with Osiander who, as we have
seen, insisted that scientific hypotheses were only attempts
to "save the appearances". Copernicus, Rheticus, Galileo,
and Kepler, on the other hand, were certain that their
hypotheses were proper reflections of reality. Hence, they
insisted that their theories were *true*.[176]

To illustrate, Duhem cites the objections which Alexander Achillini, the Italian Averroist, had made to
Ptolemy. Achillini who, it will be remembered, was the
antagonist of Ficino in the debate in which Ficino had
proclaimed a heliocentric universe in Bologna in 1492, had
objected to Ptolemy because Ptolemy had built his system
upon two hypotheses — "the eccentric" and "the
epicycle". Since, according to Achillini, these did not
accord with physics but were mathematical constructions,
they were *false* as far as reality was concerned. Taking the
point of view of Averroës, Achillini had then insisted that
"astronomy does not really deal with that which exists"; it
is simply "a suitable way of calculating the successive
positions of heavenly bodies".[177] Further, in that Ptolemy
had been unable to prove that eccentrics or epicycles
actually existed, and had used " 'fictional bodies as the
exact cause to explain the phenomena, he committed an
error of physics' ".[178] Hence his physics was false. Picking
up the argument, Duhem explained that Copernicus, too,
was not satisfied with allowing his hypotheses to "demonstrate that they were sufficient to save the appearances".[179]
Rather, both he and Rheticus had argued that the hypotheses are not only adequate to the phenomena, but "have
their foundations in nature in the same way that things
do".[180] Copernicus thus equated *theory* with *reality* and
Duhem therefore accused him of being "a realist".[181]

For Duhem as for Osiander, an hypothesis is valid if it is
capable of "saving the phenomena".[182] "If the Copernican
hypotheses succeeded in saving all the known appearances,

one could draw the conclusion that these hypotheses may be true but not that they are certainly true." For them to be "certainly true" it would be necessary "to prove that no alternative set of hypotheses could be imagined which allowed the appearances to be saved equally well". Needless to say, Duhem goes on, "this final demonstration has never been given".[183] One might add somewhat redundantly, "It never will be".

Hence, according to Duhem, logic is on the side of Osiander, Bellarmine, and Urban VIII and against Kepler and Galileo [or Copernicus] who were caught in "an illogical realism".[184] Thus, as Duhem would have it, "in spite of Kepler and Galileo [and Copernicus], we believe today with Osiander and Bellarmine, that the hypotheses of physics are nothing more than mathematical devices intended to save the phenomena".[185]

The Osiander-Duhem conception of the relationship between theory and reality, as we have noted long since, was one of the alternative views of science presented by Aristotle in his discussion of the difference between physicists and astronomers, on the one hand, and mathematicians on the other. For Aristotle, the mathematician, like Osiander's and Duhem's astronomer, is not concerned with relating lines and figures to the boundaries of natural bodies. Rather, the mathematician deals only with abstractions from physical conditions, abstractions which "are capable of being considered in the mind in separation from the motion of bodies to which they pertain". Further, for Aristotle as for Osiander and Duhem, "such abstraction does not affect the validity of the reasoning or lead to any false conclusions".[186]

There is, however, as Rosen points out so well, another alternative. Rather than accept an hypothesis as either truth or fiction,[187] or rather as "fiction" that really can never be proven to be true, we may accept an hypothesis as the best reflection of reality which is possible for the time being, and revise it when new empirical data require our doing so.[188] The Copernican theory proved to be true only in very large generalities. The planets moved around the sun rather than the earth. When, however, Kepler investigated Tycho Brahe's notations on the basis of the Copernican generality, he proved it to be true by ignoring its deficiencies. Then by modifying it in terms of his own hypothesis of ellipses, he brought about a revolution and created modern astronomy.

Kepler, thus, saved Copernicus from being one of those "fools" who thought his theory was true in spite of all the current evidence against it.[189] He saved him by "proving" that the "God" of circularity, the "God" of the Pythagoreans, Plato, Aristotle, Thomas and mediaeval theology was dead. The "God" whose nature was reflected in the harmony of geometrical symmetry of the regular circular motion of the heavens, the "God" who at one and the same time attracted the eyes of the astronomers to look heavenward and prevented their seeing what was there, was a myth created by the unwarranted speculation that his being was congruent with the classical concepts of *perfection*.

By Kepler's time, however, the God of the Bible, the God who created the world *ex nihilo*, subject to no preconceived designs of heaven or earth, had again come alive. God again became known as the sovereign Lord of all creation, the heavens and the earth. He became known as the God who gave the world its own rationality so that for Kepler the heavens were seen to conform to mathematics and geometry as designated by observation rather than as prescribed by theology. Under the God whose thoughts are not our thoughts, but in whose image we are made to know and superintend the world, seventeenth-century science, the science that saved Copernicus, was born and as a result the modern world was born. *Providentia dei, confusione hominum*, we too may be saved from gross foolishness and our limited insights may beget new truth as well.

NOTES

1. Rosen reports that although Copernicus was appointed a canon, he was never ordained as a priest. Cf. Edward Rosen, "Biography of Copernicus," *Three Copernican Treatises* (New York: Octagon, 1971), pp. 319f. Zinner, however, indicates that one record designates him as being "Domherr und Priester" (canon and priest). Ernst Zinner, *Entstehung und Ausbreitung der Coppernicanischen Lehre* (Vaduz: Topos, 1978), p. 158.

2. Rosen, *Copernican Treatises*, pp. 343ff. Zinner dates the *Commentariolus* between 1510–14. Zinner, *Coppernicanischen Lehre*, p. 185.

3. Rosen reports that the analysis of the system described in the *Commentariolus* as "concentrobiepicyclic" (epicycles on concentric deferents) while that of the *De Revolutionibus* is described as "eccentrepicyclic" (epicycles on eccentric deferents) goes back to Ludwig Birkenmajer. Cf. Rosen, *Copernican Treatises*, pp. 7, 390; Koyré, *Astronomical Revolution*, p. 87, n. 52.

4. Nicholas Copernicus, *Commentariolus* in *Three Copernican Treatises*, trans. Edward Rosen (New York: Octagon, 1971), p. 59. Cf. Rosen, *Copernican Treatises*, pp. 59, n. 5; 345.

5. Copernicus, *Revolutions*, Preface, p. 509. Rosen, *Copernican Treatises*, pp. 358–360. Cf. Koestler's account, *Sleepwalkers*, p. 146. According to Rosen, invitations were issued July 24, 1514, June 1, 1515, and July 8, 1516. Copernicus is recorded to have replied in a *Compendium* dated Rome 1516. Rosen, *Copernican Treatises*, p. 359.

6. Cf. Tycho Brahe, *Opera Omnia*, 15 vols, ed. J. L. E. Dreyer (Hauniae: Gyldendaliana, 1913–29), Vol. IV, *Scripta Astronomica*, p. 292, lines 4–20; and Rosen, *Copernican Treatises*, who translates Tycho's statement as "The copy in my possession was given to me after a second or third translation from Copernicus's own draft", p. 8, n. 15.

7. Cf. Rosen, *Copernican Treatises*, p. 407.

8. *Ibid*. Hence Rosen's legitimate objection to Koestler's phrase, "The Book That Nobody Read", as Koestler entitles one of the sections of his book. Cf. Koestler, *Sleepwalkers*, p. 191; Rosen, *Copernican Treatises*, pp. 406f. It is questionable if Rosen should describe the 1617 Amsterdam edition of the *De Revolutionibus* as a "universal manual", however, since it was printed as a direct Protestant answer to Rome's 1616 ban of the book.

9. Copernicus, *Revolutions*, Dedication, p. 508.

10. Cf. below, pp. 208f and 238ff.

11. Hence, Prowe states that "though Copernicus was a popular figure, he was not in any sense respected in the way we think of him

today". Leopold Prowe, *Nicolaus Coppernicus*, Erster Band: Das Leben, II Theil 1512–43 (Berlin: Weidmannsche, 1883), p. 244. Elbing, one of the Hansa cities known for its free spirit at the time, was also the site of a certain amount of controversy between Roman Catholics and Protestants. Gnapheus had been arrested by the Inquisition in Brussels, first in 1523 then again in 1525, before fleeing to Ermland and Elbing in 1531 where he became a teacher and later the first director of the Gymnasium there. Even Elbing, however, was not to escape the confessional tensions for long. Gnapheus was expelled by Bishop Dantiscus in 1541. Cf. *ibid.*, pp. 235–244. For Rosen's account, cf. *Copernicun Treatises*, pp. 375f.

12. Martin Luther, *Tischreden* [entries from 1538–39 recorded by Antony Lauterbach] (Eisleben: Gaubisch, 1566), p. 582.

13. The line is taken from a sermon on 1 Cor. 10:19–24 which Calvin preached in 1556. Though the statement would seem to be incidental to the main point of the sermon which is a warning against those who would pervert the truth, it shows where Calvin's sympathies were on the question of heliocentricity. Cf. Pierre Marcel, "Place et Thème du huitième sermon sur I Corinthiens 10", *Calvin & Copernic: La Legend ou les Faits? La Science et l'Astronomie chez Calvin* (*La Revue Réformée* [Mars 1980], No. 121-1980/1, Tome XXXI), pp. 15–20. Cf. also Robert White, "Calvin and Copernicus, The Problem Reconsidered", *Calvin Theological Journal* (Nov. 1980), Vol. 15, no. 2, pp. 233–243.

   In that Andrew D. White's statement: "Calvin took the lead, in his *Commentary on Genesis*, by condemning all who asserted that the earth is not at the centre of the universe," is also cited by such an otherwise careful scholar as Thomas S. Kuhn, *Copernican Revolution*, p. 192, it may be necessary to indicate that White's statement, found in his well-known *A History of the Warfare of Science with Theology in Christendom*, 2 vols. (London: Macmillan, 1897), I, 127 is spurious. White in turn took the statement from the Preface of the 1886 edition of Frederic W. Farrer's *History of Interpretation* (Grand Rapids, Mich.: Baker, 1961), p. xviii. Farrer gives no source. Thus, Reijer Hooykaas writes that for fifteen years he had attempted to show that "the 'quotation' from Calvin is imaginary and that Calvin never mentioned Copernicus; but legend dies hard". Reijer Hooykaas, *Religion and the Rise of Modern Science* (Grand Rapids: Eerdmans, 1978), p. 121.

14. Butterfield, *Origins of Modern Science*, p. 165. Cf. Hooykaas, *Religion and the Rise of Science*, esp. the chapter, "Science and the Reformation", pp. 98ff.

15. Koestler, *Sleepwalkers*, p. 165. Rosen reports that after Rheticus had, in 1539, brought Copernicus a copy of Regiomontanus' *Triangles* (Nuremberg, 1533) which Regiomontanus had written over half a century before, Copernicus made alterations in the

trigonometric section of the manuscript and added folios 23 and 26. Rosen, *Copernican Treatises*, pp. 398f.

16. For Rosen's account of the publication, cf. Rosen, *Copernican Treatises*, pp. 400–402. Rosen reports that Rheticus' fair copy of the manuscript has been lost along with a manuscript of a biography of Copernicus which he planned to have printed with a revised edition of the *De Revolutionibus* from which Osiander's Preface would have been deleted. Both Giese and Rheticus are recorded by Rosen as having taken strong exception to Petreius having included Osiander's Preface in the work, but to no avail. *Ibid.*, pp. 403–406.

As we will discuss below, the fact that Osiander's Preface was anonymous and that it misrepresented Copernicus' understanding of his theory was unfortunate. It was not a matter of ill-will. He did openly admit to one Philip Apian (1531–89), Professor of Astronomy at Tübingen University, that he added the Preface "as his own idea". *Ibid.*, p. 404. Cf. below, pp. 208f., and 238ff.

17. Georg Joachim Rheticus, *Narratio Prima* in *Three Copernican Treatises*, trans. Edward Rosen (New York: Octagon, 1971), p. 186.

18. *Ibid.*, pp. 109, 111, 186f., 192, 195.

19. Cf. Rosen, *Copernican Treatises*, p. 393 and especially pp. 403f. with reference to the correspondence between Rainer Gemma of Friesland (Gemma Frisius) (1508–55) and Dantiscus regarding the Copernican theory.

20. Prowe, *Coppernicus*, p. 277. Cf. Rosen, *Copernican Treatises*, p. 387.

21. ". . . copernicanam de moto terrae sententiam explicavi". Prowe, *Coppernicus*, p. 274. Rosen reports that Widmanstetter, as he names him, quite probably became interested in the Copernican theory through Theodoric of Radzyn (Dietrich von Reden) (d. 1559), representative of the Varmia Chapter to Rome. Rosen, *Copernican Treatises*, p. 387. Zinner names Alexander Scultetus (d. 1564), a cathedral choirmaster from Ermland who was in Rome at the time. Zinner, *Coppernicanischen Lehre*, p. 228.

22. Koestler, *Sleepwalkers*, p. 165. This, in spite of the fact, as Rosen reports, that Melanchthon had objected to the Copernican theory in terms as harsh as those of Luther. Rosen, *Copernican Treatises*, pp. 400, 407.

23. Zinner, *Coppernicanischen Lehre*, p. 243. Italics added.

24. Andreas Osiander, "To the Reader Concerning the Hypotheses of This Work," *Revolutions of the Heavenly Spheres*, p. 505.

25. Koestler, *Sleepwalkers*, pp. 166f. Cf. Johannes Kepler, *Apologia Tychonis contra Nicolaum Raymarum Ursum, Opera Omnia*, Vol. I, ed. Ch. Frisch (Frankfurt: Heyder, 1858), p. 246.

26. Cf. above, note 157 and below, pp. 208f., and 238ff. Hence, scholars report that it is well that Copernicus, who was on his

deathbed when on May 24, 1543 the printed copy of the *De Revolutionibus* was placed in his hands, did not have the strength to see the anonymous Preface which contradicted his own principles. Cf. Rosen, *Copernican Treatises*, p. 404.

27. Copernicus, *Revolutions*, Preface, pp. 506–509.

28. Some of the orthodox Aristotelians may well have been theologians but I know of no record that Copernicus' name was connected with ecclesiastical censure until years after his death in 1543.

29. Rheticus wrote to ask Duke Albert of Prussia to request permission from the Elector of Saxony and from the University of Wittenberg to publish Copernicus' *De Revolutionibus* on August 29, 1541. Cf. Rosen, *Copernican Treatises*, pp. 399, 401.

30. The thirty-six years, though no doubt symbolic, do indicate that he had conceived the theory about 1510–14, the date given to the *Commentariolus*. Copernicus, *Revolutions*, Preface, p. 507. Cf. below, pp. 219ff.

31. Rosen, *Copernican Treatises*, p. 394. Rosen reports that the citation is included in the Foreword.

32. *Ibid.*, p. 407. Cf. Koestler, *Sleepwalkers*, Part Three, "The Timid Canon", which is Koestler's interesting, if somewhat biased, account of Copernicus and his theory, pp. 119–219.

33. Koyré, *Astronomical Revolution*, p. 27.

34. *Ibid.*, p. 28.

35. Rosen, *Copernican Treatises*, p. 342.

36. Zinner reports that Copernicus' observations were accurate only within 10 or 15 minutes of an arc which in some instances was less exact than the measurements of Hipparchus and Ptolemy. Zinner, *Coppernicanischen Lehre*, pp. 241f. For a description of Copernicus' "cross-bow" or *utriquetrum* "Jacob's staff" or *Baculus astronomicus*, and "upright sundial", cf. Koester, *Sleepwalkers*, pp. 122f.

37. Copernicus, *Revolutions*, Preface, p. 507. The fact that the last observation noted in the text of the *De Revolutionibus* was made in March 1529 and that his observations made in 1532 were not considered in his theory, would indicate that the *De Revolutionibus* was finished about 1530. Cf. Koestler, *Sleepwalkers*, p. 574, n. 20 and Koyré, *Astronomical Revolution*, p. 25. Rosen points to tests on the paper of Copernicus' original manuscript of the *De Revolutionibus* which indicate that the paper used may be dated from 1512–42. Rosen, *Copernican Treatises*, pp. 390–392.

38. Copernicus, *Revolutions*, Preface, p. 507.

39. *Ibid.* As we shall see, ironically enough the Ptolemaic system was more accurate than the Copernican. For Copernicus, *gravity*, the effect of which he believed to be "present in the sun, moon, and the other bright planets", was "nothing except a certain natural appetency implanted in the parts by the divine providence of the

universal Artisan, in order that they should unite with one another in their oneness and wholeness and come together in the form of a globe". *Ibid.*, Book I, 1, p. 521.

40. Festugière, *Révélation d'Hermès*, I, 82.

41. Aleksander Birkenmajer, "Comment Copernic a't'il conçu et réalisé son oeuvre?", *Organon International Review I* (Warsaw: Mianowski Institute, 1936), p. 119, fn. 1.

42. Rosen, *Copernican Treatises*, p. 402.

43. Birkenmajer, "Copernic", 119, fn. 1.

44. This analysis is rather different from that of Professor S. L. Jaki. Cf. Jaki, *Science and Creation*, pp. 259f.

45. Copernicus, *Revolution of the Heavenly Spheres*, I. 10, pp. 526–528.

46. Yates, *Bruno*, p. 154.

47. Alexandre Koyré, *The Astronomical Revolution* (Paris: Hermann, 1973), p. 66.

48. For artistic depictions of the sun and God in the centre and in control of the zodiac, cf. the eleventh-century representation of "The Sun and The Zodiac" and Raphael's "God and the Planets" in Jean Seznec, *The Survival of the Pagan Gods* (New York: Pantheon, 1953), pp. 63, 80.

49. Copernicus, *Revolutions*, Book I. 10, pp. 527f.

50. *Ibid.*, Book I. 9, p. 520.

51. *Ibid.*, Book I, p. 510.

52. *Ibid* Plato, of course, preceded the Hermeticists in the designation in *Timaeus*, 34, p. 527; 92, p. 583.

53. Copernicus, *Revolutions*, Book I, p. 510.

54. *Ibid.*, p. 511, quoting Plutarch.

55. *Ibid.*, p. 513.

56. *Ibid.* For Aristotle's concept of sphericality and circularity, cf. above, pp. 25ff.

57. Jaki's statement is made on the basis of Birkenmajer's evidence that Copernicus had questions about the Ptolemaic system as early as Cracow. "By the time Copernicus arrived in Italy, his commitment to the heliocentric system seems to have been firmly established." Jaki, *Science and Creation*, p. 259, stands in contradiction to Rosen's statement made on the basis of a reference to Copernicus' discussion in 1508 as to "the swift course of the moon, and its brother's [the sun] alternating movements" that "Copernicus had not yet glimpsed the geokinetic cosmos in 1508", some fifteen years after he first went to Italy. Rosen, *Copernican Treatises*, p. 339.

58. Birkenmajer, "Copernic", pp. 120f.

59. The dates are taken from Zinner, *Coppernicanischen Lehre*, p. 150; cf. *ibid.*, p. 156. Birkenmajer and Rosen record his going up to the University of Cracow in 1491 but do not record his length of stay. Birkenmajer, "Copernic", p. 114. Rosen, *Copernican Treatises*, p.

315. Rosen says he did not stay the full four years, *ibid.*, p. 316. Koestler records 1591–94 as the dates at Cracow. Koestler, *Sleepwalkers*, p. 221.

60. Cf. Zinner, *Coppernicanischen Lehre*, "Die Studien des Coppernicus in Krakau", pp. 143–156. Cf. *Poggendorf Encyclopaedia*, Old Series (Leipzig: Barth, 1863–1904), II, 587; *Dictionary of Scientific Biography*, 15 vols. (New York: Scribners, 1975), XI, 348–352. Both Zinner and Koyré note that Brudzewo had written a commentary on Peurbach's *Planetary Theory*. Koyré, *Astronomical Revolution*, p. 21. Zinner, *Coppernicanischen Lehre*, p. 150. Zinner dates the commentary 1482.

61. Birkenmajer, "Copernic", p. 114.

62. *Ibid.*, p. 114, n. 2.

63. Zinner, *Coppernicanischen Lehre*, pp. 159f.

64. Marsilio Ficino, *Liber de Sole, Opera Omnia*, 2 vols. in 4 (Torino: Bottega d'Erasmo, 1959, photocopy of the Basel edition of 1576), cap. VI.

65. *Ibid.*, cap. VII.

66. *Ibid.*, cap. XIII.

67. Alexander Achillini, *De orbibus*, cited by Zinner, *Coppernicanischen Lehre*, p. 160.

68. Zinner, *Coppernicanischen Lehre*, p. 160.

69. *Ibid.*, p. 161. Rather than going directly from Bologna to Ferrara between 1501–03, Copernicus studied medicine at the University of Padua. Unfortunately, as Zinner reports, nothing is known about his study in Padua. *Ibid.*, p. 165.

70. Cf. Scott, *Hermetica*, I, pp. 36ff. Koestler's speculation that Copernicus took his degree at Ferrara rather than Bologna to escape the financial burdens of the attendant graduation festivities seems somewhat unconvincing. Cf. Koestler, *Sleepwalkers*, p. 130.

71. A. C. Crombie, *Augustine to Galileo*, Vol. II (London: Heinemann, 1979), p. 174.

72. Birkenmajer, "Copernic", p. 126. Birkenmajer also records, however, that the copy has been lost. Rosen states but does not document that Copernicus "may not have possessed his own copy of the *Epitome*". Rosen, *Copernican Treatises*, p. 324. Copernicus records just twenty-seven observations in his *De Revolutionibus*. Birkenmajer, however, gives evidence that he made more than sixty in all, "Copernic", p. 131. Cf. Dreyer, *History of Astronomy*, p. 307.

73. Birkenmajer, "Copernic", pp. 124–126. Birkenmajer tells us that Copernicus purchased the book in the second half of 1496 or the first part of 1497.

74. Copernicus, *Revolutions*, Book I. 10, p. 523.

75. Crombie, *Augustine to Galileo*, p. 174.

76. Cf. the diagrams in Kuhn, *Copernican Revolution*, p. 170, and Koyré, *Astronomical Revolution*, pp. 60f.

COPERNICAN COSMOLOGY
267

77. Hence, Rosen is quite right in calling the system "geokinetic" and "heliostatic". Rosen, *Copernican Treatises*, p. 339.
78. Cf. above, pp. 25ff., 35f., 74ff.
79. Cf. above, p. 32f.
80. Copernicus, *Revolutions*, Preface, p. 508.
81. Dreyer, *History of Astronomy*, pp. 314f.
82. Plutarch, *De Facie Quae in Orbe Lunae*, 6.923 A. Cf. Thomas L. Heath, *Greek Astronomy* (New York: AMS Press, 1969), p. 169.
83. Copernicus records respect for the "partial heliocentric system" which he knew by way of Martinus Capella, the fifth-century encyclopedist, who apparently had reported on the system of Heraclides of Pontus, saying that "Venus and Mercury circle around the sun as a centre". Copernicus, *Revolutions*, Book I. 10, p. 523.
84. Copernicus, *Commentariolus*, pp. 57ff.
85. Rheticus, *Narratio Prima*, p. 137.
86. Copernicus, *Commentariolus*, pp. 57f.
87. *Ibid.*, pp. 58f. Cf. Rosen, *Copernican Treatises*, p. 345.
88. Koyré, *Astronomical Revolution*, p. 27.
89. Copernicus, *Commentariolus*, p. 57.
90. Koyré indicates that in his Ὑποθέσεις τῶν πλαναμένων, *Hypothesis of the Planets*, Ptolemy had already attempted to harmonise the Platonic and Ptolemaic systems by adopting *real* spheres and placing them inside one another. *Astronomical Revolution*, p. 82, n. 43.
91. Copernicus, *Commentariolus*, p. 59.
92. *Ibid.*, p. 90.
93. Rheticus, *Narratio Prima*, p. 135. The explanation is of the system of the *De Revolutionibus* rather than of the *Commentariolus*. Cf. below, p. 234.
94. Koestler, *Sleepwalkers*, p. 192; p. 572, fn. 9 where Koestler enumerates the circles. Koestler's reference to Peurbach is from Peurbach's *Epitomae* on the authority of Koyré, cf. *ibid.*, p. 573, fn. 11. For the discussion of "sphere" vs. "circles", cf. Rosen, *Copernican Treatises*, pp. 18–21. For Zinner's count, cf. Zinner, *Coppernicanischen Lehre*, pp. 186f. For Koyré's, cf. Koyré, *Astronomical Revolution*, p. 89, n. 59; p. 27.
95. Koyré, *Astronomical Revolution*, p. 49. Tycho Brahe was the first to deny that the putative spheres existed. Cf. Rosen, *Copernican Treatises*, p. 289.
96. Noted by Koyré, *Astronomical Revolution*, p. 49.
97. Copernicus, *Revolutions*, Book I. 10, pp. 524f.
98. Kuhn, *Copernican Revolution*, p. 71.
99. Taliaferro, "Appendix B", *Almagest*, p. 476.
100. Kuhn, *Copernican Revolution*, p. 71.
101. *Ibid.*, Taliaferro, "Appendix B", *Almagest*, p. 476.
102. Rosen, *Copernican Treatises*, p. 390. Cf. above, fn. 3.

103. *Ibid.*
104. Copernicus, *Commentariolus*, pp. 57f.
105. Einstein, *Out of My Later Years*, p. 98. Cf. Torrance, *Theological Science*, pp. 110f. for an illuminating elucidation of the scientific method in general as well as its relationship to theology, and also the chapter, "Theology and General Scientific Method", pp. 116–131.
106. Copernicus, *Revolutions*, Book I. 10, p. 528.
107. Kuhn, *Copernican Revolution*, p. 154. There is thus a certain validity in Koestler's statement that "Copernicus was the last of the Aristotelians among the great men of science", cf. *Sleepwalkers*, p. 199. James Nebelsick has argued that Copernicus belongs to the pre-scientific era rather than that of modern science. "Is Copernicus the Last Member of the Old Era in Astronomy or the First Member of a New Era?", unpublished paper prepared for the Department of Philosophy and the History of Science, Cambridge University, November, 1979.
108. Nicholas Copernicus, *Letter Against Werner* in *Three Copernican Treatises*, trans. Edward Rosen (New York: Octogaon, 1971), pp. 94–106. The letter, written in 1522 and referred to above, is a reply to a request from Bernard Wapowski to comment on Johann Werner's astronomical treatise, *De motu octavae sphaerae tractatus primus* (*On the Motion of the Eighth Sphere*) in which Werner had called into question certain of Ptolemy's observations with regard to the positions of the fixed stars.
109. Copernicus, *Letter Against Werner*, p. 97. This in spite of the fact that Copernicus depends upon the correction of Ptolemy's notations made by Peurbach and Regiomontanus from the Alfonsine Tables.
110. *Ibid.*, p. 99.
111. Rheticus, *Narratio Prima*, p. 109.
112. *Ibid.*, p. 131.
113. Copernicus, *Commentariolus*, p. 59.
114. Copernicus, *Revolutions*, Preface, p. 507. Birkenmajer's evidence indicates that Copernicus made over sixty observations as against the twenty-seven which he records in the *De Revolutionibus*. Though the instruments Copernicus used were not particularly accurate, the observations apparently served only to support his illegitimate system of circles; hence, they do less to save Copernicus as a modern type of scientist than to condemn him. Had he been prone to believe his eyes rather than his predetermined theory, the observations might have persuaded him that his system of circles did not reflect reality. Cf. also Birkenmajer's rather chauvinistic attempt to ensure that Copernicus was Polish rather than German which imposes a nineteenth- and twentieth-century concept of nationality on a fifteenth-century situation when belonging to a Volk and one's political allegiance in central Europe

were far from being coincidental. Birkenmajer, "Copernic", p. 131, fn. 1. For other discussions of Copernicus' nationality, cf. Zinner, *Coppernicanischen Lehre*, pp. 141f. and 158; Koestler, *Sleepwalkers*, pp. 125, 129; Koyré, *Astronomical Revolution*, pp. 18–20; Rosen, *Copernican Treatises*, pp. 313–318.

115. Copernicus, *Revolutions*, Preface, p. 507.
116. Osiander, "To the Reader", *Revolutions*, p. 505.
117. Kepler, *Apologia Tychonis*, p. 246.
118. *Ibid.*
119. *Ibid.*
120. Cf. above, pp. 25ff. for Aristotle's astronomical concepts.
121. Aristotle, *Physics*, II. ii. 193b.
122. *Ibid.*
123. Rheticus, *Narratio Prima*, p. 140.
124. *Ibid.*
125. The citation is from the first Greek edition of the *Syntaxis* (*Almagest*) printed in Basel, 1538 which Rheticus presented to Copernicus. Cf. Rosen, *Three Copernican Treatises*, p. 141, n. 127. Hence, as Einstein explains, "The connection of the elementary concepts of everyday thinking with complexes of sense experiences can only be comprehended intuitively". Einstein, *Out of My Later Years*, p. 62.
126. Torrance, *Theological Science*, p. 117.
127. Rheticus, *Narratio Prima*, pp. 142f.
128. *Ibid.*, p. 186. Since Rheticus wrote the *Narratio Prima* in 1540, three years before the publication of *De Revolutionibus*, he apparently hoped to protect Copernicus by referring to him not by name but as "my teacher" throughout the manuscript. Though Rheticus was steeped in Neopythagorean Hermeticism, he was primarily a mathematician who felt that Copernicus served both his own Neoplatonic-pantheistic God and mathematics by his system. Hence it is not surprising that he could also outline the basic scientific procedure from the formation of hypotheses which, when verified by observation, constituted the principles of a system that became the basis of prediction. Koestler argues that after helping to persuade Copernicus to publish his *De Revolutionibus* and spending a year and a half copying, editing, and correcting some of the calculations of the manuscript and seeing it to the press, Rheticus said no more about the system or "his teacher" because he took umbrage at not being mentioned in the Preface. Rheticus was most generous in commending Tiedemann Giese, Bishop of Kulm, for his part in persuading Copernicus to allow the manuscript to be published. *Ibid.*, pp. 192ff. He was fully aware of the necessity of ecclesiastical loyalties and seemed much more interested in the theory than his own pride. Koestler's interpretation of Rheticus' pique seems far-fetched.

Zinner's evidence is that in later years Rheticus had nothing but praise for Copernicus and fully intended to continue his work. Indeed, though Rheticus may well have had personal problems which made him *persona non grata* in a number of contexts, the fact that after working on projects of trigonometry and planning works on geometry, knowledge of the stars, the eclipses, comparison of the planetary movements and a table of sines and, apparently after some wandering, he erected an obelisk forty-five feet high in Cracow to "prove" the Copernican theory, indicates full well his continuing interest in his "teacher". He intended to prove the theory on the basis of "the Egyptian use" of the obelisk for, as he said, "no device is better than the obelisk; armillaries, Jacob's staffs, astrolobes and quadrants are human inventions, the obelisk, however, erected on God's advice, surpasses all of them" — cited by Zinner, *Coppernicanischen Lehre*, p. 261. There is no record of Rheticus having used the obelisk. The last writing known from Rheticus (but for whom Copernicus' theory may well have died with its author) was a prophecy written in 1572 after the death of the Polish King Sigismund in which he foretold the succession of the next seven kings. Rheticus died in Kaschau, Hungary, December 4, 1574. *Ibid.*, p. 262. Cf. Koestler, *Sleepwalkers*, pp. 172–174, 187–190 for more information on this extraordinarily talented and unusual man.

129. Rheticus, *Narratio Prima*, pp. 194f. quoting Averroës, *Commentary on Aristotle's Metaphysics*, Book xii, summa ii, caput iv. no. 45. We will meet this statement again below.

130. *Ibid.*, p. 195 quoting Aulus Gellius, *Noctes Atticae*, i.9.8. Cf. above, pp. 205f.

131. Copernicus, "Dedication," *Revolutions*, p. 509.

132. Taliaferro, "Appendix B," *Almagest*, p. 474.

133. Kuhn, *Copernican Revolution*, p. 71.

134. Taliaferro, "Appendix B", *Almagest*, p. 476.

135. *Ibid.*, p. 470. To follow Taliaferro, the system is an illustration of a revolution in astronomical theory which depended less on accurate observation than "on the reinterpretation of the symbols represented by the appearances and of the numbers immediately symbolising these symbols". *Ibid.*

136. Kuhn, *Copernican Revolution*, p. 181.

137. *Ibid.*

138. Cf. above, p. 204.

139. The equating of theological doctrine with the teachings of science and the questionability of ecclesiastical control of science and opinion, to say nothing of the impropriety of the evidence on which Galileo was convicted in 1633, are all of course to be condemned out of hand. The accusations of 1633 after Galileo's telescopic discoveries became well known and after Kepler had promulgated his laws of planetary motion are of quite a different and reprehensible category from Bellarmine's formal objections to

the Copernican theory in 1616. To make matters worse, the evidence would seem to indicate that Galileo was convicted on the basis of a document, possibly "planted" in the record, which allegedly prohibited him from teaching the Copernican system at all. Cf. Crombie, *Augustine to Galileo*, II, 218f. We will discuss Bellarmine's position more fully below, pp. 258f.

140. Kuhn, *Copernican Revolution*, p. 181.
141. *Ibid.*, pp. 163f.
142. Cf. above, pp. 34f.
143. Copernicus, *Revolutions*, Book I. 6, p. 516.
144. *Ibid.*, Book I. 10, p. 526.
145. Kuhn, *Copernican Revolution*, p. 160.
146. Koyré, *Astronomical Revolution*, p. 16.
147. Kuhn, *Copernican Revolution*, pp. 200–226.
148. Rheticus, *Narratio Prima*, p. 137 quoting Galen, *De usu partium* X. 14.
149. Rheticus, *Narratio Prima*, p. 137.
150. Kuhn, *Copernican Revolution*, p. 181.
151. Zinner, *Coppernicanischen Lehre*, p. 187.
152. The moon, of course, continues to orbit the earth even in Kepler's system.
153. Ficino, *Liber de Sole*, I. 966.
154. Copernicus' own description of his work, *Revolutions*, Preface, pp. 508f.
155. Koyré, *Astronomical Revolutions*, pp. 66, 58.
156. Butterfield, *Origins of Modern Science*, "The Conservatism of Copernicus," pp. 17–36.
157. Copernicus, *Revolutions*, Book I. 9, p. 520. Aristotle, *On the Heavens*, I, ii. 268b–269b.
158. Copernicus, *Revolutions*, Book I. 10, p. 528. Cf. Koyré, *Astronomical Revolution*, p. 58.
159. Jaki's commendation of Copernicus' conservatism so as to shield him from the effects of Renaissance Neoplatonism and paganism would seem to overlook the fact that it was Aristotelian paganistic tendency to identify God with the heavens that prevented Copernicus from really being scientific. Cf. Jaki, *Science and Creation*, pp. 259f.
160. Copernicus, *Revolutions*, Book I. 10, p. 526.
161. Hence, as Koyré points out, the earth's sphere is eccentric with regard to the sun, *Astronomical Revolution*, p. 59.
162. Kuhn, *Copernican Revolution*, p. 170.
163. In order to "save his circles", Copernicus was forced to fashion the centre of his system with utter disregard for the concentricity of geometry and regular motion for which he designed the system in the first place. His rejection of Ptolemy's equant forced him to centre his system upon a "revolving equant", as I have shown. Koyré explains, "The centre of the terrestrial sphere certainly

revolves about the Sun, it is placed on a small epicycle whose
deferent has the Sun for centre, but its motion is so slow — the
epicycle makes one revolution in 3434 years and the deferent in
53,000 years — that, for practical purposes, it does not enter into
the calculations." Koyré, *Astronomical Revolutions*, p. 59.

164. Rosen, *Copernican Treatises*, p. 408.

165. Albert Einstein and Leopold Infeld, *The Evolution of Physics*
(Cambridge: University Press, 1938), p. 33. It is only in a
restricted and formal sense that we can agree with Edward Grant
that the Copernican theory represents the "function and rôle" of a
proper scientific hypothesis. Edward Grant, "Late Medieval
Thought, Copernicus, and the Scientific Revolution", *Journal of
the History of Ideas* (April–June 1962), Vol. XXIII, no. 2, p. 197.
Though it is quite true, as Grant claims, that Copernicus insisted
on the correlation of a scientific hypothesis and reality as Averroës,
Jean Buridan (d. c.1358), and Nicole Oresme (c.1320–82) did
not, that very correlation was already current with Peurbach,
Regiomontanus, and most likely with Novara from whom Copernicus learned his astronomy. *Ibid.*, pp. 205–215. Also, Grant does
not seem to be sufficiently aware of the positivistic nature of the
theory-reality correlation which in Copernicus caused him to hold
on to circularity in spite of the evidence against it and which in
Newton, whom Grant cites with approval, led to the absolutisation
of space and time, and the equating of the space-time continuum
with God's sensorium. *Ibid.*, p. 219. Cf. Isaac Newton, *Opticks*
(New York: Dover, 1952, based on the Fourth Edition, London,
1730), 3.1, qu. 31 and "The General Scholium", *Principia*
(Berkeley: University of California, 1946, revision of the Andrew
Motte translation of 1729).

166. For Polyani's discussion of a heuristic act in modifying knowledge
frameworks, cf. Michael Polanyi, *Personal Knowledge* (Chicago:
University of Chicago, 1958), p. 106; also pp. 124–131 and p. 382.

167. C. F. von Weizsäcker has rightly argued that the truly revolutionary discovery in modern astronomy was not the Copernican system but Kepler's first law. Weizsäcker, *Relevance of Science*, p.101.

168. Kuhn shows that Kepler's second law, which interestingly enough
was built upon his Neoplatonic-Hermetic intuition that the
planets were guided by the rays of the sun, was not quite accurate
but was a good enough approximation for the time. Kuhn,
Copernican Revolution, pp. 214f.

169. For Kuhn's discussion of Kepler, cf. *ibid.*, pp. 209–219. For
Koestler's perhaps over-complimentary evaluation, cf. *Sleepwalkers*, pp. 379–422.

170. Cf. above, pp. 13, 15 and 23.

171. Cf. Thomas S. Kuhn, *The Structure of Scientific Revolutions*, 2nd
ed. (Chicago: University of Chicago, 1970), esp. Chap. VI,
"Anomaly and the Emergence of Scientific Discoveries", pp.

52–65. Kuhn's thesis seems to me to be most helpful in understanding the development of science. However, like others, I have some hesitation in endorsing what appears to be his lack of emphasis on continuity in scientific discovery, his over-emphasis on the difference between "revelationary science" and "ordinary science", and his making science somewhat over-dependent on sociological factors. Cf. also Kuhn's reply to his critics in "Postscript 1969", *ibid.*, pp. 174–210.

172. Rosen, *Copernican Treatises*, p. 33. Cf. Pierre Duhem, "Essai sur la notion de théorie physique", *Annales de philosophie chrétienne*, 79e. année, t. 156, pp. 374–375.

173. Osiander, "To the Reader", *Revolutions*, p. 505.

174. *Ibid.*, p. 506.

175. Rosen, *Copernican Treatises*, p. 33 referring to Duhem, "Notion de théorie physique", p. 584.

176. Cf. Duhem, "Notion de théorie", esp. pp. 561–592.

177. Duhem, "'Notion de théorie physique", p. 354, quoting Alexandri Achillini Bononiensis, *Opera Omnia*, fol. 31, col. b.

178. *Ibid.*, quoting Achillini, *Opera Omnia*, fol. 34, coll. a et b.

179. *Ibid.*, p. 374f.

180. *Ibid.*, p. 377.

181. Rosen, *Copernican Treatises*, p. 33. Cf. Duhem, "Notion de théorie physique", pp. 373–375.

182. Duhem, "Notion de théorie physique", p. 284.

183. *Ibid.*, pp. 583–585.

184. *Ibid.*, p. 588.

185. *Ibid.*, p. 592. Bellarmine, whom we mentioned above, was the Cardinal who was in charge of Galileo's hearing in 1616. He had also featured in Bruno's trial in 1600 when Bruno was condemned and burned. Pope Urban VIII (Maffeo Barberini) was Pope in 1633 when Galileo at his "second trial" was condemned. Barberini originally favoured Galileo and Galileo dedicated to him his *Il Saggiatore*, a book on comets with explanations of experimental science and empiricist philosophy which he wrote in 1523. Urban VIII, however, later became an adversary and was largely responsible for Galileo's condemnation.

186. Aristotle, *Physics*, II, ii. 193b. Cf. above, p. 239.

187. Rosen, *Copernican Treatises*, p. 33 referring to these rival views as "realism" and "formalism" by Augustin Sesmat. Cf. Augustin Sesmat, *Systèmes de référence et mouvements (Physique classique)*, II: *L'Ancienne Astronomie d'Eudoxe à Descartes* (Paris: Hermann, 1937), pp. 105–130.

188. Rosen, *Copernican Treatises*, p. 33.

189. From this perspective Luther's statement in his *Table Talk*, referring to Copernicus being "a fool who would turn the whole of astronomy inside out", if taken in its own context does not seem so foolish after all. Cf. above, p. 203.

INDEX OF PERSONS

INDEX OF SUBJECTS

279